THE GIBSON GIRL:
Portrait of a Southern Belle

by
Langhorne Gibson, Jr.

The Commodore Press
Richmond, Virginia

FIRST EDITION
First Printing, 1997

The Gibson Girl: Portrait of a Southern Belle, Copyright 1997 by Langhorne Gibson, Jr.. All rights reserved. Printed in the United States of America. No part of this book may be used or reproduced in any manner whatsoever without written permission. For information, write to The Commodore Press, 1318 Loch Lomond Lane, Richmond, Virginia 23221.

ISBN 0-9657621-0-6 (Hardcover)

About the cover

The photographs of Irene Langhorne Gibson were taken shortly after her marriage in 1895.

My father taught me how not to bathe in the reflected light of relatives well-known and highly accomplished. A gentle, calm man, he became visibly agitated when he was labelled "Lady Astor's nephew." Whatever pride I have in being a part of an interesting family is tempered by the knowledge that those who came before me were so talented and so vital.

CHAPTER ONE

GRANNY

I envied my friends whose grandparents were a large part of their daily lives. One boy's grandmother was plump and cozy, a lady with long, white hair carefully done up in a bun which perched on the back of her head. She baked pies. Both of my grandfathers died when I was an infant, and I have only one faint memory of my mother's mother. We visited her in New Jersey, where she lived in a massive house. I remember a dinner when butlers scurried around the table and a footman stood rigidly at attention behind each adult. Obviously, she was extremely rich, but she disinherited my mother many years ago. Afterward, she never wanted to see her daughter's children. Her last husband was a man by the name of Garrett, a Palm Beach gigolo who, I think, was a hair-dresser. To my mother's irritation, my father sometimes ended our family prayers with a somber and facetious plea, "And God, please bless Grandpa Garrett."

My special grandparent, the one I remember distinctly, was Irene Langhorne Gibson, my father's mother. She was warm and loving, but not the type to wear aprons; nor did she have a wide lap to climb onto and nestle. At least, I never did. Instead, she was simply special, someone to be in awe of - - a person who periodically swept into my youth with dash and drama.

We lived on a farm in Greenwood, Virginia, just below Rockfish Gap and the Blue Ridge Mountains. In the fall and winter she came from New York City to visit us, always arriving by train. All of us - - my father, mother, brother, and three sisters - - climbed into the Ford station wagon for the short ride up to Greenwood Depot with its general store, post office, and gabled telegraph office. The wait for her train seemed endless, but finally the engine rounded the last bend, belching steam and straining mightily to pull its long load up the steep, mountainous grade. Rarely did a passenger train stop at Greenwood on its climb over the mountain, so when one did, it seemed to me as though the whole community

1

The Gibson Girl

raced to the oil-slickened, wooden platform to see who would get off.

First, the black porter resplendent in his maroon cap and white coat descended the stairs to set down the stoop. The small crowd gathered around the open door in silent expectation. My heart thumped with excitement when my grandmother appeared, her head turned backward as she animatedly said good-bye to some unseen person within the Pullman car. Then she looked down at us watching, and taking the white-gloved hand of the porter, came to us with a mixed air of majesty and openness possessed only by those comfortable with admiration and attention.

I watched as she greeted and laughed, her head thrown back, a beaming smile on her face, eyes sparkling, her teeth large and white. Even in her seventies she was a remarkably beautiful woman. Pressed away from her and unseen, I waited my turn. Finally, I got my kiss on the cheek. On the way home, tucked away in the far back seat of the Ford, I smelled the perfume and powder she left on my face.

My grandmother stayed in our downstairs guest room, but I never had the temerity to knock on her door and have her to myself. In our house she was always the center of attention, which was a place I had no way of sharing with her. She was forever on stage, and family, friends, strangers, or whoever happened to be nearby were her audience. Dinner with her was a special occasion for me because I loved to hear her lilting, animated voice as she chattered away. Special occasions were when we five children were allowed to join our parents and their guests in the evening when our grandmother played the piano and sang, her back ramrod-straight, her eyes scanning the listeners, absorbing their appreciative smiles. When no company came for dinner, we gathered around our grandmother by the fire as she told exciting adventure stories full of children performing great feats and narrowly escaping disaster and death. As she talked, her knitting needles clicked away in a rhythmic cadence which echoed the undulating flow of her words.

One afternoon with her I remember vividly. I must have been about ten years old. I went with her on a visit to a onetime servant, a wizened, ancient black woman who lived in Newtown, a settlement of cabins and tarpaper shacks precariously perched on

Granny

the steep Blue Ridge mountainside above our house. Coffee, a dignified chauffeur my father hired to take his mother around the neighborhood to call on her many friends, stopped the car on the dirt road where a rocky path began its blind ascent. I followed her up, eyes fixed on the backs of her slim calves and perfectly straight stocking seams. My young legs had a difficult time keeping up with the fast pace. We came to a clearing in the woods and a log cabin which oddly tilted to one side. Our hostess for the afternoon greeted us with a huge, toothless grin and wild cries of "Lordy, Miss Irene, I 'clare, it really is you." Inside, the walls of the cabin were lined with newspaper to shut out the drafts, the single room appetizing and neat as a pin and filled with the smell of wood smoke from the stone fireplace which dwarfed a few rickety chairs and two cots placed along the sides. They sat together on one of them, holding hands and pattering away as I sat quietly listening. My grandmother just as easily could have been in a drawing room on Park Avenue talking with one of her stylish society friends. They were so comfortable together - - not a hint of condescension on her part, nor of unease from her friend, only laughter and memories and warm smiles and hugs.

I know why this afternoon visit is so clear in my memory. I remember distinctly their conversation of shared memories of my grandmother's time at Mirador, a country house in Greenwood her father bought when she was nineteen. They told stories about her parents, Nanaire and Chillie Langhorne, and how frail and stubborn her younger sister, Nannie Langhorne, was. Lizzie, the eldest, was too headstrong for everyone's taste. They talked about how Mirador was always crammed with summer houseguests, many of them the young men who swarmed around my grandmother. Yet, the afternoon's impact on me was not their recollections, but rather the dark discomfort I felt sitting on that bed listening to them. I was envious of the unbounded attention my grandmother gave this woman. I sensed their deep friendship and history I as a child could not possibly merit, particularly from a grandmother who visited rarely and for only a few days each time.

I was the only one of five siblings who liked to go on excursions just to be with her, trips which must have been incredibly boring to a youngster. Once I drove with her and my

The Gibson Girl

father all the way to Bedford, Virginia when he took her to visit friends at an old ladies' home which reeked of stale smoke and body odors. After lunch when everyone rolled up their soiled linen napkins and replaced them in silver holders to use for the next meal, I realized I had used someone else's dirty one. Seeing her girlhood friends now so old and feeble must have saddened my grandmother because she was uncharacteristically quiet on the drive back home.

My grandmother's sister, Aunt Nannie Astor - - the notable Nancy, Lady Astor, the first woman to sit in Great Britain's House of Commons - - also came to stay with us. It was hard for me to believe they were sisters. In every way they seemed different. Aunt Nannie was short and slight, reminding me of a bird with her quick, jerky motions, her eyes darting about missing nothing. A quietness surrounded my grandmother, an elegant calm accentuated by her regal, perfectly postured height and gestures which were so slowly graceful and so deliberate they might have been choreographed.

Aunt Nannie's approach to everyone looked like a confrontation, her neck craned forward, hands on her hips, her piercing eyes looking for a weakness or a fault she could exploit. Not many could match her quickness, and the usual response was a nervous, baffled smile together with a few mumblings and polite platitudes. By contrast, my grandmother, though as direct as her sister, was a great flirt. With an ease born of years of practice she could charm anyone she targeted. It was a marvel to watch my grandmother absorb people, wonderful to see her meet complete strangers who had no earthly idea who she was, and then to see their surprised expressions gradually brighten as they were taken in by her obvious and unfeigned interest in them.

My grandmother came to live with us before she died, in a cottage on our lawn hidden from view by an old slave cabin and a clump of bushes. I do not remember her going to church, but she always joined my parents' friends who came over for after-church cocktails. On Sundays when the weather was pleasant we sat on the lawn with its panoramic view of fields and barns and mountains. I always knew when my grandmother was about to make her grand entrance because she sent one of her maids as a scout to notify her when the guests had settled into the white, wooden lawn chairs, drinks in hand. When she appeared, I cried out, "Here comes

Granny

Granny!" as she began her stately walk down the brick path toward the gathering. Conversation stopped and heads turned to watch her approach, our silent applause acknowledged with a graceful toss of her head and a light, dismissive wave of her hand. Even to the eye of a thirteen year old she was radiant, a tall, magnificent woman bedecked in a long, flowing, silk dress which accentuated her large bosom and slim waist and hips. Only her sparkling, warm eyes were fully visible, shadowed under a broad-brimmed straw hat draped with a cream-colored veil whose swirling folds covered her face and neck.

I wanted her to understand I was her secret ally and conspirator who made sure the guests noticed and appreciated her grand entrance. I longed for a private glance that acknowledged my role. It was not that she was inattentive or anything but kind and sweet to me, but I was too young and with her too seldom to be an important grandchild in her life.

I did have my chance to shine in her world when she became sick and bed-ridden, the victim of multiple strokes which gradually destroyed her brain. But when she needed companionship, someone to sit with her during the dullness of her last year of life, I was not there for her. I was too wrapped up in my teen-age interests to pay attention to a tired, old lady.

I always knew, or thought I knew, the facts of my grandmother's existence. Irene Langhorne was born in Danville, Virginia and moved to Richmond as a young girl. She was a Southern belle and married the illustrator Charles Dana Gibson, who made her his "Original Gibson Girl." They lived in a large townhouse in New York City and spent summers in a rambling house on an island in Maine. Both were superbly elegant and must have had a great deal of money to live the way they did. In our family it was enough that she was known for her beauty and it was enough that she was adored by her husband and my father, and by my aunt and first cousins. After she died in 1956, for years I rarely thought about her. No one ever talked to me - - and I never asked - - about what she did with her life or how she might have felt or how she got to be the way she was, the simple memories and reflections and opinions that perpetuate a person.

The Gibson Girl

Now I think it odd there was so little visible in my parents' house to remind us of my grandmother, only a rather bad portrait of her in the dining room and a faded photograph of her with my grandfather in a musty corner of the library. Perhaps my mother was jealous of her mother-in-law and my father did not need reminders because his happy memories of his mother were stored inside his head. However, my grandfather's presence filled our house. Its walls were covered with his talent - - pen-and-ink drawings with their bold, sweeping lines; and oil paintings of rural scenes and boats and seascapes brightly colored, the paint rough in texture as if it had been troweled on the canvas. A large, dark portrait of him hung in our front hall, which I saw every time I walked down the stairs. To my eye it was a picture of a stern and intimidating man with a bull neck, big nose, and square head. I figured he must have been a pretty important person because in our library there was a big book that told all about his career and his art, but not much about him, his wife, or his family.

Before my father died in 1982 he made a special effort to tell me everything he adored about his mother. In the process I came to see her as he did, but his picture of her seemed strangely unreal, and too much the personification of all that was right and beautiful in the world. For him she was the ultimate being, so close and dear to him, as he described his glorious, perfect childhood, an existence which seemed long ago and far away from the simple life we led on the farm. He talked of his years in France as a young boy, of backstage visits to famous actors and actresses on Broadway, New England boarding schools, summers in Maine and sailboat racing. And visits from New York City with his mother to Mirador just down the road from our farm were special to him because his mother was so radiantly happy there. After he died, I stuffed his and my own memories of her in a far corner of my mind.

A few years ago the youngest of my four children graduated from college and my cost of living plummeted. Twenty-five years in investment banking proved to be my limit, so I decided to do what I could not afford as a young man fresh out of college - - to try my hand at writing. Early retirement from established careers seems to be a tradition in the Gibson family. My grandfather tried to retire at thirty-eight; my father did at thirty-six; and the only competition at

Granny

which I ever beat my older brother was to retire before he did. We Gibson men tend to abandon the workplace as early as we are able, leaving to others the responsibility of keeping the economy primed. Anyway, after I had written two books about a prominent Richmond, Virginia family, my wife reminded me my family was interesting, and I should attempt a book on the whole bunch or pick out just one individual.

Casting around for ideas in old family documents and letters, and researching in various libraries and museums, I came across a pictorial history of Danville. One of its photographs showed Nancy, Lady Astor, at a lectern on a 1922 visit to the city. Standing beside her, statuesque and lovely and conspicuously unmentioned in the caption, was my grandmother. The photograph's caption irritated me. With a modicum of research the book's author easily could have identified my grandmother as the most popular belle of her generation, a position equivalent to that of today's movie stars and rock idols. Or he could have saluted her as the Gibson Girl, her husband's image of the woman freed from the sexist shackles of the Victorian Age, and poised to take her rightful role as man's equal. Yet, the author chose to ignore her, the same way I had when she lay dying. Suddenly all those confused childhood feelings about my grandmother surfaced - - my long-forgotten need to be special in her life and my guilt that somehow I had let her down at the end. An abrupt and intense desire to write about her enveloped me. Somehow, I thought if I paid attention to her now, and found out everything I could about her to rescue her from the shadows cast by her well-known husband and famous sister, I could atone for my past neglect. Also, I wanted to establish a relationship with her I was not destined to have when she was alive.

I started my search at my mother's house where I was raised, rummaging into flimsy, dented attic file cabinets and heavy leather suitcases almost a hundred years old. I found bundles of letters tied together with ribbon and old photographs and scrapbooks. My most exciting discovery was hidden under a pile of papers and sheet music in an antique Chinese chest of drawers in my mother's hallway. It was a short, eighteen-page typewritten memoir of her childhood my grandmother wrote in 1943, a set of

The Gibson Girl

private memories neither I nor anyone else had laid eyes on for more than half a century. I went to New York, to Maine, to Ohio, and to Rhode Island to interview relatives who knew my grandmother. I poured through old newspapers and letters and family documents and courthouse records. I dissected written accounts of cousins and aunts who knew her well. Gradually a blueprint of her life began to form in my mind and I was already at the point where I was framing opinions about her. I became particularly anxious to go back to when she was young, as far back as I could in order to discover how she came to be who she was.

CHAPTER TWO

KEENES AND LANGHORNES

There is no doubt in my mind that if my grandmother were writing her autobiography she would start with Charlemagne, the medieval Holy Roman Emperor, because she insisted we are his direct descendants. The claim seems impossible and interests me not at all, but she was true to her Southern need to establish personal worth and status through laborious genealogical study. Then she would take us through a line of ancient French noblemen until she came to the Langhorne branch. My father would have laughed at this pretentious side of his mother, reminding her that the name "Langhorne" is derived from our long-ago Welsh ancestors' propensity for stealing longhorn sheep from their more respectable neighbors. She set great store in her Virginia connections, and could trace roots which intertwine with many of the old-line families to determine she was a cousin to J.E.B. Stuart and Robert E. Lee, many times distant and much removed - - nevertheless kin.

My preference, however, is to begin with her parents and grandparents, people whose characters, whose strengths and weaknesses, gifts and burdens marked her. The geographical starting point is Danville, Virginia, the place of her birth. The house in which she was born still stands, although it has been enlarged and was moved in the 1920s from its initial location on Danville's Main Street to make way for an ugly, bilious-green apartment building. Thanks to a generous gift from my English Astor cousins and the efforts of a local historical group it is in the process of restoration.[*]

---

[*]The house was moved some eighty feet back from its commercially desirable spot on Main Street and attached to an apartment building. Very little renovation work has been done as yet, and it is not known exactly what it looked like on the outside because its dimensions were changed radically. However, experts are able to determine the dimensions and layout of the main floor rooms as they were in Irene's childhood.

The Gibson Girl

More than forty years ago, I first saw the historical marker for her birthplace. Our family was passing through Danville on a trip to North Carolina. The marker is one of thousands of cast metal, black and silver painted signs that line the Old Dominion's roads, commemorating important people and events in the state's history. It was the first time in my life it had dawned on me that there were people that important in our family. My brother, three sisters and I were in surly moods, bored and tired after a long drive from Greenwood. We groaned when my father pulled the station wagon over to the curb to read yet another marker, an incessant practice of his which annoyed all of us. Knowing we were not happy with these interruptions which elongated the time we had to spend in the car, my father usually dashed out the door and read quickly. This time, however, he just stood there, not moving for the longest time. My curiosity aroused, I climbed out the rear window to see why he was so engrossed. The prominent, street-side plaque loudly proclaimed that here was the site of Nancy Astor's birthplace, and went on at length, listing accomplishments which marked her place in history as one of the twentieth century's most prominent women. Walking around the marker to stand by my father I saw he was reading about his mother, a much shorter inscription which said she was the Original Gibson Girl and she also happened to be born in the same house.

I remember asking my father why the sign talked so much about Aunt Nannie, who was sharp and bossy and made me uncomfortable - - although I was too young to be a target of her caustic tongue - - and said so little about my grandmother. I do not remember what my thoughts were, or his reply, or even that he answered me. Today, that marker irritates me the way it must have when I was a boy. Her life deserves a fuller telling; in no way should her memory be merely the other song on a phonograph record, the "flip-side" of recognition.

My great-grandparents, Nanaire and Chillie Langhorne, were not at all sure their soon-to-be born infant whom they would call Irene would survive. The year was 1873, the day June 5th. Lumbering farm wagons and horse-drawn carts passed within a few feet of the Langhornes' cottage porch. Clouds of dust and grime swirled through the open, screenless windows into the sparsely furnished first-floor bedroom where Nanaire lay, sweating and miserable in the June heat. She was about to give birth for the sixth time. Hours before, Chillie had called for the doctor. There was nothing more for him to do except worry and keep an eye on seven-year-old Lizzie and five-year-old Keene. Now and then he shooed them from the main floor, away from their mother and the commotion, making sure they stayed in the basement kitchen or in the long, sloped backyard with its privy in the far corner. Those two were the only surviving Langhorne children because the last three babies, John, Mary, and Chiswell, had died. Three times Chillie had carried tiny coffins on his shoulder to the cemetery at Cottage Hill, his in-law's plantation - - or what was left of it - - five miles from Danville.*

Death had been a steadfast companion for Nanaire. Ever since John's death four years earlier, she had lived with the constant threat that yet another infant would be taken from her. Her only other choice was to turn away from her virile, young husband. Now she was exhausted by her long labor, and too weary to carry the fear this baby would die. Her diminutive, small-boned frame could more easily withstand the shock of childbirth when Lizzie and Keene were born. She was younger and healthier then.

If Nanaire's father had not been ruined by the Civil War, Nanaire would be at Cottage Hill then, surrounded by her parents' servants and the comfort of shade trees, high ceilings, and country breezes, not in this cramped house smelling of new paint and raw lumber. Certainly, the Langhornes would not be in this shabby, unkempt town reeking of distress, and constantly exposed to cholera, typhoid, and other lethal diseases. Perhaps their three lost children would have lived if they had not been so poor. Chillie

---

*Nannie Astor described a girlhood visit to Cottage Hill with her mother and sister, Phyllis. "We went with Mother to Danville to see her old home. The house was in ruins and the once beautiful gardens overgrown. Mother hunted for the graves of the children who had been buried there and she could not find them. She sat on the steps and cried. Phyllis and I were running around and I could not understand why she was crying. She had been a young girl there and she and her mother hastily buried the silver and what valuables they had because the Yankees were coming up the river." [No Union force got that close to Danville during the Civil War.]

The Gibson Girl

would have taken them and their mother away to safer surroundings to be pampered and coddled. Chillie could not blame himself, however. At least he had done well enough in the years since Lee's surrender at Appomattox to afford the $250 to purchase the house lot. He had enough credit to build a home so they could stop moving from one rental to the other. Nevertheless, the house with only a hallway and three rooms on the first floor and two small garret rooms for the children under the sloped tin roof was much less than he wanted for his family.

For the past decade life had offered Nanaire little in the way of choices and much in the way of hardship. Her childhood had been blessed with the comfortable rhythms of a gentle life her parents had earned for her, a world of verandahs cooled by the shadows of wisteria vines, broad vistas of field and river, and spacious rooms in an elegant house. That existence had ended with the South's defeat after four long years of mortal combat. Her privileged life had been replaced by disheartening poverty in mean and dreary rented houses on dirty, noisy streets. Each day brought with it the fear that tomorrow there would not be the money to purchase the barest necessities.

Nanaire was a Keene, born Nancy Witcher, one of two daughters of Mary Anne and Elisha Ford Keene. He was the quintessential Southern Cavalier, a large land and slave owner, a lawyer, and for years a representative of Pittsylvania County in Virginia's state legislature. Elisha bought Cottage Hill in 1849 when Nanaire was one year old. After his initial purchase of 500 acres, Elisha steadily added to his holdings, even during the war when he paid $14,000 for a large tract.

Her early life was uneventful and sheltered. The focus of her education was learning from her mother the difficult and complex art of being a plantation mistress. The basic skills of cooking and sewing first were mastered; then the management of storerooms full of foods and linens; and hardest of all, how to supervise the many slaves needed to take care of the family's needs. Somehow, wedged into the hours of each day, Nanaire had time to learn from a tutor "the three r's," a smattering of French and the classics. The sedate and solid pattern of Nanaire's everyday life at Cottage Hill was punctuated by the many friends and business and political associates who came to call or to stay, sometimes for days at a time.

Nanaire must have told her children many stories of her happy childhood, but I know of only two that have been passed down. One is a simple, idyllic picture of "darkies" home in their log cabins late in the afternoon after a long day in the fields, and singing with men playing banjos. "I listened until their song faded away," Nanaire told Irene. "I will love you till I die, Tilly Moore, Tilly Moore. I will love you till I die, Tilly Moore."

The other story, a tale of a frightening childhood experience, belies the romantic image of ante-bellum plantation life. One night, at ten o'clock, Nanaire and her young black maid, who slept in a trundle bed in her room, were awakened by a commotion. One of her father's slaves had come hurriedly in the back door, and yelled, "Massa, Rosa is sick. I wish you'd give me some whiskey." Elisha got up, filled a tumbler with whiskey, and offered it to this man who had been for years a devoted servant - - or so he thought. As Elisha approached the open door, the man drew from his pocket a pistol and shot him, nicking one of his fingers which held the tumbler. The unsuccessful killer dashed out the door and escaped from the plantation. Immediately, the white community assembled and put bloodhounds on his track. After six days he was found hiding in a gully.

Apparently, Elisha's slave had been incited by a "poor white" in the neighborhood to strike out at his owner. He said he and the man had waited in hiding beside the road to Cottage Hill several afternoons, hoping to find Mr. Keene driving home alone from Danville in his buggy pulled by a pair of piebald ponies. But, on each of those days, Elisha had a friend with him. The plotters went so far in their scheme as to dig a grave for their intended victim. Having failed in their original plan, they decided to shoot him in his house. The slave was hanged. It is not known what happened to the "poor white."

In 1862, when Nanaire was fourteen, she left Cottage Hill with her sister, Betty, and two cousins to attend Greensborough Female Institute in what is now Greensboro, North Carolina. The trip was only sixty miles, but it took two days to get there. An old friend recalled that "They came in style - - riding in a stately

The Gibson Girl

carriage, the baggage following." The devastating war brought Nanaire's formal education to an end after two years and the girls were returned to their homes in a mule-wagon with outriders guarding and directing the way back to Danville and Cottage Hill.

At the outbreak of the Civil War Elisha organized his own battalion of Confederate riflemen, but resigned from the army as a colonel in July, 1862, pleading "a frail and feeble condition, being unused to the hardship incident to twelve months of hard service and leaving me at present unfit for duty." His army record shows he had been under arrest at Suffolk, Virginia the previous February for some unknown reason. It is reasonable to assume his career as a soldier was less than spectacular. Nevertheless, his problems most likely did not involve his honor or integrity because he sat in Virginia's senate from 1863 through 1867.[*]

Fortunately for Elisha and his family, Pittsylvania County was far from the fighting, but toward the war's end it was impossible for him to work his fields because his work horses and mules had gone to serve the Confederacy's cavalry forces and to pull cannon and army wagons. The Keenes took a house in Danville, and Nanaire volunteered as a nurse in one of the army hospitals during vacations from Greensborough Female Institute. There she met Chillie Langhorne, a patient according to Irene. He worked at the large arsenal complex in Danville, and was a member of a home guard, light artillery unit.

Nanaire was only sixteen years old when she and Chillie were married in December, 1864. He was twenty-one. In spite of trying wartime conditions, Nanaire's parents were able to host marriage festivities at Cottage Hill which lasted several days. Nanaire recalled that Chillie's friends who came to "wait at the wedding" slept in the farm office, a little brick house in the yard. The day before the wedding the men went hunting so the guests

---

[*]In 1866 the Joint Committee on Reconstruction was formed in Washington to gather information on the South. In all, 137 witnesses representing various economic and social groups from eleven southern states were called, 49 from Virginia. Of the 49, 9 men represented the highly educated, experienced, and articulate portion of the Old Dominion's population. General Robert E. Lee was one of these witnesses, Elisha Ford Keene another.

would have something to eat. The partridges they shot were strung on a long line between two trees.

Chillie's sister, Elizabeth, was thirteen and struck by Nanaire's appearance the first time she saw her sister-in-law-to-be driving a small run-about. She described Nanaire's "fair hair blown about a youthful face, the sweet candor of her large blue eyes, and the youthful contour of her singularly graceful figure making an ineffaceable picture." Although diphtheria kept Elizabeth from serving as a bridesmaid, she did attend the wedding. She recalled, "The following day [after the wedding] the bridal party came to Danville where they were beautifully entertained and later they and my father and I journeyed home to Lynchburg for a large reception at my father's residence."

After the wedding, Nanaire and Chillie lived in an army camp outside Danville. Their food was military rations, and their roof was either a tent, or at best, a ramshackle hut. The first months of their marriage were a time of confusion and fear as the Confederacy started to disintegrate and Chillie was called to fight. At one point, Nanaire sold her tiny diamond solitaire engagement ring to buy a sewing machine so she could keep both of them clothed.

Chillie, or Chiswell Dabney Langhorne, was from Lynchburg, a town sixty miles north of Danville. He was the eldest of five children and the favorite, an adored, spoiled child according to Nanaire. After being discharged from the army because of recurring health problems, he arrived in Danville in 1862 to find work at the Danville Arsenal, one of the largest storehouses of munitions in the Confederacy.

At seventeen, he had enlisted in Lynchburg's Home Guard troop days after the fall of Fort Sumter. He went by train to Richmond with his company - - a hundred men strong with ninety-nine servants - - to become a part of Virginia's 11th Infantry Regiment, which heroically fought in a number of battles beginning with First Manassas, or Bull Run. However, Chillie was not with his regiment during these engagements. Soon after his enlistment he had been sent home from Richmond to recover from, most probably, a severe case of boils. He rejoined his regiment for a short

The Gibson Girl

time at its winter quarters at Centreville, Virginia, but was discharged permanently in February, 1862.

Although Chillie had no part in perpetuating myths about his military career, and was indignant when he was referred to as "Colonel Langhorne," some of his descendants embrace the need to establish family honor through glorifying his exploits. They have him gallantly fighting with the Army of Northern Virginia through all its campaigns until just before Gettysburg. Taken in by the myths, I spent one Spring bicycling through the Virginia battlefields - - The Seven Days, Five Farms, Chancellorsville, Fredericksburg, and more - - picturing my brave, young great-grandfather charging headlong, time and time again, into carpets of shrapnel and Yankee rifle fire. The truth about his army career, however, was quite available in the Confederate archives housed in The Library of Virginia, where a little research revealed enough of his war record to disprove the lore and to give clues to his actual service. With more digging I uncovered the facts of his wartime record which were known to Irene and her siblings. Chillie's children placed great value and took enormous pride in their father's role in the "War Between the States." Although his combat experience was not nearly as extensive as succeeding generations have believed, it was respectable enough for his immediate family.

In June, 1864, six months before Nanaire's and Chillie's wedding, his Danville unit, Captain Kirkwood Otey's Company, was called to defend an important railroad bridge near South Boston, Virginia some forty miles east. In the Battle of Staunton River Bridge, Chillie, as a second lieutenant, stood with his men, their backs against the river with retreat no option, and repulsed four frontal assaults by a Union cavalry force four times greater in number.* Chillie spent the first months of his marriage as a first

---

*Admittedly, I share my relatives' need to believe Chillie had a respectable war record. The regimental musters in the Confederate archives prove Chillie left the 11th Virginia early in the war and returned to Lynchburg. I got my first clue concerning Chillie's activities in Nancy Astor's unpublished memoir. She wrote that Nanaire pasted a newspaper report of the Battle of Staunton River Bridge in a family scrapbook and noted above the clipping, "Your father, C.D. Langhorne, was in this battle." I know that Otey's company

lieutenant in Company A of the 21st Virginia Infantry, a part of the Confederate army in retreat from Petersburg to Appomattox, but Confederate officers had more on their minds than maintaining muster roles and no record exists to document his service.

Chillie's military experiences were impressive compared to those of his father. At the outbreak of the war, John Scaisbrooke Langhorne, a miller, must have been an admired citizen because he was elected a captain in Lynchburg's Wise Troop. According to his adjutant, Charles M. Blackford, a Lynchburg lawyer, John fought bravely at the Battle of First Manassas. Blackford also wrote, "Captain Langhorne . . . knew nothing of details or how to look after the thousand wants which arise and must be met when a hundred men are leaving home under such circumstances. . . ."

John was noted for a flashing temper, which got him into a row with his superior officer. Apparently, a colonel said something to John he did not like, and John, forgetting he was in the army and a subordinate, replied inappropriately. In a court-martial proceeding, John was reprimanded for conduct unbefitting an officer, but was not cashiered. Nevertheless, he resigned his commission and returned to Lynchburg. He re-enlisted in May, 1864 as a private in Booker's Regiment of Virginia Reserves, but was immediately detached from the unit to continue milling.

With a partner, John had bought the family mill from his father's estate in 1858 for $50,000, and renamed it the Lynchburg Milling Company. It was the second largest milling firm in Virginia, and sold flour under the brand names of Indian Maid Meal and Old Virginia Water Meal. Although John owned one of Lynchburg's major businesses, he never owned his own home, and moved his family in and out of a succession of rented houses.[*] After the war,

---

fought in the Battle of Staunton River Bridge because Danville's Town Council commended it, and gave a burial plot in the municipal cemetery to the family of Thomas Wilkerson, the only Danville man killed. Although I have no concrete evidence that Chillie actually was in the field that day with his company, I think Nanaire's statement is proof enough.

[*]Chillie spent much of his childhood at Point of Honor, a large, brick house that John rented. It has been restored and still dominates a steep bluff overlooking the James River.

The Gibson Girl

John was the target of criticism from his Lynchburg neighbors when, in their opinion, he became too friendly with the Yankees while waging a campaign to be appointed the town's postmaster. He even went into debt to buy a silver tea service to properly entertain his northern masters. John's financial troubles intensified when he lost a great deal of money speculating on a wheat shipment to New York. He was wiped out completely by the James River's Great Flood of 1877.

The basis of ante-bellum aristocracy was land ownership, and as millers, or people "in trade," Chillie's Langhorne family branch did not belong to the upper echelon of Southern society. Nevertheless, more than one of my relatives valiantly has attempted to place the Langhornes with the Southern elite. Irene, and in particular, Nannie, were loudest about the superior qualities of their Langhorne blood, although both attributed the family's stubby, square hands to the Langhorne side, and acknowledged the looks in the family were inherited from the Keenes. Irene's great store of self-confidence was rooted in the belief she was as good as anyone else because her background was superb and second to no other. She had a passionate love of Virginia and believed her family's persistent progress through the generations was interrupted only temporarily by the Civil War. She took great pride in her father's financial success, seeing him as a flesh-and-blood illustration of survival and prosperity in a land and in a time when most others had failed to recover from the Civil War.

Pride in family is a matter of perspective anyway, and I am sure there are many people not as impressed with the Langhornes and their marriages as Irene was. One of them, Mrs. William Meade Lewis, a descendent of Meriwether Lewis, when asked her relationship to Lady Astor, was quite outspoken, declaring, "The Lewises were making history when the Langhornes were making moonshine and the Astors were skinning rabbits."

Chillie's mother, Sarah, whom Irene described as "one of those strong-minded Dabneys, conceited and bumptious," was the daughter of Chiswell Dabney, the most important influence on young Chillie. He was a vibrant, dignified man, a successful lawyer who owned a handsome estate on the heights above the James River directly to the north of Lynchburg. Whenever he could,

Chillie hiked across the covered bridge that spanned the James and trudged up the steep bluff to enter his grandfather's world, a picturebook plantation with its large, brick manor house surrounded by dependencies, slave quarters, and long, low fields.* At the Dabney plantation Chillie experienced the elegance and grandiosity of the South's Cavalier culture, and learned the rigorous code of Southern males, a morality based on gallantry, honor, courage, and devotion to women. There he got a strong taste of life as he thought it should be lived, a heritage the war had seized from him, and one he was determined to take back.

To make sure Chillie had a playmate, his grandfather bought him one when he was six, recording his gift in the books of the courthouse, "For and in consideration of the natural love and affection I bear to my grandson Chiswell Dabney Langhorne I have given and delivered to him one negro boy named Henry, January 1, 1849." Pouring through the deedbooks in various Virginia courthouses I was continually shocked by the impersonal and detached recordings of purchases and sales of human beings alongside notations of land transactions and miscellaneous legal items. The discovery that my great-grandfather, a man my father knew when he was in college, actually owned a slave was particularly unnerving.**

---

*The house Chiswell Dabney built still stands on its hill, surrounded by fast food restaurants and ribbons of concrete near the intersection of Route 29 and the 29 bypass north of Lynchburg in what is now Madison Heights. It is known as the Moorman place after a man who subsequently purchased it. During the Civil War the infant daughter of the famed Confederate cavalry commander, J.E.B. Stuart, a Dabney cousin, died in Chillie's grandparents' house when she and her mother visited there.

**The deedbooks in the courthouse in Chatham, Virginia, the seat of Pittsylvania County, record Colonel Keene's purchases of slaves from estates of his neighbors, one entry in 1856 for "the Negro woman Matilda" and her five children - - price, $200.

The South's agricultural system was founded on debt; as long as a man held slaves and land he possessed the collateral to borrow money. Many masters avoided the unpleasant and sometimes guilt-ridden act of selling slaves during their lifetime, and built up debt which would be settled after death by their estates' sale of human assets.

Some realities of slavery are rarely discussed in Virginia and local

The Gibson Girl

Chillie was one of thousands of Confederate soldiers who expected to regroup further south to continue the futile fight after Lee's retreat from Petersburg. Fortunately, the war ended at Appomattox Courthouse, eighty miles north of Danville, and he returned to Cottage Hill and Nanaire. Danville was in chaos. As soon as the surrender was announced, widespread looting of warehouses and stores began. Fourteen lives were lost when someone blew up the Arsenal. Terror, dismay, and confusion reigned until an advance guard of the Union Army restored order and discipline. Three hundred pickets encircled the town to keep Federal stragglers out and citizens in. Under martial law Confederate soldiers without official pardons were subject to immediate arrest, but were allowed to wear their uniforms if all insignia were stripped from them. The citizenry feared reprisals by the occupation troops because 1300 Federal prisoners had perished from starvation, exposure, and sickness during the eighteen months the six Danville prisons had been in use.

After order was restored, the young couple moved to Danville because the Keenes were destitute. Chillie could offer his in-laws little help. With few tools and no slaves or livestock, crops could not be planted. If there had been a place for Chillie in his father's milling business, the newlyweds probably would have traveled north to Lynchburg to begin their life together. John apparently had nothing to offer them, so they faced the challenge of

---

histories. During the four years prior to the Civil War farming in Virginia was not profitable for most landholders because the soil had played out and over the generations large plantations had been divided up again and again among heirs, the resulting fragments too small to be economical. However, in the Cotton States of the Deep South, rich loam and huge tracts made slave labor very profitable. From Richmond, Virginia, the largest slave market in the Upper South, the many surplus slaves from Virginia and Maryland passed through the hands of traders and auctioneers and were shipped to New Orleans and to other markets in the cotton belt. Virginians do not admit to their forebears "growing slaves" for sale. Yet the economic benefit was huge - - and irresistible. A white artisan in ante-bellum Virginia was paid $1.00 a day. Therefore, a field slave sold in Richmond's market for $1700 had the same economic value as five years of skilled labor by a bricklayer, stonemason, or carpenter.

survival in Nanaire's hometown. Perhaps Chillie believed business contacts resulting from his marriage to the daughter of one of Danville's leading citizens would help him to get started.

Danville was fortunate. The town had been a hotbed of secessionist sentiment, the chief supply depot for the Confederacy, and the site of prison camps that rivaled the infamous Andersonville, Georgia complex in squalor and privation. The Union forces had every justification for burning the town down. Instead, Federal authorities went out of their way to display courtesy during the occupation. They showed compassion and comradeship to a population rendered destitute by the war. Although Nanaire and Chillie reared their children against a background of ante-bellum and Confederate nostalgia, they never taught them vindictiveness against the former enemy. The hate and bitterness the Langhornes could have carried with them for the rest of their lives were swept away by the generous and fair treatment they and the community received from their conquerors.

After the war the economy of the South was completely shut down. Factories were idle, stores were empty, credit was hard to get, and the currency worthless. Chillie barely was able to provide a living for the two of them, and their existence was literally hand-to-mouth. Chillie, the inheritor of family names respected throughout the state, the son of a reputable businessman, and the grandson of a prominent lawyer and large landowner, was reduced to night-clerking in a local hotel and working in a clothing store. Nanaire, raised on a large plantation, a lovely young belle, the daughter of an important politician and lawyer, now had the grave responsibility of stretching a few dollars far enough so they would not go hungry.

Poverty did not stand in the way of having children, however, and the Langhorne family got off to a fairly fast start with the arrival of Lizzie in 1866 just eleven months after Chillie's return from the army. Two years later Keene was born. After the first five or six years of their extremely meager existence in Danville, Chillie gradually began to get on his feet. He worked hard and took any menial job, willing to try anything to support his family. He sold pianos. He purchased, on credit, a wagon and a mule and loaded up a sample piano a St. Louis firm sent him to travel Danville and its

The Gibson Girl

adjacent counties. He could not play a note, but memorized a chord Nanaire taught him. When asked to demonstrate the instrument, he said, "I'd be glad to play more for you, Madam, but I recently sprained my wrist and the doctor has forbidden me to play. But the tone of the piano is what counts! Just listen!" In Danville's courthouse records an entry gives details of his sale of a pianoforte "with stool and cover" for $250 to a Mr. Dugger who agreed to pay $125 of the purchase price in three months, and the rest in six months.

Danville's major industry was tobacco. Having learned the intricacies of trading in the staple, Chillie became a dealer. He used borrowed money to buy at what he hoped was a good price, warehoused his inventory, and with luck sold at a profit when and if the market turned stronger. The only documentation of his tobacco dealing I uncovered is an entry in a courthouse register detailing his limited partnership with a R.D. Fitzpatrick for the "purpose of transacting and carrying on a general auction and commission business in the Town of Danville, under the name of C.D. Langhorne." As an auctioneer Chillie found a way to put more spark into the process of selling tobacco. He is credited with inventing the "gobble-gobble" style of auctioning that became a fixture at all tobacco markets, and has been heard by the many who remember the American Tobacco Company's radio and television advertisements.

Because the partnership traded under his name, he probably put up most of its capital of $1600, a substantial amount in those days. He may have borrowed the money, or he could have accumulated it from business dealings. A good bet is some of the money was poker winnings. Throughout his life Chillie was known as an excellent poker player. One story dates back to these Danville days when he came home to Nanaire early one morning with tobacco juice spattered all over his shirtfront. Nanaire, shocked by his slovenly appearance, demanded to know what he had been up to. Chillie's responded, "I was playing poker with my friends and I did not want to turn my back to them."

After a career in the securities markets and as an avid card player I know luck and good fortune do not always run true. It was an extremely difficult time for Nanaire, because the family's security one day would appear to be bright when Chillie's risk-taking paid off, and dismal when he suffered losses. With feast and famine as constant guests it was a proud and hopeful moment for the Langhornes when, in the year of Irene's birth, Chillie made the downpayment on their Main Street house.

CHAPTER THREE

THE FAMILY DRAMA

By the time Irene was old enough for memories the family's days of hardship were over. She remembered, however, the pain of wearing shoes too tight for her, shoes from an oddly assorted batch Chillie purchased at a bargain price because nobody else wanted them. She also remembered being upset when she had no hat to wear to church because there was no money for such luxuries. Grandma Keene fashioned one for her out of a palm leaf fan and a bit of pink ribbon.* Nevertheless, the Langhorne children were deprived of little. Food was simple, but plentiful. The Main Street lot was large enough for a vegetable garden and a cow, chickens and maybe a pig. They were well clothed because Nanaire was an excellent seamstress, and had servants to help her. Former slaves like Mammy Harriet, "a wonderful old lady with lovely silver hair, no kinks," had to be content to stay on for pitiful wages and leftovers they could take home to their own families.

Although Irene did not make an issue of the family's lean years, her sister, Nannie, enjoyed exaggerating her humble beginnings - - perhaps because she was married to one of the world's richest men. She talked of plain suppers at home with no meat, only "corn bread and eggs, raw tomatoes, wheaten biscuits and molasses." Nannie was born six years after Irene, and by the time Nannie was able to recall, the Langhornes were eating very well.**

---

*Grandma Keene lived in Danville when Irene was a small girl. Irene remembered the candy pulls at her house, and Hannah and Tom, "two of her darkies who made everything bright and gay." Her grandmother had a little china dog on her mantelpiece which Irene coveted "above all things in the world." Irene finally was given the dog when she was in her thirties. She, in turn, gave it to her daughter, Babs.

**Irene described her father as a great gourmand, planning the menus and grocery shopping - - as was the custom for husbands to do in those days. Irene recalled the basement of their Richmond home "covered with terrapin." She wrote, "We ate terrapin as people eat hash." After breakfast, Chillie's habit

The Family Drama

Nannie could have made a better argument in dramatizing the difficulties of the family's life if she had described their cramped living conditions in Danville. Although the house has undergone numerous renovations, the Langhorne's original floor plan is still evident. The front door of their Main Street cottage opens into a hall which seems wide only because the two bedrooms on the left and the front parlor on the right are small. By the time they left Danville three more children were born - - Harry in 1874, Nancy, or Nannie, in 1879, and Phyllis in 1880 - - so eight people had to share this living space. A narrow stairwell climbed to two closet-like bedrooms under the sloped roof where the youngest children slept. Another set of stairs went to the basement, where the kitchen, dining room, and storerooms were located. Because the kitchen was the territory of servants and the parlor in Victorian days was the show room, reserved for special occasions and guests, the only area where the family could gather together on a daily basis was in the hallway. Irene thought it completely normal to share a small bedroom with at least two other siblings. The only observation she made about her house was to compare its shutters to those of her cousin, Jenny Belle Bethel, who lived across the street in a commodious, elegant house. "It had inside shutters. Ours were outside. That impressed me much."

Irene's first memory of her mother was one Christmas Eve after she had been put to bed trembling with excitement. With all but one eye under the covers, she watched her mother tiptoe into the room, her arms full of mysterious bundles. Behind Nanaire was someone else carrying a doll's house. The two of them arranged the presents, quietly exited the room, and Irene fell asleep. "The next morning I found the most beautiful doll's house in the world, with the father, mother, and children all dressed up by her [Nanaire]. To cap the climax, there was an old colored mammy." Irene marveled that her mother had the excess energy to create such a wonderful gift. "How had she had time? I believe there was nothing she couldn't do." To her, Nanaire was full of vitality and youth. "Think

---

was to discuss at length the food for the day. He concocted his own recipe for sherry garlic sauce which he put into soups and vegetables, and directed great attention and ceremony to the making of cherry bounces and mint juleps.

The Gibson Girl

how young she was, at the time only twenty-nine! . . . I also remember when the doctor came one day and found mother and Aunt Lou, father's youngest sister, on roller skates. Evidently the child the doctor had been summoned for couldn't have been very ill!"

Irene recalled parties at their house when friends crowded into the small parlor to sing and laugh. Babies were placed in one corner, swathed in mosquito netting, "kicking, laughing, crying." Nanaire was musical and played the organ at church. "She had a lovely voice, as did father, and I'm sure they added to every event in town." Nanaire performed in local musicales, one of which in 1878 was described by the Danville *Register*. It was reported that an appreciative audience attended the opening night's performance at the Odd Fellows Hall, and Nanaire, singing "Solo, Contralto," rendered Luther's "In Night's Still Calm." According to the local music critic, " . . . she performed her part well."

Parties were glorious early memories for Irene. One of her friends, Janie Smith, was the granddaughter of the Sutherlands, the richest family in town, whose house Jefferson Davis had requisitioned on his flight from Richmond in 1865. On its front lawn stood a magnificent play house where Janie gave birthday parties to which Irene was invited. "To go to her parties was Heaven." One year, Mammy Harriet picked Irene up before the party was over and before Irene had eaten her ice cream, so they wrapped it in a handkerchief. "By the time we got home it was all melted. But I was glad to have gone to the party."

Irene revealed her life-long love of attention in her description of a Sunday School Christmas party. To receive her gift, she had to walk down to a Christmas tree at the front of the room with everyone's eyes upon her. " . . . I recall my mingled fright and enchantment when my name was called and I walked down the aisle, which seemed to be a mile long, to get my present, a china doll, her body stuffed with sawdust." To Irene at the time, the promenade down that Sunday School aisle was "the most thrilling moment of my life."

By the late 1870s the remnants of the South's defeat were giving way to industrial expansion, commercial building, and a sense of hope. National demand for tobacco products soared and

The Family Drama

brought prosperity to Danville, the leaf market for south-central Virginia and the mid-counties of North Carolina. Money began to flow into the economy and the town's citizens built houses on lots purchased from residential land speculators who bought up areas surrounding the central commercial district. Chillie ventured into this speculative spree in a small way, buying housing lots from large speculators, usually in partnership with one or two others because of his limited resources. Already he had gained a measure of respect in the community by being elected as a trustee of Danville's Mechanic's Building and Loan Association. But, financially he was floundering, still selling pianos while many of his contemporaries were enjoying a standard of success that continued to elude him.

Chillie realized his haphazard, entrepreneurial approach to earning a living in Danville was getting him nowhere. He began to cast around for stable, salaried employment. He traveled to Richmond and was offered a job as superintendent of the state penitentiary, which he turned down. On his visit there he began to see the state capital - - the target of heavy amounts of Northern investment, a railroad hub, and the center of cigar and cigarette manufacturing - - as a mecca of opportunity. William Henry, a successful Richmond tobacco man, and, according to Irene, "long anxious to have Father join him," talked Chillie into working for him as a tobacco dealer. The family packed up their belongings in late 1881 and moved in with the Henrys for six months while Chillie started work at 107 South Twelfth Street in Shockoe Bottom, the commercial center of the city. Their first rental - - the first of three - - was at 5 South Third Street, where they stayed for six months. The house proved too small, and they moved to 311 East Main Street. There a son, William Henry, or Buck, was born in November, 1882, named for Chillie's partner.

The adjustment was difficult for Nanaire. Stripped of her hometown security, she was faced with having to make a succession of rented houses home for her large brood. She had to find a place for herself in a community not noted for welcoming strangers, however interesting and charming they might be. Compounding the family's difficulties was Chillie's continued lack of success. He had left Danville with the highest hopes but found the tobacco business in Richmond intensely competitive. His

The Gibson Girl

extroverted nature was of little use there because the staple sold solely on price, not personality. Only with money could he protect his wife and children from the harsh environment in which he placed them, and so far, there was little of that. The Langhornes' only security was Chillie's potential to do well.

Just a few dollars of income separated the Langhornes from the rude existence of the hordes of immigrants - - the Irish, Germans, and Italians - - who had recently swarmed to Richmond, settling in crowded tenements in the hollows and on the edges of ravines below the city's hills. Richmond had recovered from the economic depression of the early 1870s. Sprawling new brick warehouses, factories and mills had grown from the ruins of the devastating fire of 1865, when the Confederate army torched supplies so they would not fall into the hands of the approaching Union army.

Richmond's more privileged citizens lived above the factories and the slums on tree-lined streets and cobblestoned avenues, protected from the din and stench of the industrial ghettos. But even in the best areas of the city there was a frayed, rundown look. A few expensive residences had been built by the handful of local men who had found success in recent years, but, by and large, Richmond families had not been beneficiaries of what progress had taken place since the war. Most were scraping along financially, valiantly trying to keep up appearances. Railroads and new factories were being built by northern capital, and most of the money made in the South went into bank accounts in New York, Boston, and Philadelphia. A depressed region with low labor costs and excellent natural resources, the South was exploited by outsiders.

Church Hill to the east, the site of St. John's Church, where Patrick Henry gave his "Give me liberty, or give me death" speech, was no longer the choice residential area. Most Richmonders of any means long since had moved westward, past the courthouse and the magnificent Capitol designed by Thomas Jefferson, to a narrow ribbon of streets three miles in length stretching from Capitol Square toward Lombardy Street. Both Main Street and Grove Avenue were respectable, but Franklin and Grace were the most desirable west-end streets: The former, with its tall linden trees

The Family Drama

gracefully arching above elegant Victorian facades and iron verandahs, was the preferred address.

The Langhornes' provincialism was poor preparation for the deplorable living conditions they encountered in Richmond. Danville might have been a backwater, country town in comparison to the relatively cosmopolitan capital, but at least it had the airiness of open space. People were not clustered tightly together as in Richmond, the victims of inadequate sanitation facilities and appallingly low standards of hygiene. Even for the privileged in the finest neighborhoods, everyday life was stained by discomfort. In spite of the romantic aura associated with this period in our country's history, a hundred or more years ago life in any American city was very uncomfortable, even for the rich - - and it could be deadly.

Richmond was one of the South's largest cities with a population density greater in 1882 than in 1997. Its 65,000 people were packed into boundaries much smaller than today's. City mains pumped to the better parts of town water often so thick with mud that alum had to be sprinkled in bathtubs and sinks to clear them. Backyard wells a few paces away from outdoor privies were the prevailing source for water for most Richmonders. In the Shockoe Slip area at the base of the city's hills where Chillie worked during his first years in Richmond, the streets were open sewers. The stench on a hot, summer's day was overwhelming. Vacant lots throughout the city were repositories for garbage and offal. There was no central, controlled abattoir, and the slaughtering process at neighborhood meat markets spawned waves of flies and foul odors. Horse dung caked the streets, and coal dust filled the air, blackening lungs and buildings. Every surface was covered with its greasy film.

Housewives and servants struggled to keep homes clean. The task was almost impossible because dirt swirled up from bare, ragged lawns, unpaved side streets, and avenues which were watered down only occasionally. The oppressive summer heat was sometimes unbearable. Relief from open, screenless windows and cross-drafts was spoiled by attacking insects. Although mothers tried to protect their children from disease by stringing around their necks asafetida bags full of acrid smelling herbs, little could be done

The Gibson Girl

to combat the recurrent epidemics of typhoid, scarlet fever, influenza, and dysentery. Tobacco juice crusted sidewalks and covered floors and walls in commercial buildings. Public places were particularly objectionable. No responsible, loving husband and father wanted his wife and children to be subjected to contact with the ragged hordes.

But concerns over living conditions and health and financial worries were all problems for adults, not for an eight-year-old child whose recollections by no means included the ordeal of city life, but continued to center primarily on the things that interested her the most - - clothes, her appearance, friends, and adventures. Richmond was not a strange place for Irene, because the year before the family's move she journeyed from Danville to spend a long visit with the William Henrys. Mrs. Henry, or Beppie, whom Irene described as "a lovely person, very delicate, and she loved me," enjoyed having her stay with them on Linden Row, a set of stately and almost identical row houses on Franklin Street. Irene remembered her trip to Richmond. Her parents were afraid to have her sleep alone on the train from Danville, so they deposited her in a lower berth with "old Mr. Ayres." In the early morning hours, Irene awoke to find herself ensnared in his beard.* At the Henrys, their black maid, Mahalie, took Irene in hand. Irene remembered she wore a hooped skirt, long after that fashion was out of style. Irene pleaded for her own hooped skirt, and Mahalie made her one.

The only clue to Chillie's business efforts during the first three years in Richmond is that he is listed in the city directory as a tobacco dealer with an office on 12th Street. The leaf tobacco business was seasonal, and he must have taken on other work to supplement his earnings. His big opportunity finally arrived in 1885. A number of versions describes this most momentous event in the Langhorne family. A popular rendition pictures Colonel William Douglas, a railroad contractor who had been a chief engineer in the Confederate army, being impressed with Chillie's skill in supervising a gang of black workmen who appeared to like Chillie and easily

---

*Obviously, Irene's parents saw no risk in her sleeping in the same bed with an adult; nor did Irene when she wrote her short childhood memoir in 1943. Times have changed.

The Family Drama

accepted his authority. Needing someone to supervise his work crews, Colonel Douglas took Chillie on. One story has Chillie running into Douglas and pleading for a job. Still another version is Douglas asking Chillie to go on a business trip with him to entertain some railroad men. Chillie's role was to make the party a success, and to get the men in a good mood so they would sign a contract for a job Douglas was trying to land.

Irene recalled that Colonel Douglas was a close friend of her father, and for a long time had been trying to get Chillie to join him in the railroad contracting business. She was twelve when Chillie agreed, and she remembered the day vividly. Her father ran up the front steps to Nanaire and said, " 'Nannie. I'm going in with Colonel Douglas . . . and I think till it's all settled, I'll ship you all off to Mechum's River [To stay with Cousin Charlie Price].' Hastily the packing was accomplished, even the billy goats were made ready, and the van was at the door when father returned suddenly and said, ' I've taken a house on Grace Street.' " Everything was unpacked, and the family stayed in Richmond.

Chillie knew nothing of engineering, but his cousin and first partner, Stanhope Bolling, was a civil engineer. Within months the two men became sub-contractors to Colonel Douglas, delivering rock, fill, and cement to construction sites. It was a boom time for railroad construction in Pennsylvania, West Virginia, and Virginia because competing lines were being consolidated. The growth in coal and iron business required the construction of spur roads from mines to main trunks. Later on, Chillie with another partner, Major W.J. Wharton, did contracting work for the Baltimore & Ohio in the Philadelphia area. A B&O superintendent described the two men as being "not grasping" and "ask all" types, but rather "gentlemen" and "friends."

Success for Chillie was almost immediate, and in 1886 he could afford to purchase 101 West Grace Street, a spacious house on the southwest corner of Grace and Adams Streets. Included in the purchase were three adjacent lots - - total price, $22,000. Three years later he sold one of the lots for $7600. The house burned in the 1940s, having passed through the hands of a number of owners. It was remodeled substantially before 1906 to accommodate the Hygeia hospital.

The Gibson Girl

101 West Grace Street needed extensive renovation, the most important improvement for the Langhornes being a bathroom, which was fully equipped with running water, a commode, and a zinc-lined tub. In the 1880s, indoor plumbing had become a widespread convenience for people of means, and to have one upstairs for the large family's use was a wonderful luxury. A basement furnace room provided heat in the winter. Warm air rose through ducts into the rooms on both floors, a comfort the Langhornes had not enjoyed in Danville. Electricity was new, but not fully trusted. Chillie likely retained the gas fixtures when electrical outlets were installed. It is doubtful they had window screens. Vacuum cleaners had not been invented so Nanaire's battle with dust and dirt was constant.

Irene saw 101 West Grace as a lovely house with a beautiful garden on one side and five enormous oak trees. "It was a large, square brick house with a big hall running through the center, double parlors on one side, sitting room on the other and a dining room in back. Above, the bedrooms were all very attractive. Of course, we had a lot of doubling up. Lizzie was mad when I had to room with her, though I don't believe I was too inquisitive. But she was then grown, going to be married soon, and I reckon wanted to be left alone."

She described how the house was decorated. "The front parlor furnishings were most fashionable. Mother always kept up with everything. In those days people had over their mantelpieces lambrequins, made of velvet with deep fringe and put on a board which rested on top of the mantelpiece. Over each mantel in the front and back parlor was a huge mirror. In every parlor there was always kind of a loveseat, but not what is called a loveseat now. Ours was shaped like the letter S, evidently so that lovers could look in each other's eyes. Tea tables came into fashion, stationary and fully equipped for tea, and at the right of the tea table, a two-paneled screen, the frame covered in plush with silk shirred at the back of each panel. Also on each panel were two narrow shelves on which saucers were placed, while the cups dangled from hooks above. Each cup and saucer was of a different color. Nearby on a table shaped like a three-pieced clover rested the tea kettle and other paraphernalia for tea. This was the fashion of the time, but we never had tea! The reason - - we had dinner at three and supper at eight - - and everyone was out all afternoon."

According to Mary Wingfield Scott in her book, *Old Richmond Neighborhoods,* Grace Street was "about stolidity and industriousness" in contrast to Franklin Street, which was "about expense and pretension." There was a sameness to the Grace Street houses which, though substantial, sat close together with no expanses of front lawn and trees to soften the dark and morose-looking brick facades. The Langhornes' neighborhood may have lacked architectural charm, yet it possessed a small-town intimacy where everyone knew each other. Neighbors kept in touch with sidewalk meetings and notes delivered up and down the street by servants. Vendors with their carts and wagons selling all manner of goods and services plied the streets. Wild duck and sora hung in bunches from their covered wagons. Men knocked on doors, offering, for a price, to sharpen knives or clean chimneys. At two o'clock husbands came home by horse and buggy to eat their big meal of the day. A nap usually followed. While the men ate and slept, their horses patiently stood by front gates, tethered with leather straps attached to iron weights. After school, boys and girls safely played in the streets, their games interrupted by the occasional wagon.

Swarms of children filled the streets in the early evenings, lost in the rhythms of their games of hop-scotch and jump-rope as harried mothers called for them to come in and wash for supper. Fathers arrived from their offices, greeted by panting dogs and the soft odor of baking bread mixed with the stale smell of goats and sweating children well in need of their evening baths. There was no traffic noise in the evenings or at night. In summer, people sat on their front porches to escape the heat of their darkened rooms inside, talking to their next door neighbors and watching the street activity. The day on Grace Street ended with the arrival of the lamplighter, who, with his ladder or climbing stirrup, ignited the gasposts that stood on every corner.

In Irene's childhood days there were no soda fountains, no neighborhood hangouts, no Girl Scouts or other organized activities for children. Their fun was roaming through streets and yards searching for amusement and mischief. A big excitement was

The Gibson Girl

having a penny to buy licorice root, slippery elm, or rock candy at Mr. Fitzgerald's grocery store on Main Street. "They say he was so stingy that he'd bite a grain of corn in two to make the scales weigh properly," Irene recalled. "But oh! that barrel of sour cucumbers into which he would delve and then draw out a big cucumber which we'd wrap around with brown paper. Often when we got to the bottom, we'd nibble some of the brown paper, not wishing to lose any of the pickle."

Irene and her friends were not above escapades that could have gotten them into serious trouble. "Above . . . [the] store was the Masons' Hall. We broke into it one day, put on their regalia and feathered hats, and marched around the room, but were unable to solve any of their secrets. I've often wondered had they found us what they'd done with us. We were free lances and we got away with it." The children also broke into neighborhood houses. "Hide and seek was more fun. We used to play in a house on Fifth Street and Main where Poe [Edgar Allen] lived. On one occasion we got into Mr. William Haxall's house. I remember his beautiful silver. We went where angels feared to tread but they were all friends."

Each year the Langhorne children impatiently waited for the traveling circus. "One spring the circus came to town and only a field between it and us. It is needless to tell you that Harry and I loved peeking in and at one time contemplated joining up, but I suppose all children have done that. When we attended the circus we took with us a little box in which was a stout pair of scissors to cut our way out in case the tent fell. This a friend told us was the proper thing to do. When Mother saw the box, she was aghast and considered not letting us go. But we did."

The most coveted possession for any boy or girl was a billy goat. There were so many goats in the neighborhood that one day ten of them climbed to the upper back porch of the Langhornes' house and ate all the children's school books. Chillie knew an inmate at the state penitentiary who built a two-seated wagon which the Langhornes' two goats pulled all over town. "He was a wonderful provider - - my Pa. Always we had what everyone else had."

When one of the goats was sick, Lizzie and Keene took it upstairs to a bedroom. Irene found them giving it an enema, tattled,

The Family Drama

and they were severely punished. Anatomical curiosity was not confined to pets. "A great game was playing mother and children. Annie Lee was the mother - - and I think she knew little about babies and whence they came. She stuffed a pillow under her dress, wanting to be in a family way. We were very much excited. We were clean-minded children. It was an innocent game."

Nanaire and Chillie enrolled the children in what Irene regarded as the "best schools." Lizzie went to Mr. Merrill's, and Keene to Mr. Knolly's. In her memoir, Irene said she and Harry first entered school at 110 Third Street. Then, Harry went to Mrs. Annie Colston Camm's school for boys, and Irene attended Mrs. Raleigh Colston's school for young ladies at 710 East Grace Street. From Mrs. Colston's school she went to a boarding and day school run by Miss Augusta T. Daniel. Her texts were Mrs. Magill's History of Virginia, Westlake's 2000 Practice Words, and The Scholar's Companion, but in her memoirs she made no comment on her studies. Instead, she chose to recall what was in the lunch basket the Langhornes' cook handed her when she left each morning for school. "I can see the basket now and smell the beaten biscuits with ham in the middle, cake and fruit, all pretty well mixed by the time we got to school."

Irene's lifelong friend and constant girlhood companion was Bessie Martin, whom Irene first noticed skating at school recess, and was struck by how pretty she was. Her other close friend was Emma Barksdale. Both girls lived in beautiful, large houses on Franklin Street with enormous gardens. "Most of the time she [Emma] wore a Scottish chief's dress which I thought too beautiful for words. Her party was the first one I went to in Richmond. It was magnificent. Spun candy in pyramids of nougat, Mrs. Barksdale, the beautiful music, bright lights - - never will a party again seem so magnificent."

Two older girls who dressed flashily intrigued Irene. "There were two cut-ups in Richmond, young Mamie Hayes and Tittey Thomas. They were good girls but considered a little gay. To us they were wonderful. I remember their legs well. The tops of their boots were scalloped, with tassels in front. How I longed for fat legs! So much so that at the age of fourteen I got Mammy Liza Pratt to sew cotton wool in my stockings to give me calves. The

The Gibson Girl

tops of my stockings were colored, generally striped. When I walked up Franklin Street, Legh Page,* with whom I was desperately in love and whom I wanted to impress, passed me by and murmured, 'The calf's in the wrong place.' My stockings had twisted! I gave up then and continued with skinny legs, of which I am now proud."**

Grandma Keene and both Langhorne grandparents spent a great deal of time with Irene's family. Irene was fond of Mary Anne Keene and observed her closely, amazed her grandmother's black maid spent so many hours brushing her mistress's hair. "Old ladies do queer things. Grandma Keene had a great collection of what at that time were called advertising cards, very pretty, and what pleased me most was that those advertising cologne were soaked in it. I think that gave me my weakness for perfume." Irene's feelings toward Sarah Langhorne were not at all generous, believing the old woman was jealous of Nanaire because she had stolen her beautiful son. When Irene told Chillie her theory later in life, he became very

---

*Irene said Legh Page was her first love. For years he was the Langhorne family lawyer. He courted, unsucessfully, three of the Langhorne sisters and died a bachelor.

**Two of Irene's anecdotes I find to be pathetic. At 101 West Grace Street the Langhornes had a black maid named Mattie. Although Irene said she knew little about such things then, she knew there was something wrong with Mattie. "One day Mother came rushing upstairs and said to someone, 'Mattie is having a baby!' Such confusion and busying around you can't imagine. The doctor arrived and into the world came a bouncing mulatto baby. Mattie was not married, but I found out later on that she had said, 'Miss Nannie, 'twas a drummer boy who came up to Mechum's River when we was there and he ruint me." I'm sure the right thing was done by us, but her departure was felt by everybody. I don't remember that she ever returned, and I don't know what became of the little drummer boy."

And the story about an unfortunate neighbor: "There was a very rich lady called Mrs. Caldwell. She had an erratic daughter, a poor little humpback called Co. Co got it into her head that her mother loved me better than she. On one occasion I found Co patting our horse, Kate, which most of the time was in front of the house hitched to the buggy. And this is what I heard. 'I'm prettier than Irene. And don't you love me more?' I kept clear of Co most of the time after that."

upset and said, "Irene, you're crazy!" Chillie's father was sick and feeble, and the entire family doted on him. Irene and Harry made potato chips for him, and Nanaire read to her father-in-law after his eyesight failed. Irene recalled Chillie coming home tired from a trip to Baltimore, and his father asked him what he had been doing. Chillie answered, "Oh Pa, I'll tell you tomorrow. I'm very tired." The old man was visibly hurt. Nanaire said, "Dab, tell him now. He's so interested. He's been waiting so long." Irene believed she inherited her patience from her grandfather Langhorne.

Only two accounts describe Langhorne family life when Irene was a girl in Danville and Richmond, her own memoirs and Nannie's. Neither offer any hint of family tension or unhappiness. Irene ended her eighteen pages after covering her life up to the age of fourteen. Nannie continued her narrative beyond childhood, to Mirador, where the family moved permanently when she was eighteen. Nannie's recollections, together with those of Lizzie's children, my father, and family friends who often stayed at Mirador, detail the years after Irene was married and gone. They weave a romantic tale of magnolias, black servants and mint-juleps, an idyllic world full of content children looked over by a strong, yet sweet mother, and a loud and boisterous, but benevolent, father.

My inclination at first was to accept the altogether pleasant childhood picture painted by women whose memories obviously were selective. Families, however, do not work so perfectly, and knowing how the lives of the Langhorne children played out, I have had a difficult time swallowing the sometimes saccharin stories my relatives have written and my father told me as I grew up. It strikes me that all of their memories revolve around Chillie. They cast him as the central character in a family drama - - for some Langhorne children, a tragedy - - that was being staged beneath Irene's pleasant, uncomplicated memories of a youth seemingly so placid and protected.

To my father, Chillie was "Umpty," the kindly and benevolent, though gruff, grandparent, the "roly-poly" old gentleman with a white, bushy mustache who dressed flamboyantly in a swallow-tail coat with a vest cinching in his expansive girth, a flower in his lapel and at least two rings on his fingers. The Chillie whom my father remembered had undergone a radical mellowing process in the years since he had been a young father.

In his prime Chillie was a short, muscular man who held himself sharply erect. He was loud and demanding, stubborn and overbearing. He was a martinet who bulled his way through life, "all smiles when he was getting his way, but raising hell when he didn't," according to one granddaughter. Nanaire knew how to handle him. Soft-spoken and gentle, she was a petite, fair-haired woman with huge blue-sky eyes and a trim figure which amazingly regained its shape after each pregnancy. She stood by unruffled while his temper flashed and his moods turned rapidly from utter charm to blustering rage and back again.

Chillie is recalled primarily in a succession of anecdotes which to me have a harsh ring beneath their intended humor. They excuse his behavior, making the point that a man on the move, a successful man, must be forgiven his egotistical arrogance. For example, a favorite family story recalls his behavior in church. If the choir was singing too loudly, he waved his hand and the decibel level dropped; then, when he felt the minister's sermon was going on too long, another slight wave sent the cleric into a quick summation and ending prayer.

Irene described an incident when Chillie became violent. The family was seated in the dining room awaiting the presentation of a fine oyster stew by their butler, Ben, a black man with a feminine voice whom Irene thought was a "fairy" because he used "a slight bit of paint on his cheeks." Ben meekly entered, and announced that he had fallen with the tureen and the stew was no more. Chillie jumped on Ben and threatened to cut off his ears with a carving knife. Nanaire screamed, "Oh Dab, please don't kill him!"

Although Chillie did not slice off Ben's ears, he was not about to be told what to do by his wife - - at least in the company of others. Once at the dinner table Nanaire directed him to swat a bee away or it would sting him. Instead, he rolled up the offending insect in a piece of bread and defiantly ate it. After they moved to Mirador, he built a tennis court, but showed no concern that a tree was left growing on one of the back lines. When his children protested the tree's presence, he haughtily replied, "You tell me that tennis is a game of skill. Very well. Avoid the cherry tree!"

The Family Drama

Irene believed her mother had Chillie "wrapped around her little finger." Nanaire was by no means a passive person. Beneath her acquiescence as the outwardly compliant wife to her cigar-smoking, tobacco-chewing, whiskey-drinking, rough-hewn Victorian autocrat-husband was a resourcefulness and strength which Irene admired. Although Nanaire was a mother who gave to her children the gifts of love and understanding, her ire quickly could be raised if she were not obeyed or shown respect. Stories which describe Chillie's bluntness also portray Nanaire's resilience. One morning at breakfast, after he had been particularly difficult, she announced that in her dreams a young woman had come to her and said, "I am going to marry Mr. Langhorne. What do you think I should wear at my wedding?" Nanaire told Chillie and the children present that her reply to the young woman in the dream was, "Knowing the gentleman as well as I do, I would advise sackcloth and ashes!"

Nanaire was not above going to great lengths to put her husband in his place. Buck's delivery was particularly difficult. She was very ill and was not expected to live. Irene recalled a morning when Chillie was sitting by her bed, afraid his wife would die. Nanaire opened one eye and saw his distressed face. She had no intention of dying, but in a pathetic, wispy voice recited lines from "Abide With Me" and "Hold Thou The Cross Before My Closing Eyes." Chillie burst into tears and Nanaire immensely enjoyed his grief.

Although she was a match for her husband, Nanaire's subordinate family role as wife and mother was not powerful enough and her voice not loud enough to protect those of her children incapable of standing up to their intimidating father. Lizzie could because her nature was as combative and as cantankerous as her father's. She stood toe-to-toe with him her entire life. Lizzie never got along with her father, because she believed her position as eldest child and almost equal partner to her mother entitled her to criticize him freely. Only seventeen years younger than Nanaire, she was more of a sister than a daughter, and an overbearing one at that. Lizzie was quick to find fault in her mother's behavior, thinking Nanaire unsuitably young and frivolous.

The Gibson Girl

Chillie's daughters had wistful, nostalgic memories of him. In their later years they wrote fondly of their girlhoods under his roof. Their reminiscences were tinted with large doses of respect and awe rather than with the deep feelings of love and devotion they reserved for their mother's memory. Somehow, the combination of a demanding, austere father and a mother's love which gave them confidence worked well for the daughters. Bestowed to them were qualities which enabled the girls to fashion lives which were for the most part productive and meaningful.

Nanaire was able to shelter the girls from Chillie's blind need to repress and dominate, and to his credit he did give them a measure of approval and support. However, if any of his sons had left with us their honest emotions of their father, I doubt they would be as charitable. Chillie was a poor father to the boys, burdening them with disapproval, intimidation, and unrelenting pressure. As a result, his sons, in particular Keene and Harry, though attractive, intelligent, and popular, never developed the drive to make their lives more distinct. Chillie professed that he wanted them to go out into the world and form their own lives. In fact, he was incapable of letting them go, unwilling to relinquish his control over them. He solidified their dependence on him with large gifts and regular allowances, and unmercifully scolded them as adults, even taking pleasure in denying them the manly prerogative of drinking whiskey in his presence. One letter he wrote to Buck long after his youngest son was married and a father was particularly belittling. In it he assailed Buck for borrowing and riding another man's horse, a practice Chillie deemed beneath any Langhorne.

Keene, as the eldest and the son from whom Chillie expected the most, was the first to feel his father's wrath. Keene seemed to have made his life work a constant revolt against his father's authority. His teen years were full of low moments, one when he and a friend ran away from their day school in Richmond. Chillie somehow heard the boys had taken the train to Danville, so he followed and tracked them down to their hotel. Early in the morning he knocked at their bedroom door. The boys, thinking it was a waiter, called out, "Bring us two lemonades." Chillie strode into the room, gave each a sound whipping, and brought them home.

Keene's secondary school record was anything but exemplary. Chillie refused to send him to college. Instead, he put Keene to work in his railroad construction business, and sent him out to supervise construction jobs at remote railroad junctions. On one assignment Keene made filial rebellion an expensive affair for his father. After Keene returned to the Richmond office, horrendous bills totaling over a thousand dollars started to arrive by mail. How could he have possibly spent this huge amount of money in a backwater locale that boasted no more than a general store and a post office? As it turned out, a circus had come to this small town, and Keene had taken it upon himself to entertain the entire troupe. Sparing none of his father's money entertaining his new friends, he had sent away to Washington, Richmond, and Baltimore for the finest foods and beverages.

As a young man Keene must have possessed a bright spark which was slowly extinguished by whiskey and tuberculosis. At one point in his life he made a rather sizable wager that he could travel across the country, starting off with only a dollar in his pocket. He won the bet. Phyllis considered him the most amusing man she had ever known. To Irene, Keene was one of the kindest and most lovable boys, but a teaser. She was an easy mark for him because of her admitted gullibility. She described an incident during her childhood days in Danville as one of the saddest moments in her life. The Langhorne children often stood in their yard close to the dusty street to watch the world go by. Country women walked by carrying berries in their sunbonnets to sell at the town's produce stands. "Here comes Irene's mother," Keene teased Irene when one of the ladies, a Mrs. Marshall, passed the Langhorne's house. Irene wrote, ". . . he used to make me feel that she was really my mother, and I used to go away in fear and trembling and weep my heart out."

Chillie is blamed, perhaps unfairly, with causing his son's alcohol addiction by not allowing him to drink socially at home. Whatever the cause, Keene drank heavily to the point he could not manage his own life. He was banished to a farm Chillie bought him in the wilds of Buckingham County, Virginia, where he spent the

The Gibson Girl

rest of his short life. One - - perhaps final - - indignity Keene suffered at his father's hands shortly before his death, but most likely knew nothing of, was Chillie's refusal to treat him as an equal in his will. He left Keene his share in trust while the other children were given their portions outright.

A schoolmate described Harry as ". . . a slender blond youth with a beaming smile, always ready for any form of harmless fun, and one who was greatly liked." Only seventeen months younger than Irene, he was by far the closest sibling in age to her. She vividly remembered the smell of the trees and the white rocks strewn on the ground in Danville's pine groves where they played. Harry always was having mishaps, three of which occurred after they moved to Richmond. ". . . On a hot Fourth of July morning," Irene recalled, "the door bell rang and Harry was brought in as black as coal, having been down at the Capitol when a cannon or something exploded and all the powder seemed to have gone on his poor little face. . . . Mother plunged Harry into a hot [cold?] bath which saved his face from the burns, but the doctor was surprised it hadn't killed him. When he was recuperating, I decided one day to pull him across the floor, playing horse, and into his bobo went one of the longest splinters, which took some time to get out and prolonged the convalescence. As soon as he recovered, he went down to Mrs. Miller's house on Third and Cary Streets, climbed the tallest tree in the yard, from which he fell. This made a dimple in his chin, which always remained."

Irene thought Harry a "funny little boy" whose taste for "good old Bourbon whiskey" originated when he bought rock and rye candy over on Broad Street in Richmond. Like Keene, he was an alcoholic and developed tuberculosis at an early age. He stumbled through life, drinking and sporadically employed by his father until his health completely failed. As a young boy my father knew both Keene and Harry, and in his diary wrote he felt sad when Keene died, describing him as "cozy." Neither he nor any other family member, however, had anything kind to remember about Harry, probably because he turned difficult and eccentric before his early death. The only connection I had to Harry was playing in the wreck of the deserted house on a small mountaintop above Mirador that Chillie built for him so he would have clear air to breathe. My

The Family Drama

father hiked up there with me once, and pointing to a brick path overgrown with boxwood bushes, told me a story about Harry. Evidently, Harry looked out an upstairs window and saw a large rooster strutting down the path. Enraged that the rooster thought himself to be "the cock of the walk," he grabbed his revolver, and shot the poor bird. Uncle Harry needed more than mountain air.

Buck was about twenty years old when, like his older brothers, he contracted tuberculosis.* Whatever desire he may or may not have had to go out into the world and carve a place for himself was obliterated by his disease and his father's giving him everything he needed - - a large allowance and a six hundred acre estate in southern Albemarle County. By nature Buck was relaxed and easy going, and had the gift of making friends wherever he went. He was the character of the family, a gentle man with the knack of weaving long tales which kept his listeners in stitches.

His sisters never took him seriously, and called him their father's "Baby Boy." They criticized him for being "full of Negro Stories," and never making anything of his life. Buck had his way of getting back at them, particularly at Nannie. On his visits to the elegant Astor country place in England, Cliveden, he made a point of affecting his deepest Southern drawl and wearing his rattiest old clothes around her stylish and titled guests. But he was always there for Irene when she came to visit at Mirador, rushing over from his farm to spend as much time with her as he could.

Buck took full advantage of his father's munificence and lived an uncomplicated, peaceful existence until his tuberculosis recurred later in life. His greatest effort was to run for election to Virginia's House of Delegates from Albemarle County in 1920. Much to everyone's surprise, he won, elected on the strength of his principal tenet, "To hell with Prohibition." When asked his view on any other important issue, he responded, "That's a question every man must decide for himself." Buck had an unremarkable legislative career that lasted one term. However, he successfully pushed for

---

*No one I interviewed has even a theory why the three Langhorne sons contracted tuberculosis but the girls escaped. Keene's and Harry's heavy drinking certainly wore down their physical resistance to disease, but Buck never had a problem with the bottle.

The Gibson Girl

the money to pave Albemarle County's Route 20, the road from Scottsville to Charlottesville.

Buck was in his second year at the Virginia Military Institute when he stole a trained pig from the sideshow of a traveling circus performing in Lexington. He was able to keep the animal hidden in his barracks room for two days despite inspections twice daily. The pig's owner was furious and vowed to stay in town until the thief was captured. The only clues the authorities had were the culprit had a shaved head and was a cadet at the Institute. All the cadets knew who had pulled the practical joke, but because Buck was so well-liked, no one turned him in. Even the upperclassmen shaved their heads so he could not be fingered. The ruse did not work, however, and Buck was expelled.

Years later, Buck was with his good friend, Sam Goodloe, in New York City. They were staying at the Roosevelt Hotel awaiting the arrival of Buck's sister, Nannie, from England. The speech patterns of both men were indistinguishable from those of the blacks they employed in Virginia, particularly when they were agitated. One evening in their hotel room Buck and Sam got into a loud argument. The woman next door, shocked that the hotel took "Negroes," complained to the front desk, vowing never to stay at the Roosevelt again. The manager was a friend of Buck and figured out what was going on. He went up to their room, got some clothes on the men, knocked on the woman's door, and presented Buck and Sam to her. "I want to introduce to you Colonel Langhorne and Colonel Goodloe who are rooming next to you. Colonel Langhorne is up here from Virginia to meet his sister, Lady Astor, who is coming in on the boat in the morning, and we all regret very much that you have been disturbed."

Irene observed her mother's patience as Nanaire weathered Chillie's storms, and saw how after his rages had subsided, Nanaire always seemed to get her way. She watched Chillie's furor when Lizzie challenged him, and sensed the tension between Keene and his father. She felt the weight of Chillie's disapproval and scorn when the eldest son did not meet his father's exacting requirements. At an early age she absorbed these reactions to her father, and intuitively knew her method would be her mother's. She was not good at confrontation, and sensed in battling him she would be the

The Family Drama

loser. Fortunately for Irene she started out in life as her father's favorite child; to both parents her infant survival was nothing short of a miracle. With survival came an unqualified approval which was easy to give considering Irene's naturally quiet manner and beauty. Irene knew that to maintain her favored status she must continue to please and to cater to this man who already doted on her. She would give in to Chillie's explosions and his postering.

It is debatable whether Irene escaped - - unmarred - - a childhood dominated by her father's intemperate behavior. Certainly from coping with him she learned the stressful art of pleasing people and how to use her charm and femininity to achieve goals for herself and others. But the lesson must have been a painful, exhausting one for a child in constant fear of her father's displeasure as she tiptoed through the tension and unease within the Langhorne family. I like to think of Irene softly nestled against the protection of her mother's bosom, but the visual image which stays with me is the picture of a small, bewildered child silently standing in the shadows, carefully planning how to stay out of harm's way. I marvel at Irene's childhood intuitiveness, her refusal to be a victim of the confusion and uncertainty her father generated, and her sense that had she stood up to her father, he would have bowled her over. I am thankful she had the childhood wisdom to focus on the love and understanding of her mother and take with her these qualities into her later years.

Nannie was desperate for attention and approval from her father. Her problem was how to make a place for herself when she knew she could not compete with her older sister, Irene, the peaceful, endearing child who could do no wrong and was the apple of their father's eye. Craving the attention and approval Irene so easily enjoyed, Nannie decided the only way to be noticed was to be what her sister was not - - pugnacious and rebellious. Even though she was tiny and small-boned, as well as frail and sickly throughout her youth, she determined to take whatever risks necessary to impress Chillie. In the process she became both exceedingly outspoken and a reckless horsewoman. No comment was too outlandish for Nannie to utter; no fence was too high for her to jump. She refused to be cowed by the arbitrary way he handled all his children. She did not allow herself to be beaten down by his

The Gibson Girl

sometimes unreasonable responses to her oftentimes combative and challenging conduct - - and received more than one beating as a result. One moment she infuriated him, and the next instance she sent him into gales of laughter with her sharp mind and wit and mimicry. In reacting to her father, Nannie developed the power of aggressiveness, the root of both her remarkable public career and her later personal and family problems. Throughout her life, Nannie often spoke and acted before she thought, perhaps concerned about the hurt she caused, but most of the time oblivious to it.

To varying degrees Irene's three younger sisters - - Nannie, Phyllis, and Nora, born in 1889 - - were affected by her disposition and role in the family, but Irene was too old, too far removed from their childhood struggles to play a part in them. None of them was an important influence in Irene's own development. Lizzie as the disciplinarian was the larger force in their lives and someone against whom they could react. Irene they remembered as the sister who nursed them when they were sick. Nannie may have beat her head against the wall striving to compete with Irene, but Phyllis did not bother. Eighteen months younger than Nannie, the two were inseparable. Phyllis was closest in temperament to Irene, but Phyllis's age and Nannie's domineering possessiveness were barriers to any youthful relationship Irene and Phyllis might have enjoyed. It was not in Phyllis's nature to challenge anyone, particularly the assertive Nannie. She was Nannie's opposite, the introvert of the family, an extremely sensitive, wistful person who loved playing music, painting, and sculpting. Phyllis coped with the family turmoil surrounding her by escaping to her bedroom to read or to the stables to clean and polish her saddles and bridles for hours on end.

Nora was the surprise birth in the family and only six years old when Irene married and left home. She never seemed to have had the status of sister among the Langhorne siblings, and even when Nora was an adult and a parent, Irene viewed her as an irritating and bothersome child. Nora was the afterthought, the lost and somehow forgotten offspring curiously deserted by parents who were tired of the rigorous process of raising children. Probably the neediest of all the Langhorne children, and even slighter in build than Nannie and Phyllis, she craved affection and respect, and was set further adrift with the untimely death of her mother, her father's inability to cope with a teenage daughter, and her sisters' intolerance.

The Gibson Girl

CHAPTER FOUR

THE BELLE

At fourteen, Irene's lighthearted days of childhood freedom, full of games and goat carts, juvenile intrigue and devilment, dress-up, and dolls, were over. Physical maturity came early, and already heads were turning in appreciation of her beautifully proportioned figure, perfect posture, and the way she sat a horse in a finely tailored whipcord habit. By the age of sixteen Irene's figure was voluptuous, the perfect body for the style of the day. She had a rounded, large bosom and ample hips, their shapes accentuated by a tightly corseted waist. She was tall - - five feet, eight inches - - and she held herself superbly, her chin thrust ahead and the upper half of her body tilted slightly forward. Her features all were prominent, a firm jaw with a deep cleft in her chin, a large nose, and a wide forehead fully exposed when her light brown hair, thickly luxuriant, was swept backward and above her ears.

From her memoir, it is apparent Irene had been aware of her comeliness for a long time, her "beautiful, golden hair" one of her first memories. Her interest in herself and in her clothes sometimes bordered on the extreme. When she described her mother's alarmed reaction to Keene's running away from school, she made a point of noting in clear detail the hat she was wearing at the time, "a green felt affair stitched all around in yellow silk and on one side a yellow parrot." Her first bustle was a momentous occasion. "It was called 'shawl drapery' and consisted of a piece of linen a half yard long, in which whalebones starting small at the top and growing bigger at the bottom fitted inside the drapery and gave a great air."

Although Irene now gets the credit for being the loveliest of the Langhorne sisters, she and Nannie in their memoirs gave that accolade to Lizzie. They saw her as a classic beauty, attractive, beautifully proportioned, popular with numerous beaux, and the best dancer in Richmond. As a small child Irene idolized her older sister. "Lizzie was a handful, full of life and spirit. One day there was a great rumpus at the front of the house. Lizzie had come running home and leaped over the porch, five boys behind her.

The Belle

What she'd done, I don't know, beaten them up, perhaps. When they caught up with her, they hung onto her wonderful long braids. But I don't think she was defeated."

Irene observed intently Lizzie's courtships and was thrilled when one of her beaux, Charlie Bohmer, gave her sister a Dresden china slipper with a Cupid perched on the toe, to Irene a romantic present. Irene was enthralled with the attention Moncure Perkins paid her and particularly remembered the buggy rides he took her on when Lizzie was not invited. On one occasion he slipped his ring on her finger, and running to Lizzie, she proudly flaunted this token of her "conquest" in Lizzie's face. Irene absorbed the subtle nuances of her sister's mating dance; in the process she learned how to control men with flattery, and how with deft feminine maneuvers, a shy smile or a coy toss of her head, a girl could get her way.

For a long time I was confused by Irene's and Nannie's descriptions of Lizzie's beauty and vitality. The only photographs I had of her depicted a plump matron dressed in black or another dark color with, if not a sour, an unhappy expression on her face. Lizzie has always been included as one of Virginia's "Five Langhorne Sisters," all lauded for their beauty and grace. Her sisters, who retained their slim figures and handsome looks throughout life, certainly deserved the accolades, but why was Lizzie included with them?

I had a number of facts about Lizzie, particularly from her daughters, who wrote lovingly of her. She had a flair for clothes and a taste for inexpensive eighteenth century antiques when her contemporaries were decorating with ugly Victorian pieces. Her marriage to Moncure Perkins, a poor Richmonder from a good family who was not a successful businessman and who had a drinking problem, was not a happy one. And I knew Lizzie died suddenly in New York City while visiting my grandmother. I also read that after her sisters had achieved a measure of recognition and even fame she referred to herself as Mrs. "Obscure" Perkins, a sad commentary on her own life with undertones of resentment and envy.

Then, well into my research I stumbled on an old photograph of a young woman, perhaps eighteen or nineteen years old, with jet-dark hair pulled tightly from a high forehead, perfectly

The Gibson Girl

matched features, deep-set eyes under full eyebrows, a strong nose, graceful mouth and bold chin. Pencil scribbled on the photograph's back is the one word, "Lizzie," in my grandmother's handwriting. Lizzie as a young girl and woman was all her sisters described her as being. To my eye she was prettier than the rest. So why was it, I wondered, that Irene, not Lizzie with all her vivacity and beauty, was the first Langhorne daughter to be indulged by her parents and processed for a life of gaiety and belledom?

Lizzie's misfortune was that Chillie did not make his money soon enough. She reached her courtship years when Nanaire, overloaded with the cares and duties of children and housekeeping, was not in a position to promote or even to participate in her eldest daughter's premarital rites because of the scarcity of money. In fact, Chillie barely could afford to outfit her in the clothes and the accessories essential to the making of a good match. Not until after Lizzie's simple wedding ceremony in the Langhornes' front parlor and her move to live in a small apartment a few blocks away did Chillie's railroad contracting business become immensely profitable and the Langhornes suddenly find themselves rich.

Lizzie's loss was Irene's gain. Now that Lizzie was a married woman, both parents, especially Nanaire, looked to Irene to be the centerpiece of an intense social crusade which would last until Nanaire's death. Concealed beneath Nanaire's polished and ladylike demeanor was an intensely competitive, ambitious, and proud person, eager to take her rightful place in Richmond's strict and proper society. Even in the threadbare society of Richmond where class was much more a function of bloodlines and "refinement" than in the Gilded Age's northern cities, money meant social leverage; without some of it, dignity was difficult to maintain. The Langhornes always had possessed the most important credentials -- family and Chillie's respectable Confederate army service; now they could buy the proper clothes and entertain the correct people.

Old-line, upper-crust Richmonders probably were chary of the Langhornes' sudden insertion of themselves into their society. Certainly, as a cousin of the Lees and the Randolphs and other fine Virginia families, Chillie's pedigree was flawless, but his natural

The Belle

swagger, now heightened by the confidence of new wealth, was difficult for the more fastidious of Richmond's chosen to embrace.*
Nanaire must have spent hours with her husband - - whose idea of social intercourse was a raucous night with the boys - - instructing him in the niceties of decorous behavior.

Armed with beauty, self-assurance, and a strong desire to please her parents, Irene happily joined their campaign to excel socially. Nanaire and Irene spent endless hours selecting materials for dresses and wraps, undergarments and coats. They ordered patterns and hired seamstresses to outfit Irene in the latest fashions. Nanaire's instructions in etiquette and manners were exhaustive. Shepherding her second daughter through the intricate maze of growing up in Richmond's social whirl became the prime interest in her life. Through Irene's beauty and talent she could live those wonderful days of youth and gaiety and parties and balls the war had denied her. Nanaire's own days of belledom had ended soon after they began. Her life full of nosegays, gowns and flirtations too

---

*Pride in Southern roots and tradition for many of Irene's generation took a negative twist. The peculiar Southern phenomenon known as the Lost Cause was a tremendously destructive mind-set, a lethargic defensiveness - - particularly found in Richmond - - that grew out of the loss of economic vibrancy. After the post-war boom of the 1880s, Richmond lost a good portion of its port commerce to Norfolk and West Point, Virginia and most of its iron manufacture to Birmingham, Alabama. Discouraged and disheartened, the leaders of the city began to look backward instead of ahead. The Southern heritage was embraced with a new fervor as Confederate heroes were glorified, and nostalgia for what could have been preoccupied many. The intense antebellum pride Southerners had in their culture and tradition was reawakened, and they directed their fear and hatred to Yankees and Afro-Americans. Conceit and poverty do not mix well and strong feelings of resentment, bitterness, and insularity sprouted.

Although Irene's life-long pride in her "Southernness" was a result of this environment, she escaped the negative influence of the Lost Cause syndrome because of Chillie's business and financial success. She saw and respected him as one of the few who were able to persevere and succeed against overpowering odds.

Irene was not the only Langhorne child who stayed close to her Southern roots. Nannie Astor, after decades of British citizenship and allegiance, asked that a Confederate flag be placed in her coffin.

The Gibson Girl

swiftly had become one of survival in war-torn Danville. Her youth had been spent in nursing the sick, living in army camps, and bearing children. Exquisitely petite with a sultry beauty and a quickness of wit that delighted her contemporaries, Nanaire would have had a joyous reign as a leading belle. She knew she had missed out. Irene would not.

But Richmond was merely a training ground, a provincial locale in which Irene could hone her skills. Richmond's stage was too small for the Langhorne daughter whom Nanaire and Chillie believed had the potential to become the South's next great belle. Marriage for Irene was not too many years away, and she had three younger sisters. Nannie and Phyllis were children and Nora an infant, but their time would come soon enough. Nanaire and Chillie wanted to do more than position their daughters for the best matches Richmond could offer. Fine young men abounded in their town, but Irene and her sisters would do better than marry into a distinguished but poor family like the Perkinses. They saw a larger world for their girls to conquer beyond the constrictive limits of their provincial community, a world of fabulous wealth, elegance, and social prestige.

The place to take them was to one of the spring resorts. So in the summer of 1888, just after Irene's fifteenth birthday, the entire family set out for the most fashionable one, the Grand Central Hotel at White Sulphur Springs - - better known as The White - - in the mountains of West Virginia. Each summer at The White wealthy families from all parts of the country gathered not only to escape the heat and disease of the cities and lowlands and to partake of the medicinal waters, but to parade their daughters among the young men there in hopes of an eventual and advantageous marriage. Summer spas were the belles' arenas because they were the places where large groups of the elite classes from still a predominantly rural American society gathered. The resorts of the Virginias were the most popular because of their elevations, limestone spring waters, and central eastern seaboard location.

Any young lady with the prescribed family background, some money, and the will to enter the fray could declare herself a belle. If a girl's parents could not afford The White or another spa,

The Belle

oftentimes she banded together with her friends and shared the same chaperone. One belle came to the spa "in one black silk dress and her grit." Another belle had the cheek to ask Mr. W.W. Corcoran,* an old and wealthy habitué of the White, for $100 to finance her season there. He sent her the money.

To escape Richmond's humid, sultry summers, the best Chillie had done to date was to bundle off his family to the homes of country relatives. Now he could afford the lavish expenditure - - an $800 tariff for two adults, five children, and two servants, equivalent to $20,000 today - - for the best and most costly of summer spas in the Virginias. Though The White boasted a gambling house - - where Chillie spent most evenings playing cards - - and the hotel was convenient to his railroad work in West Virginia, he in no way was inspired by idle spa life, the mountain air, or the medicinal qualities of the water. Thirty-odd other spas dotted the mountains of the Virginias, springs named Red, Warm, Sweet, and Rockbridge Alum. For the Langhornes they were not grand enough, and their clientele not cosmopolitan enough to satisfy their desire to launch Irene and eventually her sisters into a wider sphere among the best and wealthiest families in the land. Not this first summer, but perhaps the next, or the summer following, Irene would meet and fall in love with a rich and socially prominent young man.

According to *Harper's* magazine, the Grand Central Hotel was the quintessential Southern resort, "a place of wide galleries and big pillars, a rendezvous for important people attended by troops of servants, the meeting-place of politicians, the haunt of the belles, an arena of gaiety, romantic intrigue and fashion, where fortunes nightly were won and lost." Since Colonial times some form of lodgings had been near hot-water springs in Greenbrier County to house the many people who believed waters full of sulfates and gases could cure most human maladies, from dyspepsia to malaria, from bladder diseases to asthma. In the spa's early years, crude shanties were erected for the infirm who had endured tortuously long wagon or stagecoach rides to find health from

---

*Corcoran was a banker and a philanthropist who built Baltimore's Corcoran Gallery of Art and contributed his collection to it.

The Gibson Girl

bathing in and drinking the water. As the decades passed, better facilities were built - - cottages and a hotel. By the 1880s, railroad service to the Grand Central Hotel was excellent, with three trains arriving daily from Cincinnati, Ohio and Washington, D.C.; guests from the states to the south arrived via the Atlantic Coast Line railroad or the Louisville and Nashville.

The train ride from Richmond to The White was an exciting adventure for Irene because she had never traveled so far from home. The long day's trip took the Langhornes through the pine forests of Virginia's Piedmont, up the Blue Ridge mountains, across the patchwork-quilt fields of the Shenandoah Valley, and over the rugged Allegheny foothills. They finally arrived at the White Sulphur Springs depot in the early evening. Exhausted from their long day, grimy with coal soot, and stiff from the uncomfortable passenger car benches, the family climbed aboard a carriage for the short ride to the resort. As the winding, graveled road passed over a low ridge, the Grand Central Hotel suddenly came into view.

The sight must have awed Irene, the size of the main hotel dwarfing any building she had ever seen. Just having undergone a major renovation, the vast, wood-framed structure glistened brightly in its fresh coats of white paint. Its great colonnades and porticos seemed to rise to the sky. Away from the hotel ranged cottages lined in rows, all facing a narrow, grassy valley with paths converging on a stately, domed springhouse. The hotel itself housed 1500 guests, and its ballroom and parlor were proudly advertised as being half again as big as the East Room of the White House in Washington. The dining room, which seated 1200 guests, was as long as a football field. Two large wings had just been added to the hotel, and the whole place was illuminated by electricity.

The Langhornes - - Irene, her mother and father, Nannie, Phyllis, Buck, Harry, Keene, Nora the baby and a nursemaid - - crowded into Bruce Cottage on Virginia Row. Cottage accommodations were more fashionable than rooms in the main hotel, and they particularly suited the family's needs because the goats and goat cart brought for the younger children could be kept nearby. Irene described Bruce Cottage as primitive. The room she shared with her sisters was tiny, with no plaster on the walls, only

The Belle

bare framing. If there was indoor plumbing, it was not in their small cottage, but in a separate toilet facility shared by other guests.

Little notice was taken of Irene during her first summer at White Sulphur Springs. The Richmond *Dispatch* in its minutely detailed reports of spa activities mentioned her only once. Along with Nancy and Phyllis, she attended the Children's Ball, an extravagant annual event for the youngsters elaborately dressed in period costumes that took place directly after dinner at eight o'clock. Irene was still considered a child, and she participated in the romantic maneuverings around her only as a spy. Young men bribed her with boxes of candy to go out on the paths and come back and tell them which belle was with which beau.

The following summer was a different story altogether. During the first half-hour of the almost nightly balls the girls considered too young to join in watched the intricate dances of their elders from the sidelines. One evening in July, William Wright, a young married man from Philadelphia, noticed Irene sitting on one of the window openings, and approached her. He asked Irene how old she was, and she replied, "Sixteen." "Then it's time you were out," he said, and he took her to the dance floor. For the social chroniclers of those times, Irene's dance that night was an important occasion because it signaled the arrival of the "last great belle" into society. The Golden Age of Belledom is said to have begun when Mary Triplett starred in The White's Grand Fancy Mask Balls of 1868, and ended with Irene's engagement, an event that "removed the last of the great belles from circulation." Irene's reign lasted for six years. They were sparkling, joyful years for her, free of care and full of attention and delight.

Although the South's pride in the rightness and the invincibility of its civilization was destroyed by the Civil War, the Southern need to magnify and glorify its culture remained. Its onetime icons, the swashbuckling Cavaliers personified by the great Confederate generals - - men such as Lee, Jackson, and Stuart - - were dead or grayed and old. Though admired, they were irrelevant symbols of a past now vague, obscured by hardship and resentment. Now, Southerners turned to their women as guardians of their heritage. They exalted their beauty and graciousness and invested

The Gibson Girl

the fairest of them with qualities protected and preserved by a severe code of manners and social restrictions.

The tradition of Southern belledom had been around ever since the first decades of the nineteenth century, but now it became almost a cult as men placed a chosen few on pedestals and then went about worshipping them. Belles became the Southern equivalent of royalty, their every move and nuance of behavior observed by their elders. Little girls waited patiently for them to appear on sidewalks and followed them. Young men pursued them and old men bowed in their honor. Newspapers reported on them often with headlines as large as those announcing the top news stories of the day.

Oddly enough, physical beauty was not the prime prerequisite for being a leading belle, but Irene's face and figure in combination with her vivacious personality was a recipe for certain success. Of course, a girl had to be pleasant-looking to garner a measure of attention, but the first requirement for being a belle was to be - - or act - - "well-bred." As one analytical social reporter put it, "Some women are beautiful, some are brilliant, but all may be charming." His definition of charm was the "priceless gift of tact," the talent of "harmonizing their surroundings and smoothing difficulties for all who are fortunate enough to come within their reach."

This self-proclaimed expert, an anonymous writer for *Harper's* magazine, defined a strict code of conduct for belles. The belle must be "observant to the rules of propriety, giving attention and deference to her mother or chaperone, who does not permit young men to be careless in her presence, nor accept the attentions of the dissipated men because she is afraid to be seen without an escort, who does not talk or laugh loud in public corridors and reception-rooms and who is not desirous of cheap notoriety, does not 'forget' her engagements when someone or something more agreeable is presented, and who does not refuse to dance with one young man on the plea of being tired and let him see her a few moments later wheeling around the ballroom with another. In a word, the girl with even modest attractions and accomplishments who has command of her temper and tongue and who has the delicacy and consideration of the feelings of others may be at the White Sulphur what is termed a success."

This social authority also wrote that the belle must be able to withstand criticism by people who are not friendly, and be able to be politically adept by making enough friends in order to silence a number of the inevitably envious tongues. The belle was expected to be a coquette; but it "is a clean, sweet coquetry, as different from broad flirtation as is milk from *creme de menthe*." This innocent flirtation between belles and their beaux in today's context would be bold sexual invitation. Then, the propriety of a "nice" girl was undisputed, and many a belle went to her wedding-night bed without much of a clue as to what was supposed to take place.

To be a leading belle, there were other very important qualities needed - - wit and the gift of repartee, and the ability to hold one's own in a verbal sparring match. Irene had these qualities. Without them she would not have taken over the reigning belle's mantle from May Handy, a girl from Richmond whose mother schooled her for a career as a belle the way a thoroughbred is trained for the track. Before May there had been Mattie Ould, known for her pomegranate lips and her clever reposte to an elderly admirer by the name of Page who had written her this couplet:

> *If from your glove you take the letter "g,"*
> *Your glove is love and that I bear for thee.*

Mattie's reply:

> *If from your name you take the letter "P,"*
> *Your Page is age; that will not do for me.*

When Irene first visited The White, the first of the great belles, Mary Triplett, was very much of a presence there. Now a handsome matron, she took new belles under her wing. Many years had passed since a duel had been fought over her, and one man tragically killed as a result.[*] May Handy was there as well, the

---

[*]Dueling was illegal, but considered to be an honorable redress for insults until the last years of the nineteenth century. In Richmond the practice

The Gibson Girl

featured player, much talked about and admired, and soon to be unseated by the new arrival.

The belle's daily schedule at The White was exhausting. Her stamina was legendary. Having gone to bed in the wee hours of the morning after one of the six nightly balls held each week at The White, she could be up at eight, horseback riding or taking the waters with a beau. After a large breakfast, she made morning calls or she honored her appointments to stroll with various young men on one of the hotels paths, each with its own name - - Lover's Walk, Courtship Maze, Hesitance, Acceptance Way, Paradise, or Rejection. Now it was time to get ready for the morning dance at eleven o'clock. If no dance was scheduled, a champagne and fruit party was held on the lawn.

The morning's festivities lasted until one o'clock. After an hour's allowance to change, dinner was served at two o'clock, a huge meal with five or six courses. There may have been time for a short nap before she played a light game of tennis, or watched the men at mule races - - the slowest one winning, or cheered them on at their baseball games, amused by their costumes. Oftentimes, they played dressed as women in long, crinolined dresses, their beards and mustaches ridiculously protruding from their bonnets.

Supper in the great dining room was early, beginning at six-thirty and lasting until eight. After supper, a peculiar activity took place at The White - - the Treadmill. Back in the 1830s, Henry Clay offered his hand to a Mrs. John Preston after supper and they promenaded around the big *fanteuil* in the middle of the salon. Other guests thought this a sensible way to work off their meals and rose from their seats to join Clay and Mrs. Preston in their stroll

---

came to an end when Joseph Bryan, a newspaper publisher noted for his bravery during the Civil War, refused a challenge. He stated dueling was both absurd and against the law, and he would have no part in it.

A strong link exists between the strict rules for the treatment of women in those days and the practice of dueling. Because a deadly affair with pistols or swords was a constant risk to a gentleman, he needed to know precisely what conduct was acceptable, and what was not. No wonder our male forebears treated ladies with the utmost decorum and respect. Any breech of protocol - - an unwanted romantic advance or a suggestive innuendo - - could result in a challenge at dawn by an irate relative or a rival suitor.

The Belle

around the room. Thus, the custom was born. One observer described the ritual. "Over in the ballroom the children were dancing, and the music strains gave the promenade a rhythm. Trains were in vogue and voluminous draperies, fans, belles passing in review, bright eyes flashing. Coquetry, even flirtation, received approving glances. Courtship was the source of universal interest." The belle's day ended with a dance, either put on by the hotel or a private party. A late-night breakfast followed.

"I loved it, loved it, loved it," Irene said when interviewed by Cleveland Amory in the 1940s. "I never wore a speck of make-up of any kind - - not even powder - - and I ate everything. Big breakfasts, big dinners, and big suppers. Hot breads and beaten biscuits too." Irene's only sporting exercise was "gentle" tennis or riding side-saddle. Yet, she managed to keep her twenty-inch waist. "The beaux were supposed to be able to put their hands around it, but my father never let them." Nevertheless, Irene was not immune to the miseries which sometimes beset young girls. Writing to her sister, Phyllis, in 1931, she told of memories as her train passed through White Sulphur Springs and she glimpsed the cottage on Virginia Row where the Langhornes stayed so many years before. "I was coming [to The White] from Asheville having visited Alice Connally and had gained fifteen pounds and had bobbed my hair into a terrible shingle of bangs. Mother had told the Northerners how pretty I was and I couldn't show my face for several days."

During Irene's second summer at White Sulphur Springs, the Richmond *Dispatch* began to feature her and the Langhornes in its social columns. "Mrs. C.D. Langhorne is remarkably bright and vivacious and her pleasant company is greatly enjoyed by her friends." And, "Among other pleasant and popular ladies are . . . Miss Irene Langhorne." The descriptions became more dramatic as the summer wore on; for example, "The bewitching Miss Langhorne, in crimson satin, with eyes glowing with liquid light and seeming like some morning sunbeam that had lingered to cheer the night. . . ." In the world of The White, full of balls, courtship, and social merriment, the Langhornes had arrived.

There would be two more full seasons at The White for the family. Nanaire loved it there. She reached summer distinction in 1891 by serving on the executive committee for the season's

The Gibson Girl

grandest event, the Colonial Ball. The minuet was danced that year, and Nanaire was chairman of the Dancing Committee. Even the Langhorne boys were featured in the society columns. Harry was victorious at a game of Newmarket Stop, but probably was not too excited by his prize, "a handsome flower photograph frame."

For Irene, those two summers were a never-ending round of hayrides with fruit and punch served at country homes, lawn parties, dances, bowling parties, luncheons, and riding parties. "I remember who I was in love with," Irene recalled. "I was in love with Nicholas Longworth." He was a member of a prominent Cincinnati, Ohio family, and came to The White in 1890. In spite of Irene's feelings as a seventeen-year-old, and her father's later efforts to marry his daughter to this heir to an old fortune, nothing materialized. Nicholas, who one day would be Speaker of the House of Representatives, nearly twenty years later married Alice Roosevelt, President Theodore Roosevelt's daughter.

Chaperonage in the South was a very serious matter, and the reputation of a girl who, even inadvertently, found herself alone with a man, could be seriously compromised.[*] Mothers were required to spend long hours patiently observing and monitoring the activities of the young set. To memorialize this social institution, the guests put on the Married Ladies' Ball one Friday night. The dance's purpose was to reverse the roles of chaperone and daughter. Irene with her young friends sat against the wall, on the sidelines, while their mothers and fathers danced. Modestly dressed as befitted their pretended duties as chaperones, they were given a lesson in endurance. Bored at the start, then getting into the spirit of the party, they continually left their seats, scolding their elders unmercifully about loud and careless manners, and warning them about sitting in dark corners. Nanaire was one of the "Married Ladies," dressed "in white-and-gold brocaded satin, with pearl ornaments."

---

[*]Rules of chaperonage were not always consistent. It was perfectly proper for Irene to take morning walks on the paths at The White without a chaperone, but in Richmond she had either to be escorted by a chaperone or be in the company of another couple.

The Belle

Irene's days at The White as a Summer Girl - - "the bird in the gilded cage, the perfume of the flower, the plot of the story, and the savory condiment of the season" - - lasted only three seasons. It was fortunate for her and the other young people from Richmond that they had a stage at The White and at the other summer resorts on which to perform and to hone their social skills, because at seventeen Irene was too young to participate in Richmond's adult life. Life at home for young and old alike was far more restrictive than the relaxed, vacation atmosphere of the summer season. The arbiters of etiquette and propriety in Richmond took more to heart the strict regulations for which the Victorian Era was known, and lives were governed by the countless books of etiquette existing at that time.

She had triumphed during the summers of her sixteenth and seventeenth years, but when she arrived home in early September, she was still a schoolgirl and under the watchful eye of her mother. Only after her last full season at The White in 1891 was Irene old enough to enter completely into Richmond's social activities. She was now considered a young lady, fully eligible for marriage. Having been well grounded in the three "r's" with a little French thrown into her curriculum, Irene's formal education was over. Chillie did not expect his girls to acquire that much knowledge, and college educations for them never crossed his mind, nor theirs.

Richmond could not offer the broad scale of entertainment served up at The White and other spas because its citizens could not afford to offer expansive affairs for their friends and children. The Langhornes, though they had the money, conformed to the prevailing practice of modest entertainments. If Irene had lived in the North, she would have been a debutante, but in Richmond the girls as yet were not formally introduced to society with elaborate balls. Even receptions following weddings, by tradition, were simple affairs. Close friends and family came to the bride's house for a wedding breakfast after the church service.

Nanaire, the wife of a prosperous man, the mother of Richmond's premier belle, and conscious of her position in society, was now in the midst of Richmond's social whirlpool beside her daughter. Seldom mentioned in the social columns before Irene's passage into society, now the Langhornes' every activity was a keen

The Gibson Girl

subject for the city's society writers who related in tedious detail the comings and goings of the fashionable - - every tea, luncheon, dinner, dance, and ball. Even when families, or a child, went for weekend visits to cousins in other cities the "news" was flashed to all the literate citizens of the city. In Sunday columns Nanaire's innumerable card and tea parties were covered together with her activities as chaperone, patroness of charity balls, and benefactress of Confederate Memorial Association events. The newspapers even commented on Chillie, complimenting him for his excellent voice and his ability to liven up a gathering or a dinner party.

Nanaire and Irene together had "at homes" - - a wonderful illustration of the complexities of Victorian social life. Women had large, complicated households to run, servants to manage, and no modern conveniences. Nevertheless, each day they had been expected to drop whatever they were doing to receive callers in proper dress and be prepared to offer refreshment. These continual invasions into their daily routines became too much to bear, so the institution of the "at home" was founded. The fashionable residential areas of the city were divided into sections. The homes of each lady were listed in the newspaper together with the day of the week - - the only day of the week - - when she received callers. Nanaire's and Irene's "at home" day was Tuesday.*

---

*"At home" hours were usually between eleven and five o'clock. The hostess sat in her best room prepared to receive visitors, dressed in a tea gown, a loose fitting garment with cascades of lace down the front. Strict rules of etiquette delineated what could be discussed, and what could not. The five "d's" - - domestics, domiciles, descendants, diseases, and dress - - should be avoided in conversation. Taboo topics included sex, prostitution, illegitimate children, birth control, homosexuality, insanity, suicide, underclothes, illness, and hygiene. The caller was expected to stay no more than fifteen minutes, a rule which seems reasonable because there were few topics left to discuss!

Quite a ritual was attached to the proper use of a calling card for other types of social visits and acknowledgments. The card had to be the correct size, not too large, and therefore ostentatious; yet, not too small, either. If all corners were unbent, the caller had not come in person. If the right-hand upper corner was bent, the person had come to pay respects, but did not expect to be received. A bend of the left-hand upper corner signified congratulations; condolences were expressed by a turn of the left-hand lower corner. If the right-hand lower corner was bent, the caller was indicating that he or she would be

The Belle

Women's clothing was as restrictive as the rules of etiquette governing their wearers' lives. Although the hoop skirt with its eleven-foot diameter was out of vogue in the 1880s, the bustle, a device at one's backside that made sitting almost impossible, was popular until the 1890s. Wire forms and whalebone and steel corsets pinched waists and flattened internal organs. Hip padding and India rubber bosoms molded figures, producing implausible shapes. Skirts dusted the pavement, picking up all matter of dirt and grime. Under the ornate dresses were multiple petticoats, a chemise, a corset cover, hose supporters, cotton or silk stockings, and underpants or drawers. Clothing was changed often throughout the day, not solely for reasons of fashion. Rather, washable undergarments wet with perspiration had to be replaced with dry linen before expensive dresses made of fragile fabrics were ruined. Imagine the incredible discomfort for a woman on a hot summer's day!

Of course, it was impolite to blow one's nose or make bread into little pellets while dining, but it was also improper to adjust a comb or even touch one's hair. The word "stomach" could never be used in proper discourse. French was very fashionable, it being very smart to interject a French phrase into a sentence. Otherwise, the speech of the upper class was deceptively unaffected; overfancy words and euphemisms denoted pretentiousness, and only the person obviously attempting to climb to a better station in life used them.

This was Irene's world, and she excelled in it. She was happy to embrace its customs. Her entire energy during those last years in Richmond before her marriage was devoted entirely to the pleasure of being one of the most sought after belles of her day.

The social season started in late November and ended in February, when the Lenten period granted a rest time after the almost manic business of keeping up socially. The main occasions every week were the germans, or dances, which were held on three

---

leaving town for an extended period of time. Calling cards could even be used to insult. If it was delivered in an envelope, the sender wanted to end a relationship.

The Gibson Girl

nights - - Monday, Tuesday, and Thursday.* The highlight of every german was a succession of elaborate and complex dance figures which required rehearsals and repetition to perfect. Each city had its leader, a social gallant who orchestrated and controlled the entire process, assisted by as many as six floor managers who guided the dancers through their steps. Richmond's was "General" Jo Lane Stern, a perennial beau and social doyen. At one german, Jo Stern guided his skillful dancers into the shapes of five Maltese crosses and then unwound them like a variegated ribbon. For his finale, he produced a star, the center figure holding a basket from which were drawn out three ribbons in different colors, on them the names of the ladies who had originated the entertainment. Two popular figures were the Butterfly, in which the women fluttered around the floor waving large wings made of chiffon while the men pursued, wielding long-handled butterfly nets, and the Coach-and-Four, in which the men drove the women around the dance floor - - harnessed four abreast and covered with jingling ornaments.

Irene's typical week during the high social season included the germans as well as luncheons and teas. She started a Friday "lunch club" with her friends - - Bessie Martin, Eugenia and Anne Tennant, Fannie and Hattie Ross, Bessie Addison, her cousin May Jones, Callie Ryland, Lelia Myers, and Mary Cameron. Nanaire and Chillie's friends, the Brydon Tennants and the Richard Piersons, gave dinners for Irene before the germans. Her clothes were described carefully in the social columns, ". . . an accordion pleated white organdy and chiffon gown," or "green satin brocade with violets." On "off" nights Irene helped her mother entertain at dinner and card parties at home. There was also the theater to attend, and musicales.

---

*The institution of the german had come from New Orleans to Richmond some years before. At first they were small affairs held in a residence after which the participants dispersed to other houses where hostesses served supper. Then the germans moved to halls; first Levy's Hall on Main Street, then St. Alban's Hall at Third and Main, and in Irene's day, in the Masonic Temple at Belvidere and Main. They started at nine o'clock, and ended with a midnight supper, typically of raw oysters, partridges, salads, and a chocolate dessert accompanied by sherry.

The Belle

Irene reminisced about a luncheon her mother gave for Mrs. Fitzhugh Lee, the wife of the governor. "Mother decided it would be a violet lunch. The flowers, the mints, the luncheon set were all in the same color scheme. The shades were all drawn in the dining-room and the candelabra lit on the table. But Nannie and Nora, my sisters, stood in the pantry and ate most of the food before it could get on the table." One luncheon Nanaire gave for ten ladies had a Valentine's Day theme. All the decorations were crimson and heart-shaped, from the hand-painted cards to the double-heart of carnations in the center of the table.

One of the activities Irene loved best as a belle was walking up and down Franklin Street. "On Sunday every girl simply had to have a beau and nosegay to sport on Franklin Street after church." Nanaire, however, felt her girls were walking along Franklin Street too often, and attempted to restict their outings. Invariably, as soon as her mother left the house, Irene grabbed her hat and parasol and joined the parade. Sunday night was the time set for the beaux to come calling. The girls competed to see who could attract the most young men to their parlors. Monday morning they asked each other the question, "How many came to your house?"

After Lent, the parties started again, but the Richmond scene was quieter than during the winter season. In the Spring of 1893, Chillie reserved a private railroad car to travel to a dance at the Hygeia Hotel on the shores of Hampton Roads near Norfolk. He, Nanaire, Irene, and Lizzie, together with a number of young friends - - Daisy Rives, Bessie Martin, Martha and Parke Bagby, and Nettie Potts among them - - climbed aboard in the afternoon, attended the ball, and returned to Richmond late that night. Interestingly enough, *Beau Monde*, a society magazine in Richmond, made no mention of Irene, reporting that Bessie Martin and Daisy Rives were the prettiest girls in attendance.[*] During the spring months, house parties at country homes were a diversion for the young who were glad to be free of severe parental restriction

---

[*] On a trip to Norfolk, perhaps this one, Irene was aboard a ship with a group of young naval officers clustered around her. Wind swept her hat from her head. She was mortified, because sewn to her hat, for everyone to see, was a curl of her hair.

The Gibson Girl

and more at liberty to pursue ardent infatuations and courtships. In May of the same year, Irene went by train for a long weekend visit to "Algoma," a farm and rambling house in Buckingham County on the James River west of Richmond owned by General T.M. Logan.

As a result of the friendships and conquests Irene made at The White, she was asked to dances and parties in other cities. Her first trip was in October, 1891 when she was gone for two weeks visiting friends in Hartford, Connecticut and Philadelphia. Two years later, she was given a crowning social honor, the invitation to lead the cotillion at New York's Patriarchs' Ball. In 1872, Mrs. William Backhouse Astor, Jr., the self-proclaimed Queen of New York Society, the guardian of its citadel against the "unwanted and unfit," and Ward McAllister, her right-hand man, a dedicated snob, and a figure of derision even in his own day, composed a list of the twenty-five foremost gentlemen in that city. Mrs. Astor designated them "Patriarchs," each man's task to ask four ladies and four gentlemen to a subscription ball to be held in the elegant rooms of Delmonico's restaurant. For over twenty years the Patriarchs' Ball had been the primary event for New York society, and every year the most attractive and enchanting young matron in that society's midst was selected by McAllister to lead the main figure. In December, 1893 it was Irene's turn. Only one time before had an unmarried girl been asked; never had an outsider been the central attraction.

Irene's invitation to lead the Patriarchs' Ball was the culmination of all Nanaire's and Chillie's social ambitions for their daughter.[*] The preparations for her entry into New York society were hectic, and for the first time Irene was allowed a hair-dresser who piled her hair tightly on the top of her head. Her ballgown was cream satin, stiffly boned. A pleated ruffle, eight inches wide, made of pale green silk with little rosebuds and lace, was draped around her neck. "My, it was pretty. . . .So was I."

Irene recalled with shame her impatience during the long, tiring dress fittings in Richmond. Irene and Nanaire made many

---

[*]Irene never was sure why Ward McAllister chose her. She speculated he knew of her because his cousin was the head of the boarding school she attended in New York City.

The Belle

trips to the home of her seamstress, Mrs. Crump, "a poor tired little soul" according to Irene. Both Mrs. Crump's children were in cribs, one "smelling of wee-wee, and the eldest always had a roach of wet hair trying to be a curl." Irene had no concern for the woman's hard life, and pressed her. "Please finish so that I can wear it." Mrs. Crump looked sadly into Irene's eyes, saying, "Well, I'll do my best."

Chillie went with Irene to New York to watch over his daughter's triumph.* Although her presence to some people was a vivid symbol of the relaxation of tensions between the North and the South, Irene was not interested in the sectional significance of this honor. She only wanted to look beautiful. "I could feel the critical glances of the New York mothers and daughters as I sat in my box at the Metropolitan Opera before the ball. At the ball, however, the men were lovely to me."

The Richmond *Dispatch* picked up the New York wire reporting the ball, and printed its description in the center of the front page with the headline, "She Leads The Cotillion And Is Greatly Admired. " The article gushed, "Richmond has reason to be proud of her beautiful representation at the Patriarchs' Ball and McAllister dinner. The New York papers have made very handsome much of Miss Langhorne and given us occasion for pride and pleasure. Our belle is better than handsome, for she is winsome and lovely in character, as well as person."

The Ball began at midnight. "The rooms at Delmonico's were transformed into bowers of roses. The rarest exotics were used for floral screens. Bases of mirrors were banked with flowers. Vine palms and roses predominated. The Four Hundred engaged the whole of Delmonico's. Supper was served at small tables on the ground floor. The cotillion was led by Miss Langhorne, the celebrated Southern Beauty, who was greatly admired by the ladies present."

---

*Nanaire might have gone, but the newspaper accounts do not mention her. It is hard to believe she would have missed out on her daughter's crowning achievement unless she was not invited or was sick.

The Gibson Girl

One society reporter was particularly enthusiastic. "She was so conspicuously handsome that she straightway became the toast with the appreciative gentlemen of the glass-of-fashion-and-mold-of-form contingent, who know a pretty woman when they see one, and the masculine intelligence from that day to this declared her delightful to look at, witty to talk to, and dangerous to think on. The girls of her set, too, have yielded her admiration for her good looks, not with the damn-with-faint-praise variety of tribute, peculiar to the envious female, but the Simon Pure thing, warm, genuine, because she was so winning."

But, one observer had not such a rosy view of Irene's evening. "At the Patriarchs' Ball," he recalled some years later, "her reception was cold, critical, and snobby from the disgruntled audience that was miffed that a local girl was not chosen, even if she had been Helen of Troy. McAllister's experiment to revive the flagging interest in this institution was not repeated, and Irene, the innocent victim of an internecine row, went back to Richmond bearing the empty honor of this single achievement."[*]

The next Spring, Irene went to Philadelphia to lead that city's Assembly. The following year, in February 1895, she was invited to New Orleans by Judge and Mrs. Thomas J. Semmes, who had met Irene and her family at The White, to be a part of the Mardi Gras celebrations. In the New Orleans papers she was rated as being "one of the most elegant women in the exclusive society of her brilliant city." In her honor, the Semmes hosted "a beautiful fancy-dress ball," and other "handsome entertainments" were given for her. *The Times-Picayune* reported at Irene's ball the "costumes were exceedingly pretty and in many instances unique." Irene was dressed as the goddess Diana, in white and gold as she led the figures with Judge Semmes.

Outwardly, Irene laughed at the fuss made over her. Within her family she did not reveal how important the attention was to her because she would have been teased unmercifully. True, she was the acknowledged family beauty. Yes, she was a glamorous figure

---

[*]I do not know the identity of this observer. The quote was taken from a newspaper clipping in Dana's scrapbook. Unfortunately, the portion of the article which may have given his or her name was not pasted in.

The Belle

of romance. But still she was only a big sister. Nannie remembered a time when Irene came home from an out-of-town visit where she had been the belle of every ball, and the papers had been full of flattering paragraphs about her. The children all fell on her, saying, "You may have looked beautiful at the party but people ought to see the way you look now."

CHAPTER FIVE

MIRADOR

The summer of 1891 was Irene's last full season at The White. In June, 1892, Chillie purchased Mirador, a country house at the base of the Blue Ridge mountains west of Charlottesville in the farming community of Greenwood some seventy-five miles from Richmond. As a boy, Chillie visited cousins in this part of Albemarle County, and he had always held an affection for the hills which rolled upward to the mountain's base, the hazy air that could turn the summer leaf greens to blue and purple, and the sweeping views of the rounded mountaintops cut by gaps that led to the Shenandoah Valley beyond.

At last, Chillie could recreate the country lifestyle he had enjoyed as a child at his Grandfather Dabney's farm above the banks of the James River near Lynchburg. Starting off with 181 1/4 acres, he gradually added to his holdings, buying farms abutting his property as well as mountain timberland and pastures where cattle were driven to graze in the summers.* Initially, Mirador was a summer haven for the Langhorne family, a refuge from Richmond's heat and dirt. In 1896, 101 West Grace Street was leased and Mirador became the Langhornes' primary residence. Mirador's location was ideal for Chillie because he was closer to the western Virginia construction sites where Langhorne & Langhorne graded and gravelled railroad beds.

---

*Chillie purchased Mirador for $9000 and a few months later deeded the farm to Nanaire to protect her should he be wiped out financially. In Albemarle County the old deedbooks are full of his land transactions. In 1895, he bought in Nanaire's name 344 1/4 acres of mountain land above Mirador for $700. His estate sold it for $6000 in 1920 - - a handsome return. From his neighbor, Purcell McCue, he bought in 1910 a parcel of 446 acres of farmland contiguous to Mirador for $4250. His grandson, Chiswell Dabney Langhorne Perkins, bought that piece from Chillie's estate in 1919 for $17,500. The farm I was raised on and where Irene came to spend her last years was once owned by Chillie. He bought it for $8000 in 1914, and gave it to Genevieve, the widow of his son Harry.

Nanaire was not at all happy with her husband's decision to become a country squire, nor was Irene, although the younger children were exhilarated with their new world full of animals, open fields, and creek beds for playing. Mirador was a far cry from the luxurious and elegant summers at The White to which both women had become pleasantly attached, where they were accepted as prominent players in that resort's society. Irene felt she was in exile from the summer drama in which she held the leading role, banished to a remote, desolate place with no audience to appreciate her charms.

Again, Nanaire was faced with the difficult task of making a house into a home. Again she had to create a pleasing environment for the many people dependent upon her housekeeping abilities. But this time her job was more complicated because the challenges of country life were monumental. Local blacks had to be trained as servants. Markets and stores to purchase the staples her large brood needed were far away. Well water was unreliable, and Mirador had no plumbing. In fact, Nanaire had encountered enough of country life as a girl and much preferred living in town.

Nanaire's initial resistance to life at Mirador soon waned as she brought the family's new life into order and began to appreciate the beauty of their summer place. The house had been built in the early part of the eighteenth century, of Federal style, the soft shades of its brick in Flemish-bond design. It was graceful in spite of its box-like shape ornamented with small white pillars framing the front door. There was a balcony, and a widow's walk capped the roof. The front lawn, shaded by oak, elm, and sycamore trees and fenced with stone walls, fanned outward from the front wooden porch down to a stone archway standing next to the post road linking Charlottesville to the westward mountains and valleys. Behind the house, Nanaire planted flower gardens of simple design, two squares enclosed by a white picket fence. Beyond the garden were orchards and fields with white plank fences, the steep-roofed barns, and the Blue Ridge mountains. There were outbuildings for servants, a smoke house, a brick cottage used as an office, and a guest house.

Mirador's floor plan was standard with four rooms on the main floor, and four above. Immediately, Chillie had two small

The Gibson Girl

upstairs bathrooms installed, but these were the only modern conveniences. Electricity replaced kerosene and oil lamps over a decade later, and for years the only source of heat was wood- and coal-burning fireplaces. A long, narrow hallway ran from the front door through the width of the house to the back porch. With the windows and doors opened, cooling breezes made the main floor comfortable except on the hottest summer days. Louvered shutters, closed against the sun, created inside the house a dusty dimness which was accentuated by Nanaire's dark Victorian mahogany furniture and heavy draperies. A large English basement housed the dining room, kitchen, pantries and storerooms. When Chillie added two wings a few years after he bought Mirador, the dining room and pantry were moved upstairs into one of them because the basement location was too dark and close to the servants' quarters; in the other wing, bedrooms and a study were added.

Thinking she would be bored in rural Greenwood, Irene spent much of the summer of 1892 visiting friends and cousins vacationing at resorts. But at some point she changed her mind about Greenwood and Mirador. In a letter postmarked June 25, 1894 to Philip Haxall in Richmond thanking him for magazines he sent her, she wrote, "I have become a typical hayseed now, but I do enjoy the country so much and I am willing to be thought one." She chattered on, "I have been riding quite a lot, but not on my mare, as she still has that gall so I have been driving her." The summer heat was unrelenting. "It is not good for crops and nothing looks its best. We had quite a family reunion yesterday, in-laws, relations from every part. We had a very jolly time. . . . I want you to see what a smart home we have, and I can give you a mount and a beautiful ride."

Irene came to love Mirador, her nostalgia somehow out of proportion to the time she spent in the Albemarle countryside as a young woman. Unlike her younger sisters who lived there year round, she had only four summers at Mirador before she married and moved to New York City. Nevertheless, for the rest of her days Mirador was always her refuge, the place where she came to be refreshed and comforted. Much later in life she expressed her youthful happiness and her deep yearning for Mirador. "Think of those lovely days at Home, everyone just thinking that tomorrow is coming with more joy and even those who had their problems enjoyed life. . . . The whole picture of home is Front Porch, summer nights, honeysuckle, frogs, creeks that smell of grapevine, singing, Popper giving us all the devil and then so kind. Mother working and making good dishes, pretty clothes for us all, playing my accompaniments. . . ."

During each of Irene's summers at Mirador the house continually was overloaded with guests, primarily friends from Richmond who had journeyed by train for three hours, an easy trip in those days. They were met at the Greenwood Depot by a family member in the farm wagon as well as one or more servants to handle the baggage. The road from the mountain depot was steep, winding and rutted. Driving was difficult because the proper pressure needed to be applied constantly to the wooden shoe that served as a brake. After a mile the road flattened as it veered right at Mr. Woodson's blacksmith shop before the long, straight stretch past Purcell McCue's apple and peach orchards. Mirador's pastures and barns, outbuildings and sheds soon came into view, and for more than a mile only the green-painted roof of the main house could be seen, its walls hidden by trees and flowering bushes. A short blast from a hunting horn announced the travelers' arrival, and servants and family poured out the doors to welcome and carry suitcases and trunks to the upstairs bedrooms or to the guesthouse. Before Chillie added the wings sleeping space was crowded and cramped. Guests - - of like sex - - were expected to share the same bed, even if they were total strangers.*

Irene may have had certain simple household duties to help her mother, but most of her energy was spent either entertaining her girlfriends and beaux, or at her makeup table, or near her closet changing outfits in preparation for yet another grand entrance. Each morning, before the deer flies stirred to mass around the horses' ears and before the heat rising from the parched ground below

---

*According to Irene's niece, Nancy Lancaster, when Dana came to Mirador to propose to Irene, he had to share a bed with another man also courting her. This is a good story, but I wonder. The Langhornes most likely would have put Dana in bed with his friend and traveling companion, Robert Howard Russell!

The Gibson Girl

became too intense, she rode, eager to take with her a young beau who would be most impressed by her horsemanship and, in particular, herself, attired in a tight-fitting, well-tailored riding dress.

Nanaire's day started early, well before that of her pampered daughter. She bustled through the house, consulting the butler, instructing the cleaning women, making sure the laundry was in full operation, and unlocking storerooms with keys from a curved wicker basket she carried in the crook of her arm. Chillie, loud and imperious, roared and bellowed, forever interfering with her routine with his demands. She was relieved when he finally closeted himself in his office with his male secretary and business associates who came to spend an hour or the week; or when he left the house, more than likely gone to the riding ring to instruct Nannie or Phyllis, or to the barn or into the fields to oversee whatever work was in progress.

Each day began with Chillie presiding at the breakfast table. Guests were expected to be present and fully clothed at eight o'clock on the dot. There he held court, setting out the day's schedule as black servants passed grits, ham, bacon and eggs, fried tomatoes and biscuits. Family and guests gathered again for midday dinner, the formal meal of the day. Like breakfast, it was a sit-down affair with great quantities of meat raised at Mirador, fresh vegetables from Nanaire's garden, freshly churned butter, and raw milk sometimes tasting strongly of onions.

Early afternoon was a quiet time either spent reading in the shadows of shade trees or dozing off in the coolest place one could find. When Chillie napped, any available child was expected to stand quietly by him to swat away flies attempting landings on the imperial head. Even in the heat, men were required to keep their coats on in mixed company; and women and girls were covered from neck to wrist to ankle in layers of clothing. The only proper place to relieve oneself of clothing was the bedroom.

Later on, toward five or six o'clock, when the sun had drifted below the tall, lush trees which framed the lawn, and the dust kicked up by the day's work had settled, activity restarted. Chillie either loaded everyone on carriages and buckboards to visit neighbors, or friends descended on Mirador expecting a drink laced with whiskey and cooled by ice taken from Mirador's pond the past winter. At night after a light supper there was conversation and joking on the front steps, guitars and banjos and singing and storytelling. Or the mood was quiet and it was enough to sit on the porch and listen to the beat of crickets, their droning cadence punctuated by the belching of bullfrogs. Sometimes in the evening or at night neighbors gave parties for all the Mirador people to attend. Greenwood, no social backwater for Richmonders, was one of the "beats" of the *Dispatch's* society reporters. A Mrs. India Blackburn sponsored a "casino" at Greenwood Depot. A german was held which Harry and Keene attended, and Irene was among the players in a series of "tennis evenings" given by Mr. and Mrs. Hilbers.

According to Nannie, Mirador and their house at 101 West Grace Street in Richmond was always full of Irene's suitors. Some were young. Some were old. They came from abroad, and from around the corner, all trying to win her hand in marriage. Nannie kept a count for Irene and figured, all in all, she had a total of sixty-two proposals. The newspapers were full of stories extolling Irene's beauty and grace. They reported her at this party or that, or in the hunting field, the center of all eyes, and the most beautiful belle at every ball she attended. Chillie is said to have become furious when her picture appeared in a New York paper with text that was too intimate for his taste.* An often-told family story is he threatened to get on the train for New York and shoot the editor.

In a letter she wrote many years later to a niece, Irene recalled one very persistent and rather old suitor. "Old Mr. Woodward" was rich and corpulent, a banker twenty years her senior. Chillie called him a "damned old fool," and was particularly annoyed at the man when Mr. Woodward demonstrated his youthfulness and agility by picking up a handkerchief from the floor with his teeth. Mr. Woodward always was trying to kiss Irene's hand, so Ned Craven, a family friend, lent Irene a pair of smelly riding gloves to ward off his amorous advances when she took Mr.

---

*I could not locate the article. It must have been offensive for the times, because Chillie had no problem with the publicity his daughters received.

The Gibson Girl

Woodward for a drive in the Langhorne's Kentucky brake cart. Mr. Woodward, desperately in love, offered Irene a choice between a cottage at Newport or a yacht after their marriage. One morning at breakfast, he put in her hand a note that said, "The dew is on the flowers. . . .Oh! Come my love with me." Enough was finally enough, and Mr. Woodward was banished from the Langhorne home.

Knowing their daughter could marry just about anyone whom she wanted, Nanaire and Chillie were confident of a good match. Chillie continued to push Nicholas Longworth, inviting him at least on two occasions to be the family's houseguest in Richmond where Nanaire organized entertainments for him. But, in the end Mr. Longworth became only a statistic- - one of the many suitors Irene spurned. All the careful planning of her parents, the summers at The White and the balls in far away cities had not produced as yet the right man for Irene. Then she met Charles Dana Gibson - - and fell in love.

CHAPTER SIX

THE YANKEE GIBSON

Irene had been avoiding her long bridal walk down the aisle for almost two years - - and for good reason. She knew marriage meant the end of her belledom, that as a matron she would no longer hold a tantalizing allure for the many men who constantly swarmed around her. She also knew from the experiences of her friends that marriage could mean the beginning of long years of slavish work and life-threatening pregnancies with the distinct possibility of being on the short end of an unbalanced relationship, dominated and controlled by husband and convention.

For Irene to succumb, Dana Gibson's impact on her must have been electric. Speculating about the sexuality of parents - - much less grandparents - - is not a comfortable subject, but I find it, though a bit embarrassing, highly intriguing. Somehow we forget that loved ones we know as old or elder were once filled with the spontaneity and juices of youth. I believe Irene's and Dana's initial attraction to one another was intensely physical. The best evidence supporting the argument for mutual physical entrapment is their photographs depicting two stunningly good-looking people. Irene's coquetry, incredible figure, and flirtatious posing, and Dana's manly, rugged bearing, and his immaculate and fashionable clothing all are revealed. A careful look at the picture of Dana kneeling at Irene's feet before their marriage reveals his forearm pressed against her thigh, an unusual liberty in those Victorian days - - especially for the camera's eye - - even if a strong bond of intimacy already existed.

Family lore suggests they enjoyed a strong sexual bond throughout their marriage. A much older cousin, who as a girl often stayed with my grandparents in New York, told me this story. When Lizzie died in 1914, Irene took in her daughter, Nancy Perkins. Nancy married Henry Field, the grandson of the department store magnate, Marshall Field. Henry died only months after the marriage, and Irene's duty as Nancy's surrogate mother was to go to Chicago and stay by Nancy's side until she recovered

The Gibson Girl

from the shock of his unexpected death. Irene went, but after a few days sped back to Dana and New York. According to my cousin, the reason for her hasty return was Irene could not bear to be away from her marital bed for any length of time.

The initial spark that ignited a marriage that would last for a half a century might have been physical, but beneath their passion were stronger needs each fulfilled by the other. Dana saw a flesh and bones person even more radiant than the imaginary women he produced on paper, a woman full of the happiness and grandeur of life, a woman who could rescue him from his painful shyness and bring him out into the world. And it must not have taken her long to discover Dana's warmth and gentleness, his quiet strength, and his lack of interest in control and domination - - to Irene, welcome comfort from Chillie's volcanic reactions if she displeased him.

I suspect Irene was first taken in by Dana's celebrity and was quick to realize the man already acclaimed as an arbiter of taste and fashion was the only man on earth who could keep her in the spotlight. Irene knew Dana Gibson was a good catch. Putting love and attraction and commitment - - the important foundations of their marriage - - aside for the moment, surely she was enticed by the prospect of marrying a man who regularly traveled abroad and who lived a life in New York full of balls and parties and elegant socialites. In the process of spurning the many proposals of marriage over the past five years, she had developed in her mind the life she wanted to lead. She had no interest in being stuck in a remote country house in Virginia's Piedmont. She wanted a life beyond the confines of Richmond. Marriage to Dana would not be boring. She would enter a broader world and share the limelight with her celebrated husband.

Some thirty years ago I went with my father to see the movie, *The Girl In The Red Velvet Swing*, the story of Evelyn Nesbit, a ravishing, young beauty whose husband, Harry K. Thaw, in a fit of jealousy killed her former lover, Stanford White, the most famous American architect around the turn of the century. The film was of particular interest to us because Stanford White was a friend of my grandfather's and was my father's godfather. My grandfather was portrayed - - incorrectly because he was in Paris at the time - - sitting with White when he was murdered, and later on a beach

The Yankee Gibson

sketching a model. My father was incensed by the actor's depiction of Dana. The actor, dressed in a shiny light-blue suit in the restaurant where White was shot and in an effete artist's smock and large, red bow-tie on the beach, was too slick-looking for my father's taste. On the way home my father, usually not given to talk in thoughtful detail about his parents, told me how poorly the Hollywood director captured his father. He said Dana would not be caught dead in a smock, and that he painted and drew in coat and tie, his only affectation great, soft collars that covered half his face and sometimes the lobes of his ears. My father told me of his great warmth and his massive physical strength, and how he would shake with trepidation before his many appearances as toastmaster at the innumerable banquets given within New York City's artistic community.

After that evening at the movies I no longer saw my grandfather as the seemingly austere image in the painting in our front hall. I began to picture him as a sensitive and loving man who was adored by his children and grandchildren. I never knew my grandfather. Although he knew of my existence and was pleased over my birth, I do not believe he ever saw me. My grandparents' plan was to have me christened in Maine in the Norman-like chapel my grandfather built with his own hands. In preparation, he imbedded in its brick wall a marble plaque commemorating the event. But I was a sickly baby and never made it up there the summer of 1941.

I have no personal memories to contribute to the understanding of my grandparents' relationship, nor did I learn much from my father. I doubt if my father was aware of the anxieties that filled Dana's life. I doubt if my father knew of his disappointments and the hurdles he had to overcome to provide for his family. He was too close, too much the child to understand how his mother's strength and understanding of her husband's artistic temperament underpinned the marriage. I can picture Dana's New England reticence, his unwillingness to share with anyone but his wife his fears and frustrations. I can picture the difficulty of his biographer as he attempted to probe into the core of the man. Most likely he was rebuffed gently by Dana's unwillingness to divulge thoughts or feelings that might have had a personal tinge. In countless interviews Dana stuck to two or three stories, never deviating from the narrow parameters of anecdote which protected his and his family's privacy.

Dana's personality is an integral part of Irene's story. An account of her life is incomplete without bringing him squarely into the middle of the narrative because their lives were so intertwined for so many years. Other writers in directing their attention to Dana's creative genius have kept Irene in his shadow, only casually referring to her as his wife and his Gibson Girl. Although Irene is the focal point of this story, I want him to share the spotlight. She would as well.

Dana was almost six years older than Irene. The year of her birth he was living in St. Louis, Missouri. His family had been driven from Chicago two years before by that city's 1871 Great Fire. Dana's father, Charles DeWolf Gibson, or Charley, a traveling salesman for the National Car Spring Company, a distributor of railcar parts, was gone from home much of the time. He left his wife, Josephine, or Bessie, to carry the burden of rearing their three sons, Dana, his older brother, Langdon, and the baby, LeBaron, who would die shortly after his second birthday. There was never enough money.* Charley was not a particularly successful salesman, and the Gibsons were entirely on their own financially with no

---

*Dana inherited a proud lineage of Bradfords, Marstons, DeWolfs, and other branches of fine New England stock whose members comprised a generous percentage of the *Mayflower's* passenger list. As distant cousins through the DeWolf line, Bessie and Charley shared the most interesting ancestor, Mark Antony DeWolf, a Rhode Island seafaring man who settled in Bristol, Rhode Island. He founded the family business of trading in molasses, rum, and slaves - - with a good deal of privateering thrown in. James, one of Mark Antony's fifteen children, took over and expanded the family fleet, which outnumbered the United States Navy's at the onset of the War of 1812. In spite of being widely known as a slaver until the trade in human flesh became a capital offense in 1820, James gained a measure of respect with his election to the United States Senate during James Monroe's administration. A fortune that made James the second richest man in America was destroyed by his nephew, George DeWolf, who gained control of the family assets in the 1830s and squandered them away through foolish speculations.

family income to augment his meager and erratic commission earnings.

By the time Dana's grandfather, the first Charles Dana Gibson, met his wife, Abby DeWolf, her family's only substantial asset was an expanse of beautiful farmland called simply, The Farm, the site of a good portion of modern-day Bristol, Rhode Island. Charles had lost his first wife and was the father of a daughter, Julia, when he and Abby were married in 1840. Evidently, Abby was extremely jealous of Julia's existence and insisted she stay in Brooklyn, New York, where friends of her father raised her, a requirement Charles tolerated for unknown reasons.

After their marriage, Abby and Charles lived in Massachusetts, then moved to Buffalo, New York, where he was a banker and grain broker. His business interests, together with extended trips to Brooklyn to be with Julia, kept him away from home so often that Abby decided to move back to Bristol and The Farm. Abby made it plain she liked her family more than her husband, and their marriage became one of convenience. Although his brief stays in Bristol upset her, they shared a marital bed at least occasionally because two children were born after their separation.

Charles was a successful entrepreneur, and in spite of their strained relationship, agreed to build for Abby, Longfield, a spacious frame Victorian house adorned with gingerbread decoration and only 200 yards from The Farm. There at Longfield, Charley was raised with his younger siblings, Maitland and Louisa. Charley adored his father, and spent much of his youth waiting for him to come home. Each arrival, full of bear hugs and kisses, was a special event for a boy deprived of constant fatherly affection. A sensitive boy, Charley at an early age disapproved of his mother's treatment of his half-sister, Julia. Abby may have mellowed as she became older, because Dana, having spent many happy summers as a child at Longfield, wrote of her years later, "She was very kind and never lost patience with any of us."

The Civil War broke out when Charley was seventeen. After enlisting in the army, he was assigned to Rhode Island's 14th Heavy Artillery Regiment stationed near Bristol on Narragansett Bay. After obtaining his sergeant's stripes, he applied to West Point. He was turned down despite a letter of recommendation from General

The Gibson Girl

Ambrose E. Burnside, a family friend then in command of the Army of the Potomac, and an audience with President Lincoln.* Nevertheless, he earned his commission as a Second Lieutenant, served for a time in Washington's defenses, and then was sent home to recover from illness diagnosed as smallpox, but was actually a bout of concurrent measles and chickenpox. Toward the war's end he volunteered to be an officer in a black regiment, but resigned his commission when the Confederacy's President Jefferson Davis proclaimed that white Union officers commanding colored troops, if captured, could be shot.

Charley obtained leave in 1864 to marry Bessie Lovett and to spend a short honeymoon in Niagara Falls. After the war they moved to Boston and boarded with relatives. Charley found work at Cabot & Brother, probably a railroad supply firm, and within two years his father gave him a small, brick house - - 27 Arnold Street - - in Roxbury, in those days a distant Boston suburb of open fields and woodland. Charles's last generous present to his son before his death in the summer of 1867, a month before the birth of his namesake, the second Charles Dana Gibson, was money to furnish their new home. Dana's grandfather had invested heavily in shares of western gold and silver mines which turned out to be worthless, and he had nothing of value to leave Abby except a life insurance policy which paid off Longfield's mortgage. During the years to come, she was able to eke out an existence by farming and selling off pieces of Longfield's acreage.

Tired of moving his family from city to city, Charley in 1875 saw the opportunity to settle in a permanent home by joining Ramapo Iron and Steel Works, the manufacturer of railroad car parts he had been selling at National Car Spring Company. Ramapo was headquartered in New York City, and Charley, not being able to afford the prices in suburban communities more convenient to Manhattan, bought a house in Flushing, Long Island.

In those days Flushing's particular pride was its trees. It was a pleasant town of 12,000 residents close to the waters of Flushing Bay and surrounded by meadows and commercial garden nurseries.

---

*Lincoln told him sons of Union officers were first in line for West Point appointments and Charley had little chance of being accepted.

The Yankee Gibson

The Gibsons lived in the middle of town at 100 Sanford Avenue where three daughters - - Elizabeth, Annie, and Josephine - - were born.* The frame, three-storied house with its front porch only a few yards from the sidewalk was comfortable with ample space for the large family. Today nothing remains of their street or the Flushing Dana knew to suggest it was once a place of beautiful trees shading brick houses and ornamented iron fences circling large lawns. Melancholy-looking apartment buildings now crowd together in the same space, their bulk interrupted only by fast-food restaurants and dry-cleaning establishments.

It must have been a particular sadness in Charley's life that, like his father, yet for different reasons, his destiny was to spend so little time with his family. Although he had provided a stable life for his family, his work for Ramapo required constant travel with trips to the Midwest lasting weeks at a time. He adored Bessie and his children, and expressed his emotion and longing in tender and passionate letters home. When walking along a railroad track somewhere in Minnesota soon after the family's move to Flushing, he picked flowers and enclosed them in an envelope with a letter to Bessie. He wrote, ". . . each blossom bears a kiss, a fresh kiss. Although they will be faded much before they reach you, the love that goes with them will never fade. Kiss tenderly for me the three precious blossoms that God has given us. . . . Bless them a thousand times and pray to grace to teach them holiness and goodness in their early childhood. . . . the sun always shines in my heart when I think of you and home so you may be sure few clouds annoy me. Any troubles come when I think of myself and my spirits sometimes sink down, down, down in sympathy for the miserable separation I must endure." Charley's brother-in-law, James DeWolf Lovett, wrote years after Charley's death, "By his own fireside, surrounded by his family, with a baby snuggled in his arms, he was supremely happy and there his love and devotion were simply boundless."

Charley compensated for his long absences by the attention he gave his children when he was home. Dana and Langdon

---

*Beth was born in 1876, Annie in 1878, and Josephine in 1882.

The Gibson Girl

idolized him. The brothers looked upon their father as a companion, a teacher, and an example of all that was good and kind. Charley loved the outdoors, and introduced his sons to the joys of nature. He encouraged them to examine and remember the most subtle details of the world around them - - the way a bird sets her wings when approaching a nest, or the staccato movement of a squirrel as he searches for acorns.

Although Charley had no special artistic skill, he loved to draw, and his letters home often contained pictures illustrating his words. He also enjoyed cutting silhouettes with paper and scissors. One day, when Dana was no more than three or four years old, he picked up his father's blunt scissors and began to cut. By the time he was eight years old, Dana's cut-outs showed a sophistication and meticulous attention to detail much beyond his years. His parents soon realized their child had a remarkable God-given gift. The Gibsons' friends, when shown the cutouts, could not believe a child had done them, so Dana was called in from play to demonstrate his creative talent. Dana's first recognition of his own unusual skill came on a long train ride from St. Louis to Boston. Fellow passengers noticed him snipping away, were entranced, and offered money for his work. The child experienced his first public critical accolade when his cut-outs were shown in a local art show. "Perhaps the most remarkable thing in the whole exhibition," reported the Flushing newspaper, "are the frames which contain the silhouettes cut by Master Dana Gibson."

On a visit to relatives in Boston, Langdon and a cousin got the fine idea that they, too, could profit from Dana's skill. They suggested that a partnership be formed to market Dana's silhouettes and set up a booth on the front lawn. After only one sale - - to the milkman - - over a two hour period, disappointed, they closed up shop. Somehow, they were unable to comprehend that seven o'clock in the morning was not the best time of day to sell their wares.

In 1931 Dana wrote to his children, "But I like to feel that my parents had a share [in passing along promising family traits] and that the health and happiness I saw and felt all around me as a child will be repeated in the lives of my grandchildren." Dana described his mother as "having perfect health and a buoyant nature." Attempting to explain away the downcast expression on his mother's face in an attached photograph, he wrote, "These pictures of my mother and father were taken at about the time I first began to remember. In my mother's picture her expression seems sadder than I ever saw her. . . . And I am sure this sadness was an accidental expression of the moment." Perhaps it was hard for Dana to appreciate the difficulty of Bessie's life, the unrelenting pressure of raising five children with little money and a husband gone most of the time. Bessie's constant worry was that Langdon and Dana would drown in the waters which surrounded Flushing. Only when the boys went off to their grandmother in Bristol during the summers could she relax.

At an early age Dana was a responsible son. He helped his youngest sister, Josephine, with her bath and her homework. He sat with Elizabeth, or Beth, when she was sick, telling stories of future adventures in Africa they would have together. He drew pictures of himself about to be devoured by a tiger and Beth rescuing him. According to Bessie, Dana was "a strong, healthy child, always happy, free from all taints of morbid moods, always finding amusement with his scissors, paint box and pencils." His perception and intellect were considered remarkable for a child. An uncle's assessment of Dana as a boy was "he spoke seldom but with a wit beyond his years."

One afternoon Bessie was called to his school, Flushing Institute, a few days before Christmas vacation. She was sure he had gotten into trouble or had been hurt. Instead, the principal took her to the locked door of the auditorium, opened it, and there, filling the blackboards on all walls, was a colorful and detailed scene of Santa Claus and his reindeer flying over hills and valleys and through ice and snow. Dana had found himself alone in this large room with plenty of colored chalk, and could not resist the opportunity to create something special for the Christmas season.

At thirteen, Dana was taken under the wing of Mrs. Robert L. Cutting, a well-connected Gibson cousin in Manhattan much interested in promoting his talent. Seeking advice on where to place this gifted child during his summer vacation, she took Dana to meet George B. Post, New York City's most noted architect, who in turn drove Dana to the studios of the sculptor, Augustus Saint-Gaudens.

The Gibson Girl

Dana recalled their meeting. "I was taken in Mr. Post's wagon and very soon found myself in the presence of the sculptor. I was scared half to death. He is a large man, and just then he looked like a giant. He was engaged in modeling a leg in clay from a big Italian in short trousers. After a short consultation, Mr. Post went away, leaving me there. 'Can you cut out things?' asked St. Gaudens, looking down at me. 'Yes sir,' said I, and he told me to see what I could do with the Italian as a model. The latter was as badly frightened as I was, and it is needless to say that I did not there distinguish myself." For two weeks Dana valiantly tried to model in clay, but apparently had no aptitude for working in three dimensions. "Then Mr. St. Gaudens and I unanimously concluded that I was a failure as a sculptor and I went back to school."[*]

The following summer, Charley secured a job for Dana as a messenger boy with Buttrick and Ellman, a Wall Street firm, hoping his son would become entranced with the investment world and want to be a stockbroker. Most of Dana's time was spent on a bench in the office vestibule, pen and paper in hand, waiting to be called and sketching the people around him. His one achievement that summer had nothing to do with the business of brokerage or investment banking, but emanated from the assassination of President James Garfield. As a memorial to the late President, a competition among Wall Street runners to determine who could best draw his likeness was held. Dana won - - the first prize, one dollar.

Dana knew he was not suited for the business or professional worlds, and by the age of seventeen he was finished with his formal education. Although he once said in his school days he had been a conscientious, if not a studious, pupil, he decided he learned less from books than from nature and man. His passion was art and he had his love for the outdoors. The idea of going to college probably never entered his mind. Charley was concerned about the probable direction of Dana's vocation. Nevertheless, he

---

[*]Two postscripts mark Dana's short apprenticeship to the sculptor. Dana's daughter married George Post's grandson. St. Gaudens and Dana later became close friends. Dana said the two of them often found amusement in recalling their first encounter.

The Yankee Gibson

and Bessie did everything they could to support his creative urge. They set aside the third floor of their house as his studio, and Bessie took money from her household allowance to buy Dana art supplies.

The second most influential male in Dana's young life was Dan Beard, a naturalist, author, and later founder of the Boy Scouts of America. Beard was also a prominent illustrator whose many commissions included the illustrations for Mark Twain's *A Connecticut Yankee in King Arthur's Court*. With Beard's encouragement and skilled tutelage, Dana developed his extraordinary and innate artistic talent. Beard took the Gibson boys on arduous cross-country hikes to Far Rockaway and Kissena Lake, Jamaica, Little Neck, and the site of present-day Garden City. The three of them gathered walnuts and chestnuts and carried home plants and mosses, their pockets alive with wiggling creatures which were placed in pails and buckets. Many years later, Dana told a friend there was not a bog or a water-hole in that part of Long Island he did not know by heart. At a dinner given in Beard's honor on his seventieth birthday, Dana told the guests, "Dan Beard turned over every stone on Long Island to see what was on the underside."

Dana asked Dan Beard for his guidance in building a portfolio of work to submit to the Art Students' League in New York City, the most prestigious art school in the country. Beard outlined a plan for his young friend, sending him out into the fields around Flushing and to the New York zoo to draw from life. The sketches, however, that won him admittance were of a plaster-cast bust of Voltaire in Beard's studio. For a $5 per month tuition, Dana was now among some of the best artists of the day. His fellow pupils and instructors included America's most prominent artists -- Frederic Remington, Howard Pyle, William Merritt Chase, and F.S. Church.[*]

---

[*] Student/artists gave each other pieces of their work as Christmas and birthday presents. For years a watercolor by Frederic Remington, a study of a weary Western cavalryman seated on a more weary mule, hung on the wall of my bedroom. One day I arrived home from boarding school and it was gone. Upset, I asked my father where it was. He told me he had sold it to pay my tuition.

The Gibson Girl

For two years Dana's world was divided between intensive study with charcoal, wash, and pen-and-ink at the Art Students' League and life at home in Flushing with his family. Each day he faced a tedious commute over the Long Island Railroad connecting Flushing with Hunter's Point in Long Island City, a ferry ride over the East River to 34th Street, and a long walk to the League on West 14th Street. Wanting to pay his own way, he trapped owls for taxidermists and squirrels for florists who put the creatures in cages to accent their arrangements.

The center of Dana's social life in Flushing was the Nereus Boat Club, an athletic association which gave dances and plays, competed against college and club oarsmen throughout the East, and sponsored sailing trips up Long Island Sound and beyond. A physically powerful young man with a six feet, one-and-a-half inch rugged, muscular build, Dana excelled in sports demanding strength. His youngest sister, Josephine, remembered going with Dana to watch a track and field competition at an athletic field in Flushing. The Columbia College shot-putter had no one to throw against, and Dana, invited to challenge him, came down from the stands, took off his coat, and with ease threw the shot much farther than his adversary.

Langdon and Dana were two of the Club's best oarsmen. One year they were asked to row with the New York Rowing Club in the annual Fourth of July regatta at Philadelphia on the Schuylkill River. Two hundred thousand people lined the river's banks as the New York Rowing Club came in a close second behind Cornell University.

Dana's stint at the Art Student's League was a time of hard work and frustration. He learned the techniques of rendering, but was still far away from creating an individual style. His drawings were crude and unpolished. Time and time again he trudged up the stairs to publishing sanctuaries, his portfolio clutched under his arm, hoping to sell one of his sketches. Time and time again his work was rejected. He suffered, sometimes convinced he was a failure. He often considered giving up and becoming a clerk, but kept plowing ahead in his chosen career, believing he might prove to be a worse clerk than artist. His father wrote to him, concerned about his son's progress. "Dear Papa," Dana gamely replied, "but

The Yankee Gibson

everyone who has ever reached the goal has had to start way down. You see, if I commence now to build up some sort of trade, by the time I have to make a living I will have some sort of reputation worked up. . . . if it is in me to make a great artist, it will surely come out." "Keep at it my son," Charley wrote back. "When you get out in the stream the current will be with you."

Then Dana's break came. When he first submitted his drawings to *Life*, a prestigious weekly magazine, its editor, John Ames Mitchell, recognized the poor quality of the nineteen year old's work but saw a potential he felt should be encouraged. Mitchell remembered, "It was apparent at the time that he and the Good Lord were entertaining divergent views regarding light and shadow." Nevertheless, the editor saw merit in a sketch Dana titled "The Moon and I" and purchased it for $4.00. "I was frightened out of my wits for fear he would ask me my price," Dana recalled, "but I had made up my mind to say 50 cents if he did, and when he made out a check for $4.00 I felt as if I were robbing the man." "The Moon and I" appeared in *Life's* March 25, 1886 issue, unsigned. Dana's later description of his first sale was blunt. It was "a measly, half-baked thing of a dog barking at the moon, very badly done, very foolish and pointless." Now he had reason to start an account book, and noted on its first page his $4.00 sale. He made six more entries detailing *Life* magazine purchases during the next four months - - total income $39.00!

Dana came onto the scene when the popularity of magazines had skyrocketed. From 1865 to 1885 the number of periodicals in the United States grew from 700 to 3300. The linotype machine, rotary press, and modern production systems had cut production costs dramatically. Magazine revenue increased as a result of advertisements for a deluge of brand names brought about by mass production and the standardization of consumer products. Dana took any job, drawing anything for anybody. He illustrated advertisements for railroads and medical supplies, and depicted scenes from Gilbert & Sullivan operettas. Demand for his work grew rapidly with more orders from *Life*. Then, *Tid-Bits*, another popular humor magazine, picked him up. Within a year his pen-and-ink sketches were in general demand, and he was getting as much as $30 for a large cartoon. His first literary commission was an

The Gibson Girl

illustration for a story by Sarah Orne Jewett, "Luck of the Bogans," which was published in *Scribner's, Century,* and then *Harper's,* the most respected of the era's periodicals.

Although he still lived at home, before long Dana was making more than enough money - - $400 a month in commissions, an annual income equivalent to $100,000 today - - to lease a studio in Manhattan's Alpine Building at 33rd and Broadway. The press took its first notice of him when, in 1887, *Epoch* magazine acknowledged him as an artist. Oddly, the writer seemed to be more interested in his athletic ability, describing him as a ". . . fine, strapping, well-built fellow who is an important member of the crew of the eight-oared shell that the Flushing Boat Club sends to battle for that old-fashioned village on the Harlem and in other local regattas."

With a few years of maturity and some experience under his belt Dana focused on political cartooning. He drew a series of pro-Democratic party cartoons leading up to the 1888 presidential election in which the incumbent, Grover Cleveland, was beaten by the Republicans' Benjamin Harrison. In the 1892 presidential campaign he turned his pen against Cleveland in weekly lampoons for *Life;* concurrently, Dana drew anti-Harrison cartoons for *Tid-Bits*. Obviously, Dana had no strong political allegiances of his own because he was happy to support the divergent editorial policies of whatever periodicals paid him.

His cartoons were clever, forceful, and humorous and had the sting of satire. "A funny dog was Gibson," wrote one critic, "full of original, whimsical humor, and an appreciation for the littleness of great men." Ten years later, a reviewer for the Buffalo *Times* chided Dana for wasting his talent "on the debauch of the summer girl," and stated that he could have been the greatest of American political cartoonists. But Dana abandoned his promising career as a political caricaturist when he realized he did not have the stomach for offending people. After one of his attacks on Cleveland, Dana found himself at a small gathering with the President at Marion, Massachusetts, where they were both vacationing. Dana never knew whether Cleveland linked him with his biting cartoons. Nothing was said, but he was most uncomfortable and embarrassed in the President's company. William

The Yankee Gibson

Dean Howells, the dean of American letters and a man Dana admired, was also a target of Dana's hired pen. Howells let it be known that he was "very cut up over Gibson's drawings of him in *Life*." A friend of Howells said, ". . . he does not think he deserves the sneers and abuse from every little penny a liner." Dana determined never again to draw acidly personal cartoons, a resolve he kept until World War I, when he attacked Germany's Kaiser.

CHAPTER SEVEN

THE FAMOUS ILLUSTRATOR

By 1889, Dana had proved his worth as a successful illustrator. Editors grew to depend on this young man to produce creative, imaginative drawings that promoted their magazines' political positions or helped to sell their advertisers' products. His income climbed to $800 a month, not because he was paid more per piece than his contemporaries, but because he worked incessantly. Now, confident he could support himself in a most comfortable style, his mind turned to the larger goals of learning to draw more skillfully and producing something entirely his own.

Asked years later why he began to draw women, Dana replied, "I was young and healthy, and the one thing that's worth drawing when you're young and happy is a woman. You can't spend all day with fruit and flowers." He drew picture after picture of pretty girls, but these early experiments were crude, undistinguished, and forgettable. His figures sometimes had curious, almost lumbering, appearances with broad shoulders and hips, thick throats, and large arms; little heads and faces with dainty and patrician features did not match too ample torsos. Dana's style, though commercially adequate, was tight and gloomy. His lines, minutely and laboriously cross-hatched, were not forceful enough to produce the images he wanted.

Dana knew he had a great deal to learn. He looked abroad, away from American techniques and constraints, to England and to George DuMaurier, a British illustrator and author. DuMaurier created Trilby, a statuesque upper-class maiden, "a beautiful woman beautifully attired," who not only was gracefully drawn but had character and strength. Comparing his amateurish efforts to DuMaurier's animated and resolute Trilby, Dana saw his mission - - to draw a uniquely American woman, a vision of clarity, charm, and personality, a woman whose distinctiveness would gain popular appeal.

With his accumulated savings Dana embarked on an extended pilgrimage to Europe, first to meet DuMaurier in London, and then to study somewhere on the Continent. DuMaurier recalled

My grandmother, as I knew her.

Nanaire.

Chillie.

Buck.

Chiswell Dabney's plantation house

Nora

Phyllis.

Nanaire and Nannie.

Lizzie.

101 West Grace Street. (Courtesy: the Valentine Museum)

Irene at 11 or 12 years old, costumed for a Roman or Grecian tableau.

White Sulphur Springs as Irene knew it. This view shows the Grand Central Hotel and the cottages where the Langhornes stayed.

This carefully composed group of belles and beaux was photographed at White Sulphur Springs in 1891 when Irene was seventeen years old. Irene is third from the left, staring into the eyes of Bernard Carter. With Carter on the front row are Chauncey Willey, Barkau Valle, and George Carter. Irene's great friend, Martha Bagby, is at her right. The other girls are Mildred Carlisle, Belle Bodine, and Irene's double first cousin, May Jones. The two men standing in back are Murray Bohlen and Thomas Riggs.

Irene is the girl on the left. She could have been no older than fifteen at the time. The elegant attire of the young men is impressive — particularly, the spats of the fellow on the left. Times have changed. Today he would be wearing a baseball hat, most likely turned around with the brim in the back! (Courtesy:The Greenbrier)

Gertie Camm, Mary Halstead, Irene, Helen Harvey, Margie Macgill, Pattie Taylor, Margaret McIntosh, Ellen Hobson, and Helen Bates posed behind Annie Camm's skirt. The picture was taken at The White when Irene was 16 or 17. Possibly the photographer was so engrossed in the artistry of his arrangement of Annie Camm's skirt, he did not realize he had run out of backdrop on the left side of the frame.

A detail from a photograph Irene labeled, "Miss Thomas's Lunch — August 18, 1890." A kiss was Irene's and her friend's idea of an appropriate pose for the camera.

Irene had to watch her weight when she was a young girl. After her marriage, one of her female contemporaries in Richmond was delighted to report that Irene was quite chubby. She was 19 or 20 in this photograph and appears to be a bit stocky.

Irene dressed in the gown she wore in 1894 to lead the Patriarch's Ball in New York City.

Silhouettes.

Dana, eight years old, cutting silhouettes.

A tintype of Dana, probably taken when he was 16 or 17.

100 Sanford Avenue. Dana's home in Flushing, N.Y.

Dana and Langdon.

Dana, with tennis racket, and boyhood friends.

Dana had his portrait taken soon after he began to sell his drawings to *Life* and other periodicals.

TIME!

First Case of Free Trade Fever.
Consulting Physician Dana: A case of Black, or Jungle Fever. Half the body gone already. At this rate there won't be a white spot on him by November.
Doctor Randall: Yes, yes; I warned him of it! But do you really think it's all up with him, Doctor?
Consulting Physician Dana: Oh, yes; hopeless you know — you can't stop a thing like this. And once let it get among the poor working people, and it will kill them off like sheep.

That Delicious Moment.
When you meet the Nobleman your daughter has captured in Europe.

That Delicious Moment.
When you find you are to take to dinner the girl who yesterday refused you.

A Bachelor's Supper.

Ethel Barrymore.

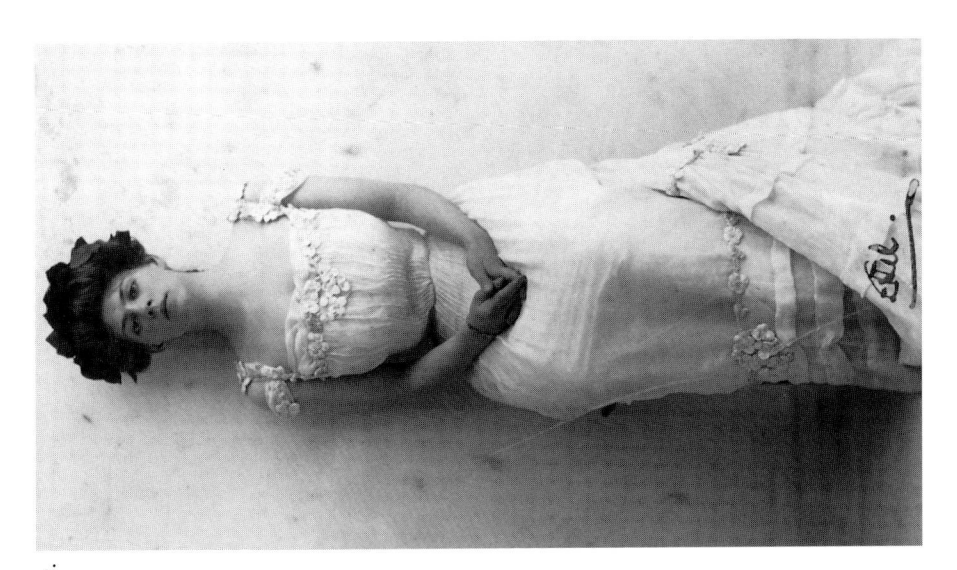

Richard Harding Davis.

Mrs. Steele Poole's Housewarming.

A Castle in the Air.

These young girls who marry millionaires should stop dreaming.

Dana in his studio.

Mirador. 1895.

Irene. The summer of her engagement.

A Parody of Dana's marriage proposal to Irene.

A Tragedy: Act I
Dana on bended knee, asking Irene for her hand in marriage.

A Tragedy: Act II
Dana, continuing his plea for her hand as she smiles down at him, perhaps more receptive.

A Tragedy: Act III
Irene turns her back to Dana, a sign of her rejection. Dana is bereft, disconsolate, a figure of canine submission.

A Tragedy: Act IV
Irene's rejection is complete. Dana expires.

Richard Howard Russell took and labeled the photographs.

Honeymoon photographs taken in England. In both pictures Irene is wearing the same dress with its voluminous "leg-of-mutton" sleeves.

After Presentation.

A Little Story. By a sleeve.

Irene at the Piano.

After their honeymoon, Dana took Irene to Marion, Massachusetts to introduce her to his aunts and their families.

Irene's and Dana's apartment on the top floor of the *Life* building. The parlor is filled with rich fabrics and ornate clutter.

An Ambassador's Ball In the Days to Come.

The
Gibson
Girl

At Longfield. Irene, Babs, and Dana with Abby Gibson, the first Charles Dana Gibson's widow.

Chillie and his poker-playing friends on Mirador's front porch.

Dana drew Irene twice in this illustration for Richard Harding Davis's novel, *Soldiers of Fortune*.

After the War.
"Welcome Home! Are you one of our heroic 71st?"
"No, I ain't no hero. I'm a regular."

Irene at Mirador with Babs, Lang, and Bobbie Shaw.

127 East 73rd Street.

Irene at 31 with her children.

A composite of Dana's pen-and-ink creations wishing him *bon voyage* as he left for Europe in 1905.

In Paris's Bois de Boulogne. Irene on horseback, with an unidentified man.

Irene. Ill and resting in bed. Paris. 1906.

Dana in his prime.

Lang and Dana.

Babs, Dana, and Irene in Maine in 1909.

Irene in her Maine flower garden.

Chillie, flanked by Babs and Nancy Perkins.

Chillie and Irene standing on Mirador's front walk.

Babs, at the time of her marriage.

In Maine. The Gibsons and the Theodore Roosevelts.

Irene with Chillie's servants at Misfit.

Dana's oil paintings of the house on 700 Acre Island.

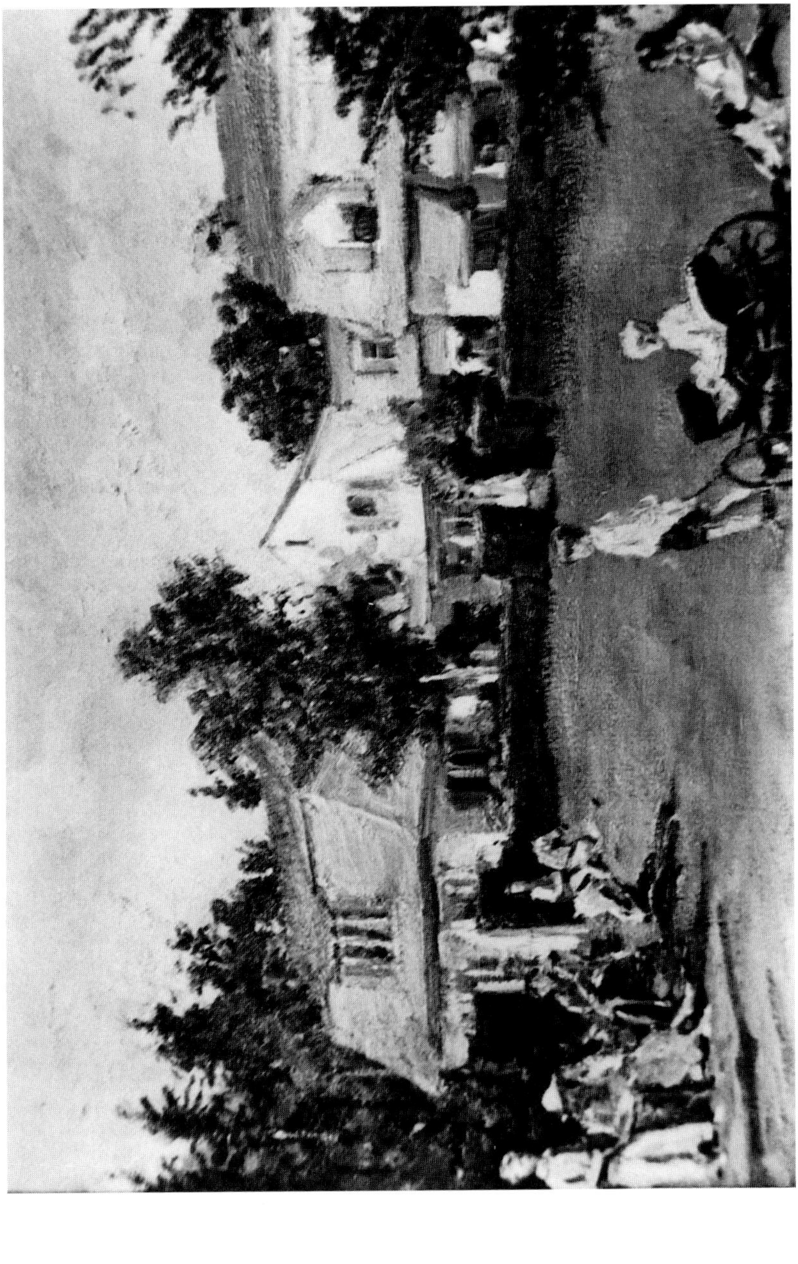

Lang in uniform.

In Irene's garden. Dana and Democratic Party presidential nominee, John W. Davis.

Dana, Irene, and Senator Claude Swanson of Virginia.

1896   1926

The Flapper ended the reign of the Gibson Girl.

Dana on the cover of *Time,* March 25, 1927.

A publicity piece for a Gibson Girl movie that never was released.

Irene in her role as chairman of New York's Child Placing and Adoption Committee.

Secretary of Labor Frances Perkins, Thomas Lamont, an influential banker, and Irene at a luncheon in 1933 opening a campaign for the Child Welfare League of America, Inc.

The chapel in Maine that Dana built.

Irene and Dana posing in front of the chapel on 700 Acre Island.

1934. The Gibsons with their grandchildren. From left, Nancy Post, George Post, Dana Gibson, Harry Gibson, Rene Emery, and Lela Emery.

In a 1942 *Life* article titled "*Life* Calls on the Charles Dana Gibsons," Irene and Dana were cited as "America's most romantic couple."

Dana working on the playhouse he built for his grandchildren.

Nancy Tree in riding habit.

Bernard Baruch and Irene were old friends.

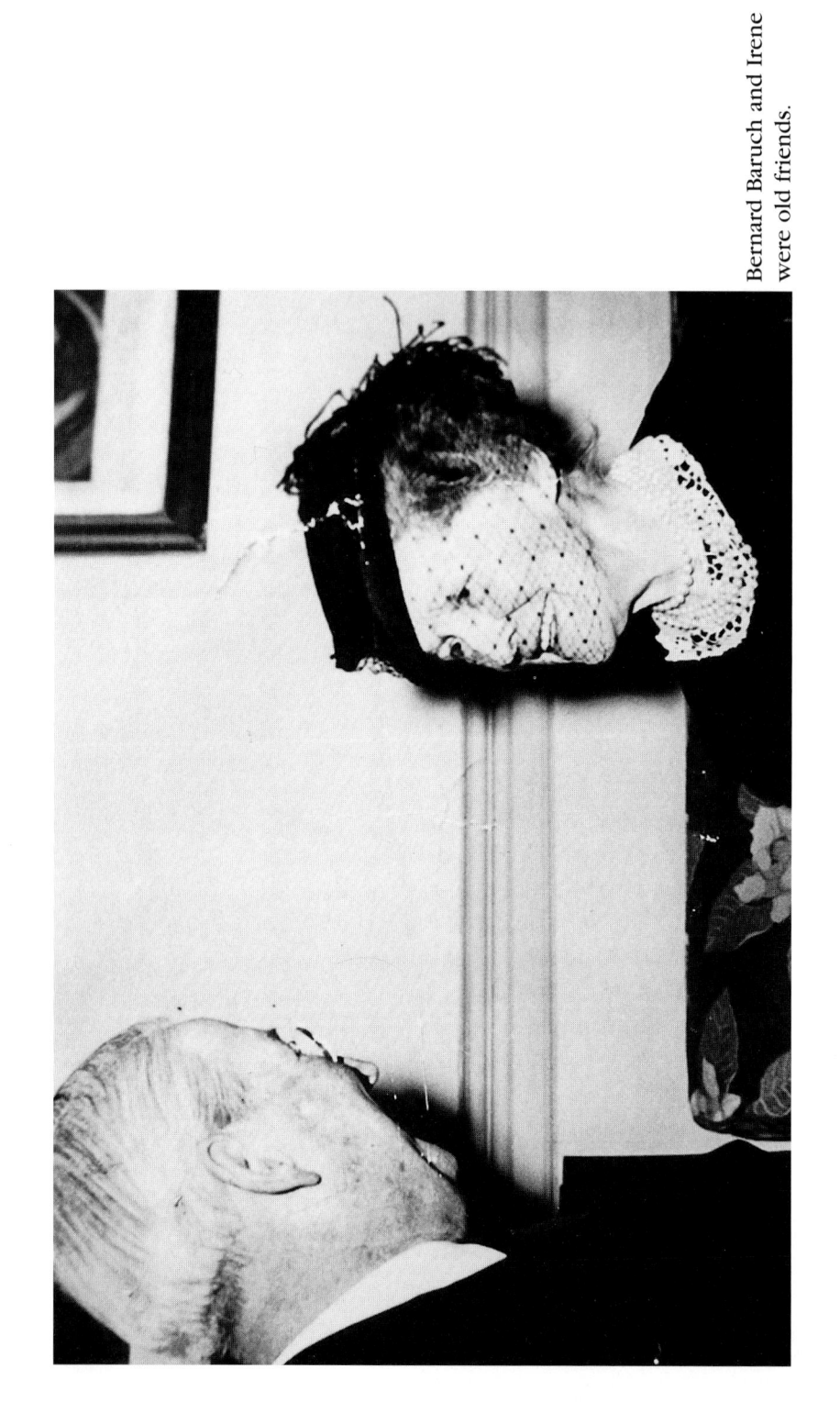

At the Gibson Girl Ball in New York City. At 75, Irene led the Grand March with Winthrop Aldrich, president of the Chase National Bank.

Irene's last home. Her cottage in Greenwood.

The Famous Illustrator

Dana's visit in an 1895 interview. "A young man came out to my house one day. He gave no name but wanted to see me in particular. He was shown into my room, a tall, brawny young fellow, very young and full of enthusiasm. He wasted no time in preliminaries. 'Mr. DuMaurier, I suppose you think me cheeky, but I was bound to meet you, and as I had no way of getting an introduction, I just came on my own hook. My name is Charles Dana Gibson. I'm an American. I draw, and you have been my master for years.' We shook hands and had a long chat together. I wished him success and he went away. We never met again until this summer when he was in London with his bride. He brought his drawings to dinner. I would not mind being his pupil."*

DuMaurier convinced Dana to go to Paris in order to walk on soil sacred to art and its masters. There, Dana applied to and entered the Atelier Julien. The French students were full of plans for rough initiation ceremonies for any Anglo-Saxon joining them. Strength tests were an everyday part of life for art students. Dana was no stranger to these student rites, having held the arm-wrestling title at the Art Students' League until Frederic Remington bested him. His physical prowess must have impressed the French because their hazing ended soon after he got there. Among his most vivid memories of his two-month stay were the sight of people lined up in hopes of getting work as nude models and the Parisians' distaste for fresh air. Being an outdoors man, Dana loathed the stuffy studio, full of body odors and the smell of garlic.

Dana was twenty-two when he returned from Paris. His savings were exhausted, but he was more confident of his direction. Encouraged by DuMaurier and invigorated by his experience in Paris, he started to include women in his commissions whenever he could. He was convinced his pen could bring forth an American

---

*Dana described DuMaurier as gracious and encouraging, ". . . a fine old man living at Hampstead Heath, which is reached by Hansom cab. You ride until the horse falls dead and then you are there. It [the fare] would have cost $50.00 in New York City. He lived in a pleasant house on an elevation in the midst of town, filled with pictures and bric-a-brac of rare interest. His studio was on the top of the house, not a studio, but a library, with original drawings not much larger than reproductions."

The Gibson Girl

ideal of femininity to match DuMaurier's achievement in Great Britain. But his ideal American Girl remained just one of his characters for another few years, and was not particularly well-received in some critical circles.*

It was quite a coup for a young lady to be selected by Dana as the subject of one of his drawings. Society girls came to his studio, chaperoned of course, and posed for him. For a time Dana welcomed their cooperation; he did not have to pay them, and because they were always dressed in the highest fashion, he could be confident his creations were properly and elegantly clothed in the latest styles. Soon the inconvenience of having his friends model for him outweighed the advantages. They took too much of his time. Too many people crowded his small space - - the girls, the chaperones, and his male friends who, attracted by Dana's models, dropped by constantly.

Dana struggled on, accepting more commissions than he could handle. He drove himself to the brink of exhaustion, and feared at one point he was going blind. In letters to editors in 1890 and 1891, he constantly asked for extensions of deadlines, apologizing when promises made were not kept. His output was uneven as he rushed through assignments. Critics chided him for drawing pictures at odd times and pasting them together, for merely aping the cartoons in *Punch*, a popular English humor magazine, and for being capable only of "clever caricatures" of stereotypes and "bitter sarcasm."

Nevertheless, most art reviewers were impressed with his output. The London *Daily Chronicle* lauded him at the expense of his mentor. "Mr. Gibson endeavors to render the effects of nature. Mr. DuMaurier ignores them." One critic commented the only difference between Dana and his imitators was that in Dana's drawings "there is a real set of legs under the trousers, and live, pulsating bodies under the low-cut dress vests." Other critics, like

---

*One art columnist as late as 1893 described Dana's women as "strapping, with big waists and untidy hair." As yet, they were nameless, except when one critic designated them "Penelope Peachblows," an unkind reference to a fat-waisted, small-necked flower vase popular at the time.

The Famous Illustrator

the *Epoch* reviewer a few years before, were as impressed with Dana's physique and personal attractiveness as they were with his art. In the April, 1891 issue of *Art and Advertising,* he received the following coverage: "No mean, nor conceited, nor small nature could draw the beautiful, noble-looking and fine-looking men he draws . . . unless he had some of the nobleness or some of the fineness of the pictures within him. . . . Dana is less like an artist than any I know. Others have Van Dyck beards, hollow-chests, and round shoulders from stooping over easels, and close their lips tightly. And then he has a smooth, strong face, and the shoulders of an end-rusher and the chest of a pugilist, and when he shakes hands with you, you wish you had your ring on the left hand."[*]

Dana's sudden burst of popularity in the early 1890s sprung not from the public's love affair with his American Girl, but from his satiric and humorous portrayal of the lifestyle of the new American aristocracy, the fabulously wealthy. A new social class - - the *nouveau riche* - - had emerged, its great fortunes made since the Civil War in oil, railroads, real estate, steel, and iron. They spent their millions with abandon, most noticeably in New York City, now the social center of the country. They erected grand mansions north of the city's old neighborhoods on lots which a few years ago had been pastures. A society founded on money and lavish entertainments, of Astors, Vanderbilts, Schermerhorns, Rhinelanders and others, was the country's new nobility. It had a name, "The Four Hundred," or the number of people who could fit into Mrs. William Backhouse Astor, Jr.'s ballroom.

Society in America was not like Europe's rigid class system, which was based on ancestry, its members, regardless of their talent and accomplishment, destined forever to remain in the same

---

[*]The San Francisco *Argonaut* reported, "He not only paints and draws, but also plays on the guitar and piano, and sings, talks well, and is an all-round good fellow." Dana even made the personal columns. "It is very true as a contemporary suggests, that Dana Gibson, the artist, is a great favorite of young women, but it is true that the young women have not yet spoiled him." And, when he was an usher at a wedding in Rochester, New York: "At the reception the women fairly tumbled over each other in their anxiety to secure an introduction, with the hope that they might appear in one of his drawings."

The Gibson Girl

stratum. Everything America offered was open to all comers, if only one was both lucky and willing to work hard enough to amass a fortune. The American public believed in this, their Dream, confident they or their children could achieve the same success. They did not resent the spectacles of narcissistic gratification, the balls given for pets, masquerades where women dressed as men (and vice-versa), gluttonous dinners, and entertainments whose costs matched the annual budgets of entire communities. Instead, the lower and middle classes were enthralled with the antics of the wealthy, and wanted in some way to be a part of the glorious display of having so much money it could be burned - - and literally was at one affair.

Dana gave his public what they wanted. He drew handsome and dashing young men escorting beautiful fashion plates who instructed their viewers how to carry a parasol, how to hold one's chin, and what to wear. He depicted the elegance of fancy balls with men immaculately clad in evening dress and ladies in lavish gowns. He drew summer picnics, fashionable Madison Square Garden horseshows, and dining room scenes full of sophisticates. With his drawings spread out on kitchen tables or framed on parlor walls, the rest of the nation fantasized about the fairy tale existence of the rich.

Welcomed for his talent and his celebrity, Dana was no stranger to society. From his advantageous, inside position he was ably qualified to make his pictorial reports to the masses. Although he was from a good family and long ago had learned about finger bowls and which fork to use for which course, it was the money and fame he earned that won him admittance to the gilded world of New York City. Only a decade earlier, as a Wall Street messenger boy waiting in the hall to deliver a note to the Cornelius Vanderbilt mansion, Dana had been admonished by the master of the house for not standing in his presence. Now he was a regular guest of the Vanderbilts.

Dana progressed from portraying the rich to lampooning them, especially the particularly obnoxious varieties - - the social climbers and the snobs with their pretensions, Americans who aped their British cousins, and the ill-mannered, coarse industrial barons and their wives whose refinement fell far short of their wealth. The

The Famous Illustrator

example of Mrs. Burton Harrison,* a displaced Virginian and well-received novelist whose books Dana illustrated, gave Dana the courage to poke fun of the world to which he belonged. An older woman, for years she had been a part of New York's society, but deeply critical of it. Her novel, *Sweet Bells Out of Tune*, was a searing attack on the life of the ostentatious privileged, depicting it as exceptionally dreary, and full of moral and mental poverty. Dana was more gentle with his pen than Mrs. Harrison was with her words.

Dana's passion about the subject of marriage was based on reasons other than love. Venting his ire at the exquisite women he drew who married old and unattractive men for money, he seemed to enjoy their unhappiness as they sat alone at massive dining room tables or collapsed over piano keyboards pining for children and young, virile husbands forever out of their reach. In particular, Dana, an ardent American, railed against the quite common practice of wealthy Americans marrying off their daughters to European peers for the privilege of a title. His central character in these drawings, his American Girl, for all her beauty and gracefulness, was more often than not a grasping, willful, and obviously shallow creature for whom he accorded little compassion.

---

*In her diary entry for February 27, 1890, Mrs. Harrison wrote, "Have just seen the drawings in illustration of the A.M. (*The Anglomaniacs*). They are done by Charles Dana Gibson, a new young artist for whom the *Century* people and others predict a brilliant future. I am simply delighted with them. I hear Mr. Gibson says drawing the society types has opened a new view to him which he enjoys greatly."

A native of Richmond and a friend of Nanaire, Mrs. Burton Harrison was Constance Cary before she married her lawyer-husband who was one of President Jefferson Davis's wartime secretaries.

Dana's bachelor days might have ended sooner if Nanaire and Irene had accepted an invitation of Mrs. Harrison in Bar Harbor, Maine during the summer of 1892, when Dana was her houseguest. About to depart for Virginia and in the process of leaving calling cards, the Langhorne women in their carriage entered Mrs. Harrison's driveway. She came out to greet them, insisting they come in to meet her guest, a handsome, young illustrator from New York, but Nanaire was in a hurry, demurred, and drove away.

The Gibson Girl

Adding to Dana's growing popularity was the sardonic cleverness of his cartoon captions. In the 1880s the magazine illustrator's task was to develop pictures to interpret jokes and punch-lines readers were encouraged to submit. Periodically, Dana and *Life's* editor, Mitchell, sat down to pore over entries, framing as many as fifty pictures in a single session. From Mitchell's lessons in written humor Dana learned the basics of clever and amusing titling. Soon he was writing his own captions and first combined his art with his wit in the Delicious Moment series. One not so Delicious Moment, "When You Meet The Nobleman Your Daughter Has Captured In Europe," features a pretty girl presenting a scrawny, decrepit, monocled old man to her shocked parents. In another Delicious Moment, "When The Narrator Has Told His Most Subtle Story To An Intelligent But Unimaginative Audience, And They Are Still Waiting To Catch The Point - - If There Is Any," four gentlemen lounge around a table, three with expectant and bewildered looks on their faces.

In February, 1890, tragedy struck the Gibson family. Dana's father died. Charley had been in Grand Junction, Colorado seeing Langdon off on the Stanton Expedition, a trip down the Colorado River to determine whether a railroad could be built along its canyon, a cross-country route that would bypass the Rocky Mountains.* There Charley caught a bad cold, came home, then immediately set out on a business trip to Milwaukee. Although Charley was still a healthy, robust man, he had put on too much weight, and his heart could not stand the strain of a prolonged

---

*Stanton's first expedition to survey the Colorado River ended in disaster. Because of poorly constructed boats and ineffective safety gear two men drowned. The second expedition, which Langdon joined, took to the river on December 10th, 1889. Langdon brought to the effort a young, strong back, but was given topographical duties as well. The party was down in the canyon away from all contact with the outside world until March 6th, when they reached Diamond Creek. There Langdon found out his father had died. He wanted to leave, but felt especially obligated to continue since three men bolted at this first opportunity. Langdon's total journey - - 985 miles -- did not end until April 30, 1890. Twelve men had started, and seven went the entire way. In his journal Stanton is extremely critical of the other men, but never once did he write anything negative about Langdon.

The Famous Illustrator

illness when his cold developed into pneumonia. Crushed and shaken by his father's untimely death at the age of forty-seven, Dana immediately assumed the duties of the family head because of the older son's absence. Langdon heard about his father's death two weeks after it occurred, but was unable to leave the expedition party and come home until May.

Like his own father, Charley had little to leave his family, only a small life insurance policy which covered the mortgage on the Gibsons' house and produced a woefully inadequate income for Bessie. On a clerk's weekly salary of $18, Langdon had no money to contribute to the support of his mother and three sisters, so the full burden fell on Dana's broad shoulders. Fortunately, Dana was making enough money for his family and himself, but at a heavy cost, as his health suffered from unremitting work and the gnawing fear that if anything happened to him, his family would be destitute.

The time was long past when he should have moved from home, but he was a devoted son. His sisters, Beth, now fifteen, Annie twelve, and Josephine four, needed a father figure. Every weekday, he rose early for the long commute to Manhattan, and hurried home in the evening after a hard day at the drawing board to help his mother. On weekends he stayed in Flushing, making repairs to the house and taking his mother and sisters on picnics and outings. Dana's lifelong role as benefactor to his mother and sisters was cast. Possessing the innate generosity of spirit to enjoy giving to the ones he loved, he provided for Bessie until her death in 1922, supported his sister, Beth, after her divorce, and was a father to Josephine, educating her, financing her trips abroad, and underwriting the expense of refurbishing Longfield when she decided to live there.

Ironically, Dana was shackled by his success, while poverty freed Langdon, whose youthful wanderlust still was not satisfied. In June, 1891, just one year after Langdon's return from the Colorado River, Dana stood on a Brooklyn quay waving good-bye to his brother, who was sailing off on an even more dramatic sixteen-month adventure as ornithologist and hunter in Robert E. Peary's first expedition to Northwest Greenland. The two brothers were extremely close, and it was not in Dana's nature to resent either

The Gibson Girl

Langdon's freedom or Langdon's inability to pitch in and help the family.

When the Gibson household stabilized after Charley's death, Dana moved into a studio/apartment in the Aldine Building on 33rd Street in New York City. His space had only two rooms, but the studio was spacious, and well-lit by large windows reaching to the high ceiling. Its walls were covered with tapestries and with pictures Dana's artist friends had given him as well as his own. The simple lines of Dana's drawing board and hardback chair in the room's center contrasted sharply with the heavy, ornate furniture and towering costume wardrobes he positioned along the walls. Finally, Dana was on his own, away from the daily family responsibilities in Flushing. The handsome, young bachelor of twenty-five, though burdened with financial obligations, was free to concentrate on his career and his art.

In 1892, the Sanchez & Miller gallery at 126 West 23rd Street in Manhattan held the first one-man exhibition of Dana's work. Fifty-eight drawings were displayed. Dana recalled the gallery owners were just starting out and were glad to have an exhibit of anything. "The black and white sketches are all good and the exhibition is a very credible one," reported one newspaper. "The sketches are attracting attention and already a number of them have been sold." In fact, $3000 worth were sold. One critic commented, "Mr. Gibson is a humorist as well, the delicate subtle kind that often borders on the pathetic." He went on to describe Dana's Delicious Moment series, ". . . the man who always has a friend he wants to present, the mother who allows you to admire the baby, delicious moments when you must discharge the cook, or waiting in vain for a laugh to follow your best story, and when you find you have married a shrew."

Pleased with the results of his first showing, the following year Dana arranged Philadelphia, Boston, and Chicago exhibitions, as well as a second Sanchez & Miller show, which received mixed reviews. One critic complained, " . . . the catalogue is unworthy, and the titles on some of the pictures are abominable, with bad grammar and evident haste in execution." One illustration was an "utter mistake." He chastised Dana for his "glaring faults" but then went on to say it was ". . . the best exhibition of black and white work that I have seen in many a day, and after one has spent half an hour in the gallery he feels that he has been in the company of some well-bred and perfectly dressed people, who, unfortunately, are unable to sport the effect of their gracious presences by talking through their noses."

Itching to return to London, Dana saw his opportunity when Langdon returned from Greenland in late 1892 and Bessie and their sisters could be left in his brother's care. Having saved enough money to support his family while he was gone, pay his own rent, and finance his travel expenses, Dana left New York when his career was in full gallop. Any financial qualms were overshadowed by the knowledge that he had a great deal to learn. Dana agreed with his critics who told him originality is a function of experience; perhaps he would find the answers he needed in London. He had to take his work to another level, to develop a technique that was new and all his own. Three years before DuMaurier had given him direction. Now he had to find a focus for himself.

This London trip was different from his first visit three years before because he went not as a student supplicant to worship, but as a well-known artist whose reputation had preceded him. For an interval he stayed at John Singer Sargent's studio, meeting and befriending his British counterparts, men such as Phil May, whose style of long, sweeping lines influenced him. Dana went to observe, haunting the streets to capture the subtle nuances of the English characters who intrigued him - - the "rat man," the "recruiting sergeant," and the "sidewalk artist." Fascinated with England's class system and its strict cultural delineations, he noted the mannerisms and the dress of the upper class, searching for their faint, but to him eloquent, facial and body expressions. He dined at the Houses of Parliament with a member of the House of Lords and enjoyed the boisterousness of the London music halls as well as the elegance of the opera. Always most conscious of his looks and now enjoying his success, he frequented Savile Row, outfitting himself in beautifully cut, tailor-made clothes in the latest fashions. Never a bohemian, Dana dressed conservatively and elegantly.

Soon after his return from London in the summer of 1893 Dana journeyed to Chicago. In the Columbian Exposition his work

The Gibson Girl

was on display in a broad exhibit of the publishing business glorifying the growth and technical innovations in that industry. The Chicago *Evening Herald's* coverage of his own one-man show at the prestigious O'Brien Gallery confirmed Dana's celebrity status. The reporter described Dana ambling through the packed throng on opening night, his presence completely unnoticed. When finally he was recognized, ". . . admiring young women attacked him. Dana Gibson is more popular than any matinee idol. A crowd of girls besieged a lucky damsel who had the good fortune to talk to Gibson for sixty minutes. She said he is just like the men he draws and he uses slang, not sarcastic, but patient and resigned."

Dana's drawing style had changed radically in 1892 and 1893. Little was left of the tight, cramped lines scratched so carefully, the greys and shadow work constructing heavy, dark spaces that dominated his illustrations. After years of learning and practice, he was beginning to master the technique of producing long, faultless strokes from the movement of shoulder and elbow rather than from his wrist. The result was bold, sweeping lines, graceful and weightless, rich in their blackness, and doing the work of many smaller ones. His subjects desperately tried to escape the flatness of the paper as his drawing became confident and assertive. The technique was new and singular, his work now markedly distinguishable and identifiable. A Philadelphia art critic described his change in style. "He suggested little or nothing. Everything was carried out to the end. Now he is all suggestion, and draws in an hour a picture he would have spent a day on. His lines are now heavy, bold and free, and it takes a couple of them to suggest a hand or a table or a bottle or a foot."

Dana now used only professionals as models for his American Girl. In his opinion, a good model had to lack all self-consciousness and possess a necessary comprehension and magnetic force, but her chief characteristic "must be to have a will of her own." As his popularity soared, his models became celebrities in their own right. The most well-known one was Minnie Clark, described in a newspaper account as having " . . .straight sweet brows and great pure eyes, a dainty, piquant nose and full ripe lips. Her hair is dark and curling. She is of medium height, of graceful proportions, and her arms and shoulders are flawless."

The Famous Illustrator

The "yellow-press" was obsessed with the notion that artists used their models for purposes other than posing and went to great lengths in the attempt to expose licentious behavior it hoped was going on within the walls of their Bohemian studios. Dana was one of the targets for the New York *World's* attempt at sensational journalism. One evening, while sitting with a group of friends at the Players' Club, among them Edwin Booth and Joseph Jefferson, both prominent thespians,* he told his story.

A young woman called at his studio to ask for modeling work. Dana had no reason to believe she was not a professional, but he began to have his doubts when she put on a ballgown incorrectly and asked him to adjust it for her. "There was something in her manner which confused me. She was smiling and allowed her eyelids to droop in a dreamy sort of way." Suddenly, it dawned on him that she was a newspaper reporter because Dan Beard had warned him of the *World's* effort at temptation. He confronted the imposter, "You are doing this for the *World!*" Admitting her duplicity, her face reddened and she blurted out, "Why the *World?*" "Because," Dana replied, "it is the only newspaper in the city that would resort to such an infamous method to get an insight into a man's private life." Dana said that if she had been a man, "I would have throttled him where he stood."**

Absorbed in his work and loath to leave his studio sanctuary for any length of time, Dana's natural penchant was to keep to himself. Fortunately, he came under the influence of charismatic and sophisticated older men who, respecting his talent and the appealing personality which lurked beneath his shy and overly modest exterior, befriended and introduced him to a world of exciting and talented people. Dana's closest friend and sponsor was Richard

---

*Booth, the elder brother of Abraham Lincoln's assassin, was the foremost tragedian of his day, specializing in Shakespearean roles. Jefferson was best known for portraying the title character in the popular play, *Rip Van Winkle.*
**One of the men at Dana's table corralled a New York *Sun* reporter sitting nearby who took down Dana's story. A long article appeared in the next day's edition.

The Gibson Girl

Harding Davis, a well-known investigative reporter when they met, and destined to become one of the most glamorous celebrities of his day. Dick Davis was Dana's complete opposite - - dashing and cocky, theatrical, and fully aware of his extraordinary good looks and the impression he made on others. Davis's literary fame was founded on a series of romantic, adventure novels, the most successful being *Soldiers of Fortune*. It was enhanced by his war-correspondent reporting in which he deftly portrayed himself as a stalwart hero clad in sun-helmet and tropical whipcord outfits.

Davis knew everybody of importance in New York, and included Dana in the group of political, theatrical, and artistic luminaries of the day who gathered around him, men like Chauncey Depew, an influential New York political figure, and Thomas Nelson Page, a Southern writer and ambassador to Italy. Davis was the central figure in a younger circle as well, among them the actresses Ethel Barrymore and Maude Adams, the actor E.H. Sothern, Arthur Brisbane, a writer and newspaper editor, the publisher Robert Howard Russell - - and Dana.* None of them was married in the early 1890s, and according to Dick Davis's brother, the members of this group were seldom apart and were "extracting an enormous amount of fun out of life." Besides friendship, a professional alliance beneficial to both men existed between Dana and Dick Davis. Some of Dana's most important commissions were illustrating Davis's novels. The author generously attributed a large measure of their success to Dana's bringing life to his romantic characters. In turn, Dana used his friend as his principal - - though unpaid - - model for his Gibson Man.

Through Dick Davis, Dana met Stanford White, the era's most gifted and prolific architect. White was an artistic celebrity in the New York scene, and taking a liking to the young artist sixteen years his junior, took Dana on as a protege. During the trial of White's murderer, Harry K. Thaw, the sordid, secret life of the

---

*Maude Adams later gained fame as Barrie's Peter Pan on the New York stage. E.H. Sothern was noted for both romantic and classical roles. Arthur Brisbane was a master of the big, blaring headline and the atrocity story.

The Famous Illustrator

famed architect was revealed. A rake and a womanizer, he kept a private apartment in the tower of one of his most magnificent creations, the Madison Square Garden, to entertain a constant flow of much younger women.

Whether or not Dana was aware of White's sexual proclivities, I have no way of knowing, but Dana was one of a group of men who often joined him for nights out on the town. They started off their evenings at the Players' Club for early cocktails, and then had dinner at Delmonico's or the Union Club or Martin's restaurant, after which they went to a music hall, a variety show performance, a boxing match, or a concert. One evening, White gave a birthday party for "Diamond Jim" Brady in his Madison Square Garden apartment, and invited thirty friends, among them Dana, Saint-Gaudens, and other artists and theatrical people. White took Dana into his confidence concerning his plans for the night. He sent a note to Dana's studio the morning of the party: "Hell is going to be let loose, but don't tell anybody about this." The men were served an elegant twelve-course dinner, and then were entertained by four banjo players and four singers. The red wine was poured by a brunette, the white by a blonde. The final course was introduced, a huge pie covered by a flaky, brown crust. Out of it flew a swarm of canaries, and out popped sixteen-year-old Susie Johnson, barely covered in filmy black gauze, as eleven other near-naked girls danced into the room.

The popularity of Dana's work grew steadily as the country descended into an economic depression, which culminated in the Panic of 1893. In search of diversion from their everyday misery, people clamored for his drawings. They were more than pleased to join with Dana in laughing at the silly players in the upper crust's comedy. Poor and frightened men looked longingly into the faces of the lovely feminine visions he created, while their wives and daughters dreamed of looking and dressing like one of his girls.

In a sense, Dana profited from the country's economic debacle. Both wealth and power were concentrated in the hands of a very small portion of the population. To make sure they retained their hold on the country's reins, the rich and the politicians they controlled kept the country on the gold standard. The money supply shrank, prices fell, farmers and railroads went broke, and banks

The Gibson Girl

failed. All the while, circulations of periodicals grew, and with them Dana's income.

Needing a break from his exhaustive work schedule, Dana again sailed for Europe in October, 1893. On the eve of his departure, Dana was feted at the Aldine Club at a sedate affair presided over by R. W. Gilder, editor of *Century* magazine. Twenty of Dana's friends came to wish him Godspeed, among them Dick Davis - - whom Dana would meet in Paris - -, Dan Beard, D. Webster Evans, C.S. Rinehart, and Arthur Scribner.[*] He planned first to visit his friend and fellow illustrator, Edwin Austin Abbey,[**] in London, and then go on to Paris. *Life* was in the process of constructing a new building at 17 West 33rd Street in New York, and Mitchell offered the top floor to Dana to lease as studio and living quarters. He could move in the next summer, so Dana timed his arrival back in New York for July, 1894.

In a newspaper interview before his departure, Dana vowed he would not draw Parisian life until he had been there six months, a strange statement because he would be gone for only eight months, and because the main business purpose of the trip was a commission from *Harper's* to illustrate Dick Davis's travelogue, *About Paris*. Dana's contract with *Harper's*, which stipulated a $200 payment for each picture the periodical published and $100 for each original drawing, was a significant milestone in his career. He was now the highest paid illustrator of his day.

At 48 Rue Fabert in one of the best parts of Paris, he rented a studio overlooking a courtyard. The French artist, Fleury,[***] had once lived there. Davis described the studio's decorations as "all in perfect taste;" its walls covered with "a wealth of tapestries and armor." Having found time to work on his own, Dana exhibited seven drawings at a salon on the Champs de Mars in the spring. His

---

[*]Scribner, Evans, and Rinehart were magazine publishers.
[**]Edwin Austin Abbey was best known for his illustrations of the works of Oliver Goldsmith and Shakespeare, as well as for decorative schemes of public buildings.
[***]Tony Robert-Fleury taught many of the famous painters of the nineteenth century. His forte was historical paintings.

The Famous Illustrator

small showing was well-received, and Dana was pleased the French considered him an artist first, then an illustrator.

In January, Dana gave a "housewarming." Among the guests were the American ambassador, James B. Eustis, and his family. His party - - no simple affair - - was covered by a Paris newspaper: "At a charming soiree in the studio of Charles Dana Gibson, Mlle. Sybil Sanderson [the prima donna of Paris's Opera Comique] was loudly applauded for her renderings of songs from Gounod's 'Romeo et Julliette.' " The reporter was most impressed by Mlle. Sanderson's presence at Dana's, commenting that she charged at least 1000 francs for private performances. Perhaps, Dana paid her. Perhaps, she was a friend who sang as a favor.

Much of *About Paris*, and most of Dana's sketches deal with Parisian night life. The two men explored every out of the way bar and bistro and often greeted the dawn. They walked the streets, absorbing the scene and mood of the place, Dana's sketchbook always in hand. They rode horses in the Bois de Boulogne, went to masked balls, and celebrated Bastille Day at the Jardin de Paris, a nightclub where men put candles on their high hats and the can-can dancers snuffed them out with their kicks. John Drew, the actor and uncle of Ethel Barrymore, joined them on some of their forays.

Davis wrote of their times together as "full of jolly dinners with such good talk and such amusing companions," and Dana described this sojourn in Paris as one of the best times of his life. It was a fertile time for Dana's art. Critics of his work attributed the influence of the French school to Dana's retreat from fine line drawing to the use of fewer broad strokes. His drawings of Parisian life received favorable reviews in American columns; however, one paper said his illustrations of the Moulin Rouge were ". . . . tame, that *Harper's* was evidently afraid of realism on a subject like the Moulin Rouge."

Dick Davis's and Dana's mission was to create for *Harper's* a light-hearted, whimsical view of life in Paris, but they came back with a few serious observations. Both men were deeply disturbed by the assassination of French President Carnot by an anarchist, which occurred while they were there, and shocked by how lightly Parisians took his death. They drank tea with the expatriate artist, James Whistler, in his garden. Despite his own frequent travels and

The Gibson Girl

long visits abroad, Dana criticized American artists such as Whistler who turned their backs on their own country. Dana felt there was much for American artists to learn in Europe, but having studied and absorbed, they should bring their talent back to the United States and enrich the culture of their own country.

Paris was full of beautiful young models wanting to sit for Dana. Some were amazed they did not have to pose in the nude. One was quite indignant when Dana drew her as Mother Hubbard, claiming her professional reputation was tarnished. Susanne was Dana's primary Parisian model and received a great deal of press coverage. Articles about Susanne stressed her stable middle-class background and her chastity, and emphasized the fact her father brought and fetched her to and from Dana's studio each day. Dana described her as winsome, her face not beautiful, ". . . but suggests so much." When she posed for him, she was twenty-two. "Her eyes were unusually wide apart, their brown irises rimmed with edges of black," according to one reporter.

Dana arranged for Susanne to come to New York, but a few days before her expected departure, she died of pneumonia. "She was the brightest, truest, most gentle little woman I have ever seen," Dana told the press. "She stayed with me all day and lunched with me. She was a sympathetic little girl, full of sentiment and grace, and there will never be another like her."

When he returned home in July, 1894, his studio and apartment in the *Life* building were ready. His sister, Josephine, who stayed with him sometimes for a week at a time, described the studio as a large room with a fireplace. A bedroom and two small rooms were off the entrance hall, one a dressing room for models, the other a bathroom with a punching bag where Dana worked out every afternoon. Emulating the lavish decorations in the Paris studio he had rented, Dana installed heavily carved furniture and rich tapestries on the walls. Influenced by the affluent lifestyle of his friends abroad, he imported an English man-servant, according to the Chicago *Record,* " . . . a valet clothed in red breeches and other imposing habiliments . . . a valet so genuinely British that upon beholding and hearing him you find it hard to realize you are in the middle of an American city and not in the heart of cockneydom."

The Famous Illustrator

His new flamboyance in no way affected his assiduous work habits. Josephine remembered the intensity of her brother's work. He spent hours at his drawing board. One model dropped from exhaustion, having held her pose for too long. He hated interruptions, and would become irritated when friends came by uninvited. Some models were easier to draw than others. After particularly frustrating sessions, the floor was strewn with sheets of cardboard filled with incomplete drawings.

Throughout his life Dana was intensely proud of being an American, and anxious to promote his country's assets, particularly her women. Interviewed by a New York paper, the *Advertiser*, shortly after his return from France, he acknowledged a beautiful woman is beautiful the world over, but in America "women had the chance to show their true worth. Not shackled by the effete customs of the Old World, they seem to develop into fine specimens of womanhood." He compared American women to those of ancient Grecian times, an era when costumes did not fetter their actions. He believed that their freedom of spirit had to do with the fine carriage of the average American woman. She was taller, more sinuous, more erect, healthy, and "imbued with snap." To Dana, English women all looked like sisters, and French women were "more or less artificial."

But when it came to the subject of marriage, Dana was not so positive about the attributes of the opposite sex. His personal fear of the hazards of marriage permeated his work. Perhaps, he was influenced by the drama in his own family, having seen how hard his father worked and how unhappy he was spending so much of his life away from home in order to support the family. Perhaps, he feared marriage would mark the end of his career. His success in illustration might be only fleeting, and he would find himself burdened with a family and no way to support them adequately. He continued to present his female characters as grasping women, intent on gaining a fortune or a title, or women who, having landed husbands, turned into shrews. His friend, Dick Davis, wondered why he took such a depressing view of matrimony and why he thought every American girl was ready to sell herself for a title.

In spite of his rugged handsomeness, his success, and his obvious attractiveness to women, there is no hint, either in his

The Gibson Girl

correspondence, or in that of his family and friends, that he was ever romantically attracted to any woman before he met Irene Langhorne. "Gibson despises dancing, and cares more about pictures than he does girls," commented one reporter. Another writer described him during this period as being "aggressively modest." Perhaps, he felt altogether safe behind his drawing table, and did not have the confidence to risk rejection. Perhaps, he was frightened of commitment, or fearful of coming within a woman's control. During the two or three years before his marriage, he was quite the young man about town, but a "man's man" rather than a "lady's man."

The gossip columnists kept a close eye on him. About the best they could do in suggesting he had a love life was to place him in the company of a young woman among a group of his friends. One half-hearted attempt was made to link him with Ethel Barrymore, but with disappointment the writer admitted Miss Barrymore was only sixteen years old. The following is a typical social column comment: "Mr. Gibson was much struck with Miss Sperry, and, I am told, invited her to sit for him. I suppose one will have an early opportunity of recognizing the features of the pretty Californienne in *Life*."

A shipboard incident on his way back from Paris made the social columns. A beautiful girl was aboard. One day while she was on deck lounging near the smokestack taking in the sun, Dana secretly sketched her. Someone caught him at it and asked if he cared to donate the drawing to the raffle being held that night to benefit the Seaman's Fund. Modestly, Dana at first refused, but finally agreed. On board a man from California and a New Yorker were vying for the beautiful girl's attention. The New Yorker opened the bidding for Dana's sketch at $10. The Californian came in from the smoking room and said $100. The New Yorker responded with $150. To wild applause the bidding ended at $400, equivalent to $10,000 today. The next day she gave Dana a private sitting.

In the autumn of 1894, Dana collaborated with his publisher friend, Robert Howard Russell, on the first Gibson book, a folio of eighty-four of his best cartoons with a sketch of his American Girl on the cover. The price was $5.00, or $10.00 with a signed artist's proof included. It was printed on Japanese paper, and for the first time his audience saw the drawings connected, not on the shiny yellow *Life* paper separated by the magazine's spine. A Boston *Journal* critic commented on Dana's capacity to make money. "Mr. Gibson may well rub his hands. He is a thrice paid man. *Life* pays him for a cartoon. The same picture in an album of his drawings pays him a royalty. Then the original brought to Boston, for instance, is bought for a fat price."

An appendage to his success and fame were attempts to take advantage of him. An automobile manufacturer sent Dana a letter offering a $100 prize if an original drawing of his was selected to advertise his product. To Dana, the award was absurd because he demanded a great deal more than $100 for a piece of his work; plus, he saw the offer as a ruse to get one of his drawings free. In a perhaps playful frame of mind Dana wrote back, "You are cordially invited to participate in my grand $10.00 automobile contest. Each participant must submit one or more automobiles and the winner will receive $10.00. The automobiles must be brand new and shipped f.o.b. New York. They must be fully equipped. The unsuccessful automobiles will remain the property of the undersigned. Charles Dana Gibson."

In 1894 the New York *Commercial Advertiser* reported on the people who made more money than the President of the United States. The head of Equitable Life earned $50,000. Top lawyers and bankers pulled in as much as $60,000. $10,000 was a very large income for a successful physician, and editors of big magazines received $10,000. Dana's and Frederic Remington's were put at $15,000. Dana was twenty-six years old.

CHAPTER EIGHT

COURTSHIP AND MARRIAGE

Irene was aware of Dana Gibson, the popular, young illustrator whose American Girl drawings were the current rage. A few years previously at Mrs. Reed's School in New York City, one of her schoolmates had the honor and pleasure of posing for the well-known artist. It is most probable that Irene, along with her girlfriends, spent some amount of time swooning over this handsome bachelor with the build of a prizefighter. At some point Irene focused on Dana Gibson. She was fully confident she could have just about any man she wanted. It was only a question of timing and strategy.

In a newspaper interview Irene gave almost fifty years later she recalled meeting Dana for the first time at the fashionable annual horseshow at Madison Square Garden in November, 1894. With a somewhat blasé air she recalled she was interested in the young artist, but during her stay in New Orleans the following February, she "fell in love with several other young men and returned home with no ill effects."

Dana's recollection of their first encounter was different. She was dining at Delmonico's with friends when one of her party mentioned the celebrated artist, Charles Dana Gibson, was at a table nearby. Irene looked up and noticed that Robert Russell, whom she knew, was sitting with her quarry. Irene wanted an introduction. Trying to catch Russell's eye, she more than once took a somewhat circuitous walk to the powder room, a route which just happened to pass by Dana's table. Russell finally took notice of Irene's loudly swishing skirts, stood up to greet her and introduced Dana.

Dana remembered asking a friend to help him arrange a tea at his studio the next day so he could see Irene again. He thought her luminous, "like a house with all the windows lit, sweet music coming from a party going on inside." A piano was in Dana's studio, brought in as a prop for a drawing he was working on. Irene sat down at the keyboard and sang "Good-Night Beloved." They arranged to sit together at the horseshow the next day.

I try to visualize these first encounters, which must have been great sport for Irene and so awkward for this bashful man who was too modest, too humble, in many respects too old for his age. Dana, in spite of the scores of women ready to succumb to any advance he made, was wary and uncertain of the opposite sex. He held women at a professional distance. There had been no raging loves in his life, perhaps not even casual dalliances. Here he was confronted with the most dazzling of creatures, a supremely vivacious and confident young women, a collector of men. For him to respond to her she must have put him at ease almost immediately. She must have broken through that dignified facade to extract his wonderful sense of humor, which before only the comfortable company of male friends or the detached safety of his drawing board could bring forth. Her self-confidence - - even cockiness - - in some way must have challenged Dana to enter the world of romance he had assembled with his pen but had frightened him in his personal life.

Irene came to New York again during the last weeks of 1894. Their budding romance was mentioned in the newspapers, one gossip columnist reporting, "A new engagement is to break suddenly on the horizon." They had dinners with Dana's friends, were seen at the theater and on an ice pond, skating one morning after a dance that had lasted all night. People were watching the young couple, intrigued that Dana was showing an interest in a young lady. The artist who had distanced himself from his own needs and from life in order to capture it - - the artist who had allowed himself only short playtimes away from his studio between long, unrelieved periods of work - - finally felt the bittersweet pleasure of passion.

After that initial time together in New York City in late 1894, Irene and Dana went their separate ways. Irene, the belle, was very much in demand with her many commitments in Richmond's social season, and there was the trip to New Orleans to plan. Dana was extremely busy, producing weekly pictures for periodicals, working with Robert Russell on an album of drawings and preparing for showings of his work in Boston and Chicago.

The Gibson Girl

During this period Dana received extensive press coverage. "Charles Dana Gibson has been touring the West," one account proclaimed, "exhibiting his pictures and his journey has been one continual triumphal march. Critics little and big have vied doing him homage, cities have feted him, men and women have bowed to him, and the columns of the papers have been filled with stories of his life, his habits, his models, and his manners." But, professionally Dana knew he was in trouble. The reviews of the important and most respected art critics he carefully pasted in his bulky, black scrapbook had an ominous ring to them. Uninterested in his celebrity appeal and his personal attractiveness, these reviewers were beginning to tell the story of themes grown stale and hackneyed. His drawings, particularly of his American Girl, had a sameness to them. She had lost her luster. Dana Gibson was in danger of losing his position as the country's favorite illustrator.

In the first two months of 1895 contact between Irene and Dana was limited to the exchange of polite, stilted letters beginning with salutations of "Dear Miss Langhorne" and "Dear Mr. Gibson." Dana knew to keep his letters formal and proper. He realized Irene was obliged to show them to her parents. Hers let Dana know she still existed, she was popular and having a grand time without him, and she would be receptive to a visit from him. She was not about to throw herself at Dana. He would have to make a move toward serious commitment..

He did, albeit a tentative one. Most likely exhausted from his frantic work pace and probably deeply worried about the direction of his career, Dana in late February went to St. Augustine, Florida for a rest. On his way home to New York City he stopped in Richmond, ostensibly to visit his friend, Thomas Nelson Page. With Page in tow, he called on the Langhornes. His respite in Florida seems to have done him little good because he was sick the entire time he was in Richmond. Although this first visit to Irene and the Langhornes could not have been that successful, at least his overture gave Irene the opening to ask him back in April.

Their relationship was not shaping up to Irene's satisfaction. Dana was far away in New York or traveling around the country, and she was not able to orchestrate the complicated, stringent, and ritualistic process of courtship - - the dance of ensnarement. She

Courtship and Marriage

knew her role, to keep the man - - the supplicant - - tantalized with her feminine mystique, pulling him close with sweet words and coy innuendo, then pushing him away just as he thought he was near his goal. The distance that separated them must have been particularly vexing for Irene because she was not able to use her considerable womanly wiles to keep his interest in her at a feverish pitch. She knew full well his desire for her quickly could be diverted or lost.

Dana knew the dance as well. Distance in one sense was a blessing for him because he did not have to endure the endless rounds of front porch and parlor social calls to Irene's family or the heavily chaperoned carriage rides, literary meetings, and teas that were so much a part of the Richmond courtship scene. Yet, even from far away he realized whatever advances he made had to be careful and well thought out. Not only must he satisfy Irene's sense of propriety, but also he had the watchfulness of brothers to think about, and particularly, Chillie's stern judgment to appease. Early on, Irene must have alerted Dana that neither parent was pleased with her interest in him because his occupation was too out of the ordinary, and his income, sizable perhaps for the time being, certainly could not be stable. Chillie did not care how talented Dana Gibson was. His eldest daughter was married to a meat packer who could barely support his family, and now, the daughter who could pick and choose from the richest and most fashionable men in the world was contemplating marriage to a New York artist, to a Bohemian. Nicholas Longworth, the wealthy Cincinnati scion, was a much preferred prospect for Irene.

Dana's April visit was planned against a background of romantic trickery on Irene's part. Because she asked him down without her parents' knowledge or consent, the arrangement was for Irene to be "surprised" he was in town. The afternoon of Dana's arrival a friend rushed into the Langhornes' house and exclaimed, "Did you know Charles Dana Gibson was at the Westmoreland Club?" Irene pretended to be baffled. A few moments later the doorbell rang and in walked Dana and Robert Russell. Nor did Irene alert Dana that Nicholas Longworth was also in Richmond, staying with the Langhornes at 101 West Grace. She knew Dana would not come if another beau was a Langhorne houseguest. Irene's plan was clever. She wanted both men in Richmond to

The Gibson Girl

watch her perform that week as the star of "The Chimes of Normandie," an amateur musical production at the Academy of Music. Both Dana and Longworth could see her in all her glory; more importantly, Dana could see for himself that she had at least one other very impressive suitor.

Irene had played the lead in other musical plays in Richmond, such as "The Widow," "Highest Bidder," and "Violets," but this role was her most important. The play was directed by her old friend and musical mentor, Professor Jacob Reinhardt, Richmond's maestro and organist at St. Paul's Church. The theater was packed for each performance of "The Chimes of Normandie," a benefit staged for three hospitals. "Miss Irene Langhorne was the bright, particular star in the stage heaven last night," the Richmond *Dispatch's* music critic reported. "She enacted the role of Germaine with great charm. Her portrayal was not deficient in poetic quality and was strongly and picturesquely done. Her really beautiful soprano, highly skilled as it is, gave the utmost captivation to Planquette's strains, and her acting was full of the most delicious expression, and if she could have given her numerous songs three times over, her many admirers in front would still have been unsatisfied. . . ." Irene "took the house by storm," the newspaper article continued, and was showered with magnificent bunches of roses and baskets of flowers.

Dana must have been impressed. Irene's message to him was that he was not the only celebrity.

The day after the opening performance of "The Chimes of Normandie" the *Dispatch* recounted the following tidbit: "On Thursday Miss Langhorne invited Miss [May] Handy and the two visitors [Dana and Robert Russell] to a drive in her drag [carriage] and to an informal luncheon at her home afterwards where they were joined by Miss Tennant and Mr. J.B. Ellerson of Philadelphia." Nicholas Longworth either had left Richmond or was left out.

In June, Dana traveled to Mirador accompanied by Robert Russell - - his ally in a strange and hostile country. Hot and dusty from a long and difficult buggy ride over the mountain from Basic

City,[*] the two men arrived at Mirador's front gate, where they were greeted by Chillie. "Hold on there a minute," Chillie called out as Dana reached into his pocket to pay off the driver. "Let him wait, because you won't be staying long; the train leaves for New York early this evening, and I don't want any damn sign painter from the North coming down here to interfere with my daughter's life." Dana replied, "So this is what you call 'Southern hospitality?'" Chillie must have liked that answer and told Dana and Russell to come into the house.

Chillie later recalled an incident from that same trip that must have further endeared him to this Yankee intent on marrying his daughter. He and Dana were walking behind two of his other daughters. The backs of both their outer skirts had come undone. "The Langhornes are good soldiers," Dana remarked. "They never look behind!" Chillie knew Irene was being courted by a man with a sense of humor.

Chillie allowed the two men to stay a few days. Because Mirador was crowded with family and friends, a fishbowl for the young couple, escape from the curious eyes of little sisters and concerned parents was difficult. Soon after he arrived, however, Dana got Irene to himself under a large sycamore tree in the back garden a few yards from the house and proposed. Although Irene did not expect Dana's proposal and said she was unprepared, she immediately accepted. A month later, Irene wrote her friend Martha Bagby, "This was sudden. I have had my mind on him for some little time, but really did not think it was so serious."

To the Langhorne family, Dana was just one more suitor at the end of a long list of beaux Irene had charmed and turned away, so they were surprised that Irene had agreed to marry Dana. Nanaire and Chillie had seen their daughter fall in love time and time again, and thought her infatuation for Dana would run its course. When faced with the reality of her acceptance, at first they withheld their approval, hoping she would change her mind. "I am having the greatest trouble in getting my good father to actually consent," she wrote Martha. "He has pretty nearly, but I can't

---

[*]Now Waynesboro.

The Gibson Girl

announce it yet." Irene knew she could get her way with her father, and I doubt if she was at all concerned.

Irene wanted Martha to know her catch was a good one. "He has a name and a good one. I am in love, engaged, and to be married to C. Dana Gibson. Really he is most attractive and you will love him. He is clever which of course appeals to me. As they say fools like those [sic] kind. As the Frenchman says, ' I am not ze dam fools zi looks.' . . . He makes loads of money (a plenty anyhow) and is the most determined soul you ever saw. . . . I am very happy and consider myself most fortunate."

Immediately after Irene agreed to marry him, Dana wrote his Uncle Jim Lovett in Boston. "I want you to be the first to hear of my good fortune. I am engaged to be married to Miss Irene Langhorne of Richmond. Va., the dearest girl in the world. She's twenty two - - the finest girl in the world covers it. And dear Uncle Jim. If you will take my dear father's place and write to her you will make me very happy."

Although she was committed to Dana, Irene had no intention of curtailing her social activities and relinquishing her role as the available belle. When she wrote to Martha, "What I say to you is a dead secret, and I stake myself in your hands. . . . please say nothing of this," Irene's concern was not about honoring her parents' wish to keep the engagement secret. Rather, she did not want her marriage commitment to spoil her fun. "Gordon Dexter came down yesterday, and I was as nice as possible. Very coquettish so I darned not say anything. He begs me to go to Bar Harbor and let him come up. . . . Tomorrow I go to Narragansett for the week. . . . Jan Richardson writes he will be there with his horses which are at my disposal. Can't you see me running away with Dana following on behind Jan."

Dana went to Narragansett to be with Irene. In a newspaper account describing August's high season there - - with its belles and beaux, the races at Wild Field Farm, hops at the Casino, polo games, and tennis - - Irene and Dana were given prominent mention as guests of Miss May Jones, Irene's cousin. In a letter to Martha Bagby, May wrote, "Irene and Mr. Gibson spent a few days with us and we enjoyed them very much. They are desperately in love with each other."

Courtship and Marriage

In August, Dana followed Irene to Mirador where, finally, Chillie gave his consent to their marriage. It was decided that the entire family plus Dana would go to White Sulphur Springs, where the engagement would be announced. The notice first appeared in the Richmond *Dispatch* on August 15, 1895, its first-page bold headline proclaiming "Miss Langhorne Engaged." Dana was a "famous American artist," but Irene got most of the coverage. Richmond was her backyard. "Miss Langhorne is one of the greatest beauties in the South, and excepting Miss May Handy, it may be said she stands unequaled and unrivaled in her regal beauty. She possesses in an intrinsic degree that charmingness of manner that is as captivating as her beauty."

Drawings of Irene which did not do her justice appeared in the northern press. She was described erroneously as being "short, undersized, a brunette with great dark eyes." Some reporters even were churlish in their coverage, seemingly pleased to believe Irene did not resemble Dana's American Girl. Other coverage was somewhat dramatic, citing waves of feminine indignation at Dana's forthcoming marriage. Did not Gibson belong to young American women collectively? "Lost was the sweet charm in the celibacy of a talented young man," said one paper. And, "Marriage was a dangerous game for him. How could a man who so often had lambasted marriage, portraying girls as callous in heart, forswear his freedom?"

Nanaire was back at Mirador on the eighteenth of August and wrote Martha Bagby. "I am very pleased with Mr. Gibson. He is the most natural, earnest person I ever saw and I know of no one [else] to whom I would entrust Irene's happiness. He seems perfectly devoted to her, and she is very much in love with him so I think they have every prospect of a happy future though it is very hard to lose Irene. I shall feel as if half my life were gone. Nanaire continued, "We have had the very nicest letters about Mr. Gibson you ever read, voluntary, of course. Irene gets at least twenty-two or three a day . . . ."

Nanaire's and Chillie's attitude toward Dana may have progressed from disapproval to resignation to pleasure, but thirteen-year-old Josephine Gibson was not at all happy her brother was marrying into the Langhorne family. Obviously, she was

119

The Gibson Girl

jealous of Irene and upset her brother/father was being taken from her. Her impressions are poignant because they so clearly show her possessiveness, and important because they may provide a glimpse into how the Langhornes appeared to other Gibsons older than Josephine.

A few weeks after the announcement of their engagement, Dana gave a reception in his New York studio for Nanaire and Irene. Josephine recalled when Dana's mother offered Mrs. Langhorne tea, she replied she would rather drink "beer-on-draft," a highly unlikely preference for Nanaire. Before the wedding Dana took Josephine to Mirador. Josephine's disenchantment of all things "Irene" and "Langhorne" came out in her description of the visit. It was like a journey to a foreign land; she could not understand what the natives said or what they did. Josephine had heard of tobacco-chewing, but had never witnessed the practice - - so she said. Whiskey, Chillie's drink of choice, to her was a drink only for day-laborers. She referred to a family argument in which a horsewhip was used. The Langhornes impolitely talked of "bedbugs." Josephine's shock continued. Mirador was in an uproar during her stay because Harry, a student at the University of Virginia in nearby Charlottesville, recently had been accused - - unjustly - - of stabbing a black man in the stomach.

In September, Irene and Dana had a serious accident that could have been fatal. Irene was driving them in the Langhornes' buggy to call on the Winns, neighbors who lived two miles from Mirador, when the horse stumbled and fell to its knees. It regained its footing, but frightened, began to run out of control. Irene could not check its speed. A turn in the road loomed, the buggy swerved, and its undercarriage smashed into a large rock, shattering the light vehicle. Both of them were thrown out and knocked unconscious. On coming to, they dragged themselves to a nearby farmhouse.

Newspapers at first reported Irene had broken her knee-cap. Yet, the northern papers were more concerned over their own speculation that Dana had broken his wrist and would not be able to draw. They were both badly shaken, but suffered only bruises and minor cuts.

The wedding day was set - - Thursday, November 7, 1895 - - in Richmond, at St. Paul's Church, where Robert E. Lee had

Courtship and Marriage

worshipped and where Jefferson Davis had sat thirty years before when he received word that Richmond must be evacuated because the Union army had broken the Confederate lines at Petersburg.

Dana arrived from New York Wednesday morning. The newspapers reported his party consisted of twenty-five people who went at once to the Jefferson Hotel, "where elegant apartments had been engaged for them." The Jefferson had been rushed to completion by its owner, Major Lewis Ginter, to accommodate the wedding party. Dick Davis, who came with his sister, wrote to his brother that the Jefferson was, " . . . a bully hotel as big as the Waldorf with prices in keeping."

Stanford White and his wife were there, as well as the many friends Irene had made on her jaunts to Baltimore, Philadelphia and New Orleans. Ethel Barrymore shared a Pullman compartment with Nancy Langhorne on their way from New York. Newspaper reporters prattled over all the elegant people, but had no way to know a woman who would become America's most famous actress was in their midst. However, Dick Davis mentioned in the same letter to his brother cited above, "Ethel had a great deal of attention shown her and was perfectly happy."

Nanaire and Chillie planned a full array of pre-wedding events. The celebrations started a week before the wedding with a dinner for twelve at the Jefferson given in Irene's honor. On Wednesday, Chillie invited the wedding party to the Deep Run Hunt Club for a foxhunt. Davis said before they drove out to Deep Run a large group gathered at the home of a friend of the Langhornes. The owner was not there, but they "drank everything loose" and helped themselves to pocketfuls of cigars. Perhaps, because the groomsmen were not entirely sober, one of them, Juan Smith, took a bad fall in the hunting field and broke his arm. Chillie was reported to be riding far ahead of everyone else, probably challenging Dana's younger friends to keep up with him. While the men were out riding, Lizzie gave a tea at her house in honor of Dana's mother. The evening before the wedding James L. Breese,*

---

*Breese was a wealthy New York bachelor who, according to Cleveland Amory, gave parties that rivaled those of Stanford White. At one affair a "Jack Horner" pie was placed in the center of the banquet table. His

The Gibson Girl

a New York friend of Dana, and the Whites gave an informal dance on the roof of the Jefferson for the New York guests, the bridal party, and other close friends of Irene. The *Dispatch* labeled it a "brilliant affair . . . followed by a chafing-dish supper."

Dick Davis described the scene before the wedding: "The next day we had to fight the biggest crowd I ever saw at a wedding. They lined the street for a mile from the Langhornes to the church and two policemen and I held the door against them for an hour." The dilemma was only a few had been allowed in when the church doors had been opened to admit the public to the unreserved seats. The newspapers reported "seething, expectant throngs" outside the church waiting for Irene to arrive. Chaos almost became calamity when a restless horse, spooked by the commotion in front of the church, started to kick and buck, scattering the crowd.

Davis described Irene as "the prettiest and most stately and altogether loveliest [bride] I ever saw." In the flamboyant journalistic style of that time, somewhat dramatic and pretentious, almost bordering on the absurd, the *Dispatch* described the effect Irene created. "As she entered the church the vast concourse of necks craned and Miss Langhorne was more than ever admired by the people of her own home. She looked pure and lovely, yet sisterly and beautiful. The bride wore a very handsome bridal robe of white satin, en train, waist of white chiffon, garniture of Renaissance lace. Her veil, a graceful creation, was fastened in her soft, golden hair by a spray of orange-blossoms and clusters of diamonds. She carried a bouquet of lily of the valley and violets. Moving up the aisle, the bride looked neither to the right nor to the left, but walked as did her father, with becoming dignity."

The ceremony began with the entrance of the choir, singing to the organ music of Professor Jacob Reinhardt. Next down the aisle came Dana's six ushers, followed by six bridesmaids and the maids of honor, Nannie and Phyllis. When the minister asked "Who gives the bride away?" Chillie broke with convention. Instead of

---

male guests pulled ribbons to open the crust, and out sprung a gorgeous creature "covered only by the ceiling."

answering "I do," he stepped slightly forward. Irene turned her face toward him, and they kissed.

Josephine might have been concerned her brother was marrying beneath him, and the Gibsons might have wondered about the bumptious and free-wheeling style of Irene's family, but the press all over the country made Irene's and Dana's marriage a front-page event of national social significance. Two-thirds of the front page of Richmond's *Dispatch* was devoted to their nuptials. Its headline was "Beauty and Genius: One of the Most Brilliant Weddings in Our City's History."

Newspaper accounts were full of glossy hyperbole and dramatic statements. Within the tortured English in the following accolade the impression is that one reporter found Irene to be something more than a pretty face. "Miss Langhorne will enter upon her new life amid a shower of such widely-expressed good wishes as is an exquisite tribute to her belleship. She takes all the adoration the press has given her with the genial and sweet unconsciousness that is not the common quality of beauty and the charm of her radiantly friendly personality will not be less missed when Mr. Gibson takes her to her new home than will her gay and handsome face."

After the ceremony Irene and Dana walked from the church into the cheers of the throng waiting to catch a glimpse of them. They entered their carriage and rode to 101 West Grace, where a wedding breakfast for a hundred guests was waiting. At the entrance a desk "of dainty design with silver furnishings" held a register for the guests to sign. Tables of four and six were set up throughout the house, even in the upstairs hall. The bridal party was seated in the dining room. Flowers were everywhere - - American Beauty roses in tall vases, and yellow and gold and white chrysanthemums. A string band played from behind a screen of palms and flowers.

A usually reserved Dana must have enjoyed himself immensely. His friend and usher, Dick Davis, recounted, " When we got back [from the church] I asked if the ushers were to kiss the bride as I saw Dana kissing everyone in sight that [sic] wore skirts and the bride said yes and held out her lips to be kissed. . . ."

The Gibson Girl

That afternoon the bride and groom took the Chesapeake & Ohio's 3:25 train for Old Point Comfort and the Hygeia Hotel, where they stayed a few days before returning to Richmond. Then they went on to Boston, where Dana wanted to check on a show of his being installed. On the way back they stopped over at Longfield so members of Dana's family who had not come to the wedding could meet Irene. From there they traveled to New York, and on the 24th of November boarded the steamship "Columbia" for the honeymoon trip Dana had promised Irene five months before.

Their first landfall was Gibraltar. They toured Spain, then called at ports along the French Riviera. They visited Rome, Florence and Naples and stayed for a time in Paris. In January they arrived in London. Their Grand Tour was over. Dana was anxious to get back to work.

CHAPTER NINE

THE GIBSON GIRL

Dana and Dick Davis, both physically attractive and sought-after celebrities in the New York City scene, had gone out of their way to avoid serious relationships with women. After Dana succumbed, Davis did not let go of his friendship with Dana, but adjusted his intense traveling schedule to be with the Gibsons whenever possible. Irene was the ideal female companion for Davis, a woman in his words "perfectly ineligible and free to sigh for and make pretty speeches to, and see as often as you can, and revel in your devotion and unrequited affection." I suspect Davis's fragile ego would have been crushed if he had known how Irene felt about him, thoughts she kept to herself while the two friends were still alive. Toward the end of her life she commented that Davis's lisp annoyed her, and he was the type of brassy, seemingly cocksure individual who was rude to doormen and restaurant waiters.

Davis arrived in London shortly after Irene and Dana took up residence in an apartment at the Albany, formerly the exclusive territory of London's elegant bachelors. Dana's fame as an artist, together with his many friends from former trips to England, produced numbers of social invitations for the young couple. Davis wrote that to reciprocate the hospitality shown them, Irene gave her first dinner party. Among their guests were John Singer Sargent, Mr. and Mrs. Edwin Austin Abbey, and Henry James.[*] Irene had miscalculated the amount of food needed, and the guests went away hungry. The story got out, and for the rest of their stay in London, Irene's friends playfully inundated her with gifts of food.

Davis joined the newlyweds on a day trip to Henley to watch a rowing regatta in which Yale University was competing against British crews. Three young Englishmen anchored near their punt became so entranced by Irene's beauty and tears of suspense

---

[*]Henry James was one of the most influential American writers of his day who wrote primarily of a society of sophistication and culture. A master of fiction and of the travelogue, today he is criticized as being a hopeless snob.

The Gibson Girl

that they too cheered for the losing Yale crew. Davis wrote that after the finish the "Brits bowed sadly and paddled away in melancholy sadness."

Some eight years later, Davis recalled, "I never saw a young couple more popular any place. They were sought after by everybody. They had charming apartments at the Albany, and every afternoon you met there the most interesting people, the very best of the social, artistic and literary worlds." Irene was in her element, a center of attraction in a world full of new friends and new experiences. She wrote her friend, Martha Bagby, about a luncheon party at the home of the novelist, Anthony Hope, whom Irene thought to be "very nice." Hope was sitting next to a Mrs. Spender, and across the table sat a Miss Nilfard, an actress currently starring in a London play based on Hope's novel, *The Prisoner of Zenda*. Hope and Miss Nilfard were having an affair. Irene overheard him whisper to Mrs. Spender, "Are you jealous?" Irene was titillated by this clandestine behavior. "Of course I pricked up my ears and caught it all."

In the same letter Irene wrote, "Honestly, you have never seen such a place as London filled with interesting people. Thomas Hardy is nice but ugly indeed. Mrs. Humphrey Ward is also nice. . . . Mrs. Craigie seems to be very much liked here.[*] Lord Alexander Thyme was to have lunched here today with us quietly, but his father, the Marquis of Bath, died suddenly in Venice." Irene reported to Martha her conversation with Sir Evelyn Wood,[**] a Lieutenant General in the British army, as they walked toward Piccadilly Circus. "He said to me, 'Come go in here with me a minute. I want to write my name in a friend's book. 'I found when in there it was the house of the Duke of Cambridge. I said, 'Sir Evelyn, why do you do that?' He said he could not leave his card on

---

[*]Mary Augusta Ward, a novelist and a vehement opponent of women's suffrage, became president of America's Anti-Suffrage League. Pearl Craigie, a novelist and dramatist, like Mrs. Ward, was against women obtaining the vote. Though seeing herself as the exception, she said she had no confidence in the honor of the average women or of her brain.

[**]Sir Evelyn had fought in the Crimean War and became a Field Marshall after service in the Boer War.

'Royalty' for no one can unless they are 'Royalty.' It shows they are not on equality with them." Irene was amazed that a person of Sir Evelyn's stature and social position must defer to an even higher stratum of society.

Dana had not decided to stay in London solely for amusement and social contact. He had come to work. The first order of business was to complete a commission for the *Ladies' Home Journal*, a series of drawings entitled *People of Dickens*. He took to the streets and into courtrooms and parks to capture London's mood and its people. Even gatherings in their Albany apartment were work sessions. Dick Davis recalled, "Dana drew everyone who came to see him. It was not uncommon to see the Commanding General of the British Army being sketched while Dana's charming wife was pouring tea and chatting with such company as Lady Henry Somerset,* Anthony Hope, DuMaurier, Lord Minto, Arthur Wing Pinero, George Curzon, Henry M. Stanley, and a host of other clever, charming people."** But sketching Londoners and his commitment to the *Ladies' Home Journal* were of vastly secondary importance to Dana. All he wanted to do was draw his wife. He had captured in marriage his Muse, the flesh-and-blood incarnation of the ideal woman for which he had been searching since he first determined to create a woman all Americans could idolize and take to their hearts. Since that first

---

*Lady Somerset became president of both the World's Women's Christian Temperance Union and the National British Women's Temperance Society. I wonder how Irene, at twenty-two and whose life had been mainly a whirl of social and romantic entertainment, related to these powerful female personalities who came to her London apartment. The only thread which joins the influence of these women to Irene's later beliefs is that she was slow in advocating suffrage for women.

**Lord Minto was a British statesman who served as Governor-General of Canada and Viceroy of India. Arthur Pinero, an actor and popular London playwright, was known as the "Enfante Terrible" of the 1890s because of his controversial themes. George Curzon later was Viceroy of India and Foreign Secretary in Lloyd George's cabinet. Stanley uttered the famous line, "Dr. Livingston, I presume?" A journalist, he was sent out to find the explorer-missionary, and in the process became the first European to explore the Congo River from central Africa to the Atlantic Ocean.

The Gibson Girl

meeting in Delmonico's he had wanted to draw her, but until they arrived in London after their Continental tour there was no opportunity for Irene to pose for long stretches of time. No doubt Irene was prepared for the tedious sessions in front of Dana's drawing board, and no doubt Dana had shared with her how critical was her modeling for his career, that professionally she could rescue him.*

Dana realized people were tiring of his American Girl. At any moment a new talent could catch the imagination of the magazine editors, then the public, and he could lose his popularity. In interviews prior to their departure abroad, Dana made a point of telling the press he was abandoning the American Girl and was replacing her with another type, according to one reporter, "the exact nature of which as yet is a mystery except to the initiated few." Another reporter who obviously had spent some time with Irene and Dana guessed what he was up to. "The great artist's bride, while a woman of striking beauty is modeled upon quite different lines from his ideal woman. Mr. Gibson's infatuation and his exceeding admiration for his new 'study' leads to the supposition that he may picture her as the new type of American girl, and give the public one which will eclipse the stately, haughty, high-bred beauty which stands so commandingly and majestically in the foreground of his best pictures."

Since 1890 Dana's American Girl had led the charge against the oppressive, sexist codes of her generation. Prevailing ideas about women included the notions that they were genetically inferior, that their smaller brains could not retain much information, and that their proper place was in their homes and forever at the beck and call of their husbands. Only the most assertive women of the era had demanded more, continuing with their educations and going into the world along the only career paths open to them - - social work and teaching at wages much lower than their male

---

*Years later, in a newspaper interview Irene admitted she was insecure sitting for Dana because his other models were professional. As she posed in London during the first months of their marriage, her only thought was "make me pretty, Dana, make me pretty."

The Gibson Girl

counterparts. Where the ideal Victorian woman was small and delicate, pure and meekly faithful, Dana depicted his American Girl as assertive and physically robust, oftentimes larger in stature than the men with whom he placed her. Victorian women blushed, cried, and fainted over trivialities; tears came to the eyes of the American Girl only if she had suffered a personal catastrophe, the loss of a loved one or a great disappointment.

The American Girl popularized the new fashions in women's clothing. The bustle, that grotesque contrivance that accented the posterior to the point a buffet luncheon could be served on it, was out, and the hour-glass figure was in. The new style, though still restrictive with an unhealthily corseted and pinched-in waist, exaggerated the bosom. Skirts were slimmed down to suggest the enticing curves of the hips. The American Girl popularized the interchangeable, economical shirtwaist and separate skirt. Now millions of women not able to afford voluminous, heavily ornamented dresses could own smart wardrobes. Under her influence, women could enjoy a new freedom at the beach in costumes which left their arms bare. The calves of their exposed legs were covered only by black stockings.

But because of his own discomfort with women and his distrust of their motives, Dana was incapable of imbuing his American Girl with much more than beauty, fashionable clothes, calculated romance and a haughtiness that approached cynicism. The American Girl was still her own worst enemy, still the pawn of the men in her life. She permitted herself to be pushed across the ocean by fathers into the wizened arms of decrepit European barons and counts. Even though she held herself aloof and was capable of wit and even caustic sarcasm, she, like her Victorian counterpart, had no aptitude for self-accomplishment. Her achievement in life was measured only by the man she married. She was perfectly willing to spurn love and the chance for lasting happiness for social standing and wealth, an overdone, demeaning theme of Dana's that he emphasized with cold body language - - stiff poses on ballroom floors or languid posture on overstuffed sofas. Dana seemed to hold as much contempt for his American Girl, in spite of her youth and stateliness, as he did for the old and unattractive man who was able to lure her into matrimony with wealth or title.

The Gibson Girl

According to a number of art critics and social commentators Dana's public resented his idea that the American Girl was ready to sell herself for a title. "She stamps out Cupid from their hearts," one said. Another acknowledged Dana's creation was charming with a world-wide reputation for beauty and elegance, but hoped that one day "she may be given a heart and sentiment." One reviewer described Dana's portrait of the ideal woman as "a muscular maiden who plays tennis and pulls a good oar and could evidently play center rush of foot ball very handily. One sees no reason why she could not blacksmith or pitch hay. She has a chest expanse of four inches."

Having met and fallen in love with Irene, Dana now understood the cold objectivity his American Girl possessed, her distance and a lifelessness that sprang from his own lack of personal commitment to the opposite sex. The first indication Dana gave that he was rethinking his attitude occurred in a newspaper interview he gave in February, 1895, only three months after he had been introduced to Irene. In his clinical description of the different types of women, I believe he was describing the various character facets he saw in the one woman he expected to become his wife. He separated women into seven classifications - - The Beauty, the Boy-Girl, the Flirt, the Sentimental, the Convinced, the Ambitious, and the Well-Balanced. To Dana Irene was the Well-Balanced woman, the combination of the six other types and the woman a man loves and wants to marry. "The Well-balanced Girl is the nearest to the ideal. She has a harmony, almost a completeness. She has been loved by many men, has refused many men, but always retains their friendship. When she loves a man, she makes him happy. She is the sort of woman a man wants to call his friend."

Obviously, Dana's growing admiration and love for Irene already had begun to tear down his defenses. She had awakened somewhere within him an innate respect for women he as yet had not been able to bring forth, an esteem that proved to be the pivot of his devotion for her and the foundation of his successful career. As an old man, Dana compressed his life-long attitude toward women into one statement: "Nowadays, some men let women have their own way. I don't agree with that. I don't think husbands should allow their wives to have their own way. I think they should insist on it."

For the first time in his life Dana began to draw with feeling. He drew Irene singing, seated at a piano with a chorus of angelic children's faces behind her. He drew her at the theater. He drew her as a young bride and as a female football player on a Vassar team battling Yale. He dressed her in military costume, in clerical robes, and as an ambassadoress. Where Dana's drawings of women had possessed a serenity that approached vapidity, they now took on Irene's personality. When Irene tired of posing and he used other models, he gave them her wasp-waisted figure and rearranged their features to project Irene's resolute, though tranquil, manner. He captured her facial expressions, her seductive eyes whose lids drooped ever so slightly, her joy of life, her enthusiasm, and her coquettish manner. And, beneath Irene's vitality, Dana captured her softness and compassion. His work became his declaration of devotion to her, and with pen, pencil, and ink he proclaimed his enchantment to the world.

Dana got an unexpected opportunity to capture Irene in a regal setting when America's ambassador to the Court of St. James's arranged for her to be presented to Queen Victoria at the first Drawing Room of the year in Buckingham Palace.[*] Court Presentation was an important part of the English class system, and only those "of society" were eligible; not many Americans got the opportunity. Drawing Rooms were held in the mid-afternoon, the presentation ceremony consisting of the ladies - - sometimes as many as 800 in number - - being ushered in a continuous stream before the royal dais. They curtsied, and Victoria or her stand-in bowed slightly to each of them. A levee was held before this parade - - lasting as long as an hour - - to which the ladies' escorts were invited, but they had to retire before the presentation itself. Nothing in the way of food or drink was served at either stage, and everyone

---

[*]Irene wrote to Martha Bagby, "The Queen will hold her Drawing Room that day (poor old lady). She must be pretty well tired out." Irene did not get the opportunity to see the queen because Victoria was unwell and her daughter, Helena, presided in her behalf.

The Gibson Girl

went away hungry and thirsty to Drawing Room Teas at private houses after the event.

With Irene's invitation as his ticket of admittance Dana obtained a commission from the *London Graphic* to make drawings of the occasion. He made background sketches before the presentation, and then was allowed to stay during the ceremony. He peered into the reception hall through a window as each of the presentees slowly paraded by Queen Victoria's daughter, Helena. Of course, Irene was the central figure in his pictures, resplendent in the bridal dress she had worn a few months earlier.

Dana was thrilled with his new depiction of the American woman Irene inspired and impatient for people to see his work. He arranged a showing of thirty of his drawings in London's Fine Art Society gallery. But his American public had to wait until October, 1896, two months after they returned to New York City from London, when his second book of drawings featuring Irene, *Pictures of People*, was published. The rave reviews Dana received for *Pictures of People* and, shortly thereafter, for his third book, *London*, were a welcome relief, powerful indications his popularity was intact.

When Dana's audience first saw Irene, the response was ecstatic. The New York *Journal* dedicated an entire page reviewing *Pictures of People*, and its headline blared, "Mr. Gibson Selects His Wife As His New Type Of American Girl." She was described as "tall and graceful, exercising her sway in a kindly manner." And, "Mrs. Charles Dana Gibson is a beautiful young woman who has succeeded in adding a great deal to the interest of her husband's artistic work." Gibson had a "wonderfully light touch," and he "successfully brings together the highly artificial aspect of American society with the natural impulses of love and marriage."

Within weeks after his first drawings of Irene appeared, the term "American Girl" gave way entirely to "The Gibson Girl." Dana's name now inextricably was joined with his portrayal of his wife, a bond with which he was never comfortable. In fact, he declared he was forever embarrassed that his ideal of the American woman was named for him. Five years earlier he saw the Gibson Girl designation applied to his drawings when he was asked to illustrate for *Century* magazine a story which dealt with a certain type of girl. When the manuscript came to him, he noticed the name "Goodrich" was typed over erasures in the article. Dana did not know that in the text of the story the authoress, Nathalie Harris, described her heroine as a "Gibson" girl, but the editors of *Century* did not think Dana well-known enough to have a girl named for him. Nathalie Harris got her way, and when Dana saw the issue in print, he saw his name attached to her heroine. Dana described his reaction: "[When] I saw what had been really done, I blushed. I have been blushing ever since." Nathalie Harris's label did not stick after this early christening, and in the years before his marriage to Irene only occasionally did a columnist or reporter refer to his creations as "Gibson's girls," but never identified one as a "Gibson Girl."

Although it was Irene's face and the boldness of her character that captured the imagination of Dana's public, Dana never publicly acknowledged the influence she had on his art. Obviously, he had no more interest in drawing attention to his wife than he did to himself. Furthermore, he deflected all speculation concerning any and all models who inspired him by asserting in innumerable interviews, "The Gibson Girl does not exist. She has been as the grains of sand in number." Nevertheless, over the years there were many claimants to the title.*

The pettiness and flippancy of his American Girl was gone, replaced by Irene's enthusiasm and vivacity. There was nothing average about the Gibson Girl. Although she was American womanhood idealized, Dana saw no need to make her perfect because Irene was not. Occasionally the Gibson Girl would make the same mistakes as her predecessor by marrying foolishly or being too haughty or too narcissistic. Irene had her faults, and Dana gave them to his Gibson Girl. The Gibson Girl was Irene, full of the juice and spontaneity of youth, daring, charismatic, and sensuous. Like Irene, she was flirtatious, reveling in the power she had over men and needing their attention, but every inch the lady. She flaunted her sexuality, but with subtlety and style. Irene loved the outdoors.

---

*On a London trip Irene and Dana were at the theater, and a girl on stage was introduced as "The Original Gibson Girl." They both were amused. Dana never had laid eyes on her.

The Gibson Girl

She was athletic, an excellent horsewoman, a golfer,* a swimmer, and an avid cyclist. So was the Gibson Girl. Irene adored elegant balls and dinner parties, the beach, the hunting field and horseshows. So did the Gibson Girl.

Dana used the Gibson Girl to champion women's inherent capabilities. His first salvos were drawings of Irene in roles and occupations not dreamed of for the fairer, delicate sex. Though tame in today's world, his statements were completely out of tune with Victorian mores and women's concepts of their own limitations. Dana's progressive approach toward women hit the perfect chord for the day because Americans were tiring of the strict prudities of the Victorian standard. They were willing to take on new attitudes in the positive national atmosphere and economic resurgence that began in 1896. Now dressed in the less restricted fashions Dana had made popular, women were rebelling against being slaves of their overbearing husbands. They began to assert themselves, and left their houses to follow challenging vocations.

Dana's work made its inroads into all aspects of American life. Ordinary shop girls, school teachers, adolescents, and housewives took the Gibson Girl as their role model. They emulated the way she dressed, the set of her neck, the way she positioned her fingers, her walk, her posture. Men were entranced by her looks, captivated by her sensuousness. Her disciples did not care that she was unreal, apart from real life, her hair rarely out of place, and her clothes invariably pressed and starched perfectly. It was no matter she never perspired or showed strain or even the slightest fatigue. They fell in love with this exquisite girl who oftentimes was outspoken and domineering, and at other times vulnerable and sentimental.

The Gibson Girl was royalty as Princess Flavia, the romantic heroine in Anthony Hope's *The Prisoner of Zenda*, and its sequel, *Rupert of Hentzau;* she was Princess Aline in Richard Harding Davis's *Soldiers of Fortune*. Taking advantage of Irene's willingness to sit for him, Dana drew her twice in one of his illustrations.

---

*Dana thought golf a waste of time, but Irene was an addict. Years later, Irene wrote to Phyllis, "I am the busiest golfer you ever saw. I would like to build on a drive [driving range] or a green and just go out and hit.

The Gibson Girl

Gibson Girl centerfolds were pasted on the walls of frontier cabins and mounted in storefronts in Japan and Spain. Eleven Gibson books were published. Kings and queens owned them. Each week the Gibson Girl appeared in *Life,* and the magazine's circulation swelled as readers bought issues if only to get Dana's latest drawing. Dana was not at all shy about commercializing his work. There were Gibson Girl pillows, calendars, leatherwork, plates, songs, and even a musical. A 1906 hit song from the Broadway show, *The Belle of Mayfair,* was "Why Do They Call Me a Gibson Girl?"

The simple, yet forceful, statement his Gibson Girl made was a woman need not abandon her central role of lover, wife and mother to take more from life than previous generations had offered her. She could stand proud and still be agreeably sensitive and wistful, needful of love and approval. Unlike her rather dour and militant contemporaries, the women aggressively active in the temperance and suffrage movements, the Gibson Girl was no threat to the sexist structure of American society. As a result, she was embraced by men and women alike. Women's movements were in their infancy, but America was not ready for revolutionary notions. Because Dana's subtle vision of the New Women was universally popular, the Gibson Girl, perhaps, did more to further the cause of women's rights than the dedicated, courageous women activists who mainly were scoffed at by both sexes.

CHAPTER TEN

CITY LIGHTS

For Irene, New York City was a giant showcase where she knew she could shine as a star attraction. Dressed lavishly and elegantly in the latest fashions so suited for her tall and well-proportioned figure - - gowns by Worth[*] covering petticoats of taffeta and silk whose rustle suggested glamour and romance, feathered fans, and cartwheel hats teeming with ribbons and flowers - - she swept into Dana's New York life full of his literary and artistic friends. Hers was a world of dinners and evenings at the theater, of ballrooms and drawing rooms populated by the affluent and the influential. Now sure of her ability to perform in a sphere more cosmopolitan than her comfortable and secure life in Richmond and at The White, she came flushed with confidence from her success with the older and more worldly society in London, where she had captivated fashionable men and established friendships with extremely able women many years her senior.

Henry James described New York at the turn of the century as a "huge, jagged city full of rancorous noises, turmoil, and conflict. . . ." Irene's city was a small one centered in today's midtown Manhattan between 23rd and 40th Streets, a world and a culture away from the stinking tenements of the Lower East Side or the market district or the river front where the bowsprits of sailing vessels hung over the streets. It was, nevertheless, raw and exciting, loud and crowded. Her city was populated by men in tall silk hats and ladies in long skirts, leg-o-mutton sleeves and fashionably plumed bonnets served by hansom cab drivers perched above their passengers and grocers in long, white aprons. Its streets were a tangle of people, carts, brightly colored trolley cars with curved roofs, and great lumbering wagons pulled by teams of dray horses. Sidewalks pockmarked with coal chute covers and covered with striped awnings were jammed with pedestrians weaving back and

---

[*]The premier couturier of the day.

forth to avoid the ever-present construction projects which were taking down six-story buildings and replacing them with skyscrapers of up to twenty floors. The din of jackhammers, street peddlers' chants, and steel-rimmed wheels against cobblestones filled the dusty, coal-soot air.

In a sense, Irene's setting - - bordered by the grand residences on Fifth Avenue and the rural beauty of Central Park and full of theaters, expensive restaurants and hotels - - was as unreal as that portrayed by Dana's illustrations. It was a world divorced from and seemingly immune to the economic and class tensions brought on by the worst depression the country had undergone. Irene was as oblivious to the larger world around her as the penned, black-and-white girls she inspired. In a time when five cents could open an account at a savings bank or buy a cup of coffee or a pint of beer, and when a laboring man earned $500 a year and a domestic servant $156 annually plus board, Dana's income brought them whatever they wished. Chillie's wealth had spun a golden cocoon around Irene ever since she was a young girl, sheltering her from the harsh, dreary life led by most Southerners. Now Dana's money protected and pampered her in New York.

Everyone was curious to get a look at this beautiful young woman from the South Dana had married. His love of the theater and his friendships with actors and artists opened up new horizons for Irene. Publishers and editors and writers were entranced by her vivacity and were more than willing to sit down after dinner to watch her play the piano and sing. Socialites always wanted an attractive young couple to enliven their parties. The Gibsons were a celebrity couple, sought after by the celebrated of the city. Irene was where she wanted to be - - in the spotlight, readily recognized on the streets, catered to in restaurants and shops, surrounded by a host of friends and acquaintances.

My mother once described trailing behind Irene as she walked around her Manhattan neighborhood in the 1930s. She knew everyone - - the grocer, every doorman, the shopkeepers, the trashman - - and had a kind, personal, and sometimes a spicy word for each of them. The men doffed their hats and the women smiled and once in a while curtsied. And Irene loved the attention, the warmth that came back to her. Transposing this mental image back

The Gibson Girl

another forty years, I can imagine the figure she cut on the streets of the city as a young matron in the 1890s, every inch of her a real-life Gibson Girl as she stood tall on a street corner, dressed in a sharply tailored, split-skirted riding dress with stiff, dark brown boots disappearing beneath her hem, whistling for a hansom cab to take her to Central Park for a horseback outing. Or picking her way through the sidewalks on a shopping expedition or on her way to market or to lunch at a club or restaurant, men ogling the voluptuous lines of her body sensually exaggerated by boned and laced corsets which encased her bosom and accentuated her hips.

The Gibsons' life-style was a great deal more expansive then their living quarters on the top floor of the *Life* building. The small rooms must have seemed even more cramped after Irene completed decorating them with the rich fabrics and ornate clutter so representative of the taste of the era. Dana worked across the hall in his studio, while Irene managed the tiny space with the assistance of a cleaning maid and a laundress. Irene would not have dreamed of doing any cooking, so they certainly employed a cook as well and often had meals brought up from a nearby restaurant. Entertainment in the small apartment was out of the question, and the problem of social reciprocity was solved in clubs and restaurants.

Shortly before Irene and Dana returned from their wedding trip, Nanaire and Chillie enrolled seventeen-year-old Nannie in Miss Brown's Academy for Young Ladies in New York City. Now that Irene was a prominent young matron in New York City, her parents considered it her duty to spring Nannie from the relatively parochial environments of Greenwood and Richmond. As far as they were concerned, it had been their long and carefully orchestrated campaign that had positioned Irene into wealth and society. Now it was Irene's turn to wave the family marital banner and present her younger sister to a more promising marriage market than Virginia offered.

Irene did what she could to make her sister happy in New York. Frequently, she took Nannie from school on outings and had her over to spend the night in their small apartment. The rebellious Nannie loathed Miss Brown's for its regimented, and to her, intellectually vapid climate. She could not stand the snobbery of the

City Lights

girls, and to counter her schoolmates' affectations, Nannie told them she came from a poor southern country family. She faked a hideous drawl and wore outlandish clothes to make believable her disadvantaged background. But the game soon was up for Nannie because she could not explain her sister who, to the girls, was an elegant celebrity. Nannie mentioned in her memoirs another irritation. She was never referred to as "Miss Nancy Langhorne," only "Irene Gibson's sister." In not too many more years those tables would turn, and Irene would be known as "Nancy Astor's sister."

Nannie did not last long at Miss Brown's and soon left for Virginia, probably because her older sister was in no condition to give her the comfort and attention she needed. Irene was pregnant before leaving London, and when she began to show, no longer able to hide her widening girth under the loose drapery of dresses, social convention required she retire to shield her delicate condition from male observation. Irene's initial flurry of intense social life in New York City had not lasted long. In February, 1897, Irene Langhorne Gibson, or Babs, was born in their apartment's four-poster bed.

Lodgings which had been ideal for a bachelor illustrator but tight for a married couple plus Nannie, the frequent overnight guest, were now entirely unsatisfactory with the addition of a sometimes squalling infant. Dana's popularity grew exponentially. His workload was enormous. Working close by, across the narrow hallway, he found the atmosphere on the top floor of the *Life* building particularly unsuitable. They moved to a larger apartment and Dana rented a separate studio.

Fortunately for Irene and Dana, but frustrating to the task of recounting their early years of marriage, they were seldom apart for long periods. Therefore, they wrote no letters to each other. The only surviving correspondence from this time is a packet of letters Babs's nursemaid, Jessie, wrote daily to Irene from Mirador in August, 1897. After six months of mothering Babs, Irene was in need of a vacation. Irene and Dana traveled to Mirador to deposit the baby and Jesse at Mirador, and then swung back north to Marion, Massachusetts with stops at Bristol and Newport, Rhode Island. Jesse's letters gave Irene a blow-by-blow account of Babs's

The Gibson Girl

daily schedule, the baby's attack of boils, and minute descriptions of infant body functions; but amid the baby-talk reportage Jesse manages to portray a lively picture of Mirador's hectic social life with family, guests and callers overrunning the place, Chillie's aggressive personality, and Nanaire's calmness.

Chillie and Nanaire coaxed Nannie back to New York in the Spring of 1897 to stay with the Gibsons. They must have been desperate to get Nannie on a road to marriage; the pickings were non-existent in Greenwood and still sparse in economically depressed Richmond. Nannie was now well within marriageable age, so the pressure was on Irene to find her a suitable - - the definition being "rich" and "social" - - husband. This she did. Robert Gould Shaw came from an excellent New England family that had made its fortune in copper mining. His parents were well-meaning people who at the time were not greatly worried about their son's growing signs of dissipation. They believed any problems he had could be cured by this strong, headstrong female he was about to marry.

Shaw arrived at Mirador in August for a long visit. He must have behaved himself admirably because Nannie's parents gave their consent. Nanaire and Chillie prepared for a grand wedding in Richmond, but the young bride-to-be, probably extremely upset by a decision she knew to be wrong, became ill. Wedding plans were shelved, and Nanaire took Nannie to Hot Springs to recuperate - - and no doubt to convince her daughter to go ahead with the marriage. When Nannie regained her health, the wedding took place at Mirador in a small, family ceremony in the front parlor. Irene and Dana were there with Babs. After the ceremony, Nannie again left for Hot Springs, this time with her new husband. The honeymoon - - for unexplained but easily guessed at reasons - - was a disaster, and Nannie flew back to her parents. They pushed her again to Shaw and the result was a disastrous marriage that lasted six years and produced one son, Bobbie Shaw, Jr..

Babs did not hamper Irene's and Dana's mobility. Dana knew trips abroad breathed freshness into his work. He needed the stimulation of unknown places - - new sights produced new ideas. He had planned to include Egypt in their honeymoon itinerary, but they had bypassed this exotic land, which had become very popular

City Lights

with American tourists. Another opportunity came in 1897, when Doubleday & McClure Co. commissioned him to make a series of drawings in Egypt to be included in a travel book. They bundled up ten-month old Babs in December, 1897, and set out. First, they stopped in Cairo, staying at the old-world and luxurious Shepheard's Hotel. They took in the usual sights around Cairo, such as the Pyramids and the Sphinx, but the bulk of their time was spent with friends on a chartered riverboat that took them up the Nile. Somewhere around Thebes they celebrated Christmas. In the middle of this far-off land Irene sat at the boat's piano singing Christmas carols and "Way down upon the S'wanee River."

A record of their trip exists because Dana's publisher suggested strongly he write the travelogue which his drawings illustrated. Taken aback by the rather firm request because he thought he had no aptitude for writing. Dana acquiesced nonetheless, and *Sketches in Egypt*, a 114-page description of their trip, was published in 1899. Dana always was timid about his writing, leery of exposing himself to the criticism of his writer-friends. Yet, he used words as clearly and economically as he used pen strokes. His account began, "Egypt has sat for her likeness longer than any other country. Nothing disturbs her composure. Financial ruin may stare her in the face, armies may come and go, but each year the Nile rises and spreads out over her, and all traces of disturbances are gone."

Dana's text in *Sketches of Egypt* reveals his attitude toward personal and family privacy; not once does he mention that his wife and child were traveling with him. They were traveling as a couple with a baby in a destitute, disease-ridden country, and no mention is made of how they coped with the intense heat or the language barrier or the logistics of having a baby along - - a hazardous risk for Babs when the everyday dangers to even an adult's health in Richmond or New York were serious enough. Dana's commentary is in the first person, and any "we" used refers to other tourists sharing accommodations with the Gibson family. Only the drawings of Irene made the reader aware of her presence. He held the strong desire to shield his family from the publicity so important to his career, and during the first six to eight years of their marriage Irene

The Gibson Girl

is rarely mentioned in interviews and in articles written about him and his work.

From Egypt they journeyed to Germany, where Dana rented a studio in Munich. He had accepted a commission to illustrate *Rupert of Hentzau,* an Anthony Hope novel set in Bavaria, and he wanted his characters to be authentic. Also, he had been exploring ideas for a series of drawings featuring Americans traveling abroad. Inspiration for his main character came when a shriveled up little Munich native knocked at his studio door asking for a modeling job. Mr. Pipp was born, the genesis of a body of work which became Dana's most popular. It is the saga of an immensely rich, but hen-pecked, man who traveled through Europe with his domineering wife and two lovely daughters.

Away in Egypt and Germany, Dana did not catch the warlike fever of many of his contemporaries. He missed the raging nationalistic hysteria touched off by the sinking of the battleship *Maine* on February 15, 1898 in Havana's harbor. America was eager to flex her international muscle in the 1890s, and our excuse to challenge European rule in the Western hemisphere finally came. The Cuban rebels fighting Spain's oppression had a measure of sympathy in the United States, but it was the "yellow press" of William Randolph Hearst and other publishers who fed the flames of jingoism. Hearst had sent Dana's friend, Frederic Remington, to chronicle Spanish atrocities in Cuba, and when Remington wired back to New York that war did not seem to be materializing, Hearst flashed back, "You furnish the pictures and I'll furnish the war." With the destruction of the Spanish fleet as it attempted to escape Santiago harbor, the "Splendid Little War" was over a few weeks after it had begun.[*]

Dana's pen did get into the act after he returned to the United States. *Life* was violently anti-imperialist and anti-war, and

---

[*]The war was a great opportunity for Dana's friend, Dick Davis, who as a war correspondent covered Teddy Roosevelt and his Rough Riders in July, 1898 when they stormed San Juan Hill. He reported the Rough Riders ". . . had no glittering bayonets, they were not massed in regular array. There were a few men in advance, bunched together, and creeping up a steep, sunny hill, the top of which roared and flashed with flame."

he drew cartoons reflecting Mitchell's position. One of them expressed Dana's irritation at the glorification by the press of the volunteer army at the expense of the regular army. "After The War" shows a young lady asking a wounded soldier if he is a volunteer hero. He replies he is only a Regular.

Shortly after Irene and Dana returned from Germany in the late summer of 1898 my father was conceived. Pregnant, hot, and uncomfortable in the sweltering city heat, Irene went to a rented house close by the water in Hempstead, Long Island to await the birth, and Dana commuted on the weekends. In July, 1899, Langhorne, their second and last child, was born. On his birth certificate the name "Charles Dana Gibson" was inked in, then crossed out. Dana balked at the prospect of a "junior" because he believed if the father's name was ever tarnished, so would be the son's. My father, in turn, sired and named three sons before he decided to forego the family "tradition" and give me his name. I was born when he was forty-one, and he determined his life was too set and he too old to get into any trouble or scandal which would make his name a burden for me to carry.

Although Irene was terribly homesick for her Virginia family, her visits were few because Dana was working hard. Babs was an infant, and her days and nights were full of social obligations. Happily for Irene, Dana decided to get away from the city to write the text of *Sketches in Egypt* at Mirador during the first months of her pregnancy. In 1896, the Langhorne family had moved permanently to Mirador. Keene was working with his father and Harry had a job as a clerk in Richmond with the Southern Railway Supply Company. Phyllis's life at sixteen was centered around horses, and Buck and Nora were children living with their parents a simple, country life. Now that he had made his money and handed over most of his business affairs to his young partner and cousin, Daniel Langhorne, Chillie could play the gruff, domineering country squire. He relished his roles as the central figure in Mirador's rambunctious and chaotic drama and as the paternalistic head of Greenwood's small society with his reserved pew - - with spittoon - - at Emmanuel Church.

In 1900 Phyllis was twenty years old, and Nanaire and Chillie were concerned that she would never marry. With her quiet

The Gibson Girl

manner, petite figure, and chiseled features, Phyllis was an interesting catch for any man. She was extremely athletic and enjoyed many sports, including tennis and squash. Her great love was horses, and she traveled from New England to South Carolina, riding in the finest hunts on the east coast. Knowing they had to separate Phyllis from her horses so she would concentrate on choosing a mate, again Nanaire and Chillie sent a daughter to New York City, where Irene could orchestrate a suitable match. On a short visit to Newport, Rhode Island with Irene and Dana, Phyllis met Reginald Brooks, a fast-living Harvard man with no vocation, whose finest achievement to date had been racing small sailboats in the waters off Newport. Although Nannie had discovered marriage to a rich playboy was no ticket to happiness, Phyllis learned little from her sister's misfortune. Evidently, in endorsing another family marriage to a man who had never shown any initiative, neither Irene nor her parents had learned much either. Encouraged by Irene and Nannie, braced with the knowledge that her parents heartily approved of another daughter's marriage into money and society, and aware a large purse was needed to finance her expensive avocation, Phyllis accepted Brooks's proposal.

A private trainload of the North's socially elite - - Vanderbilts, Astors, and Whitneys among them - - arrived at the shabby station at Basic City, an unattractive industrial town ten miles west of Mirador and Greenwood on the other side of the Blue Ridge mountains. The more fastidious must have been aghast that their personal brilliance had been subjected to this raw place. They must have wondered who these Langhornes were, to what type of family the elegant groom was attaching himself. Their fears, no doubt, were relieved when they pulled into the shaded, groomed grounds of the Brandon Hotel - - Basic City's one shining asset. Chillie had set an army of carpenters to work refurbishing the hotel so that the 350 invited guests would be comfortable and impressed. In spite of its backwater location, the Brandon had modern conveniences. It boasted bathrooms with both hot and cold running water on every floor, toilets, and radiators in every room.

Greenwood was too small to accommodate the invited throng. For Phyllis's wedding Chillie wanted to spare no expense, determined to show off the wealth he had amassed. He imported chefs and a large orchestra from Richmond, borrowed servants, carriages, and horses from his friends, and arranged for fresh meat, seafood, and flowers to be brought in from Baltimore, Norfolk, and Washington markets. He had conformed to Richmond's modest standards with Irene's simple reception at 101 West Grace Street. For Phyllis he pulled out all the stops.

The celebration lasted three days, culminating in Phyllis's and Reggie's exchange of vows in the ornately decorated Brandon Hotel's lobby. Nannie was her sister's matron of honor, but Irene and Lizzie were considered too old to be in the wedding party. Society reporters had a field day, citing Irene as the loveliest in attendance and noting her every word, agog at the splendor of the opulent gifts and the notable guests.

Babs and Lang were present in Basic City to see their aunt married. Irene and Dana doted on their children and left them in the hands of governesses as rarely as possible. Apparently, the only regular vacations they took without the children were brief summer trips to explore the coast of New England. However, in 1902 they made an exception to their policy of not spending long periods of time away. They accepted an enticing invitation of a friend - - a Mr. Smith - - to join him and a small party aboard the steam yacht, "Margarita," to sail the Mediterranean.[*] Dana wrote a series of letters to his brother, Langdon, detailing the excursion. He said the yacht was so big it dwarfed an Italian man-of-war in Rome's seaport city, Civita Vecchia. He and Irene had a hundred yards of deck to walk. A maid Irene hired in Paris and a steward on board, whose primary duty Dana described as "looking after my two serge suits," tended to their needs in private accommodations consisting of four cabins and two bathrooms.

The "Margarita" sailed through the Greek islands, to Constantinople, to Sicily, Italy and the coast of France. They visited the island of Elba and the "palace" of the exiled Napoleon.[**] Dana

---

[*]I cannot identify Mr. Smith, but the yacht "Margarita" was owned by Anthony J. Drexel. She was a steel, twin-screw schooner with a waterline depth of 272 feet and a 36-foot beam. Smith must have chartered her.

[**]"The place is simple enough," Dana wrote Langdon, "but it is evident an attempt at splendor had been made. There were eagles and bees carved in

The Gibson Girl

kept fit in the exercise room. ". . . once in a while I go into the gymnasium and jounce up and down on a leather horse and ride a stationary bicycle." He and Irene participated in ping pong tournaments, ate too much, and grew tired of their idleness long before the trip was over. They wanted desperately to go home and be with the children.

By the turn of the century Dana's income far outstripped their unpretentious apartment lifestyle. It was time to create a permanent home in New York City, and time to have a summer place so the family could spend long stretches of time away from the city stench and heat. Dana, in spite of his affluence, was helped with the two building projects by a handsome gift from Irene's father. The Gibsons' foremost need was a comfortable and larger home in New York City, so they commissioned Stanford White's architectural firm, McKim, Meade, and White, to design a house for the lot they purchased on 73rd Street.

Like its neighbors, the house, built of Harvard brick in red and gray tints, is deep and narrow, the facade Neo-Georgian-Federal in style. With cellars and storerooms beneath, the ground floor is elevated six steps above street level. A small vestibule opens into the main hall, the intended effect a gradual welcoming into the house. A large fireplace stands to the left of the entrance, and to the right, a curved staircase ascends to the upstairs hall. When Irene and Dana lived there, the first floor contained a drawing room facing the street and a dining room at the rear with connecting wide doorways so the entire space could be open. The library and their bedroom were on the second floor; a guest and children's rooms were on the floor above, with servants' quarters still higher under the eaves.[*]

---

many places, and of course the letter 'N.' The little rooms had been decorated evidently by some amateur who had followed him in his misfortunes. The walls of one room were painted with scenes and especially poorly done. It was pathetic, the whole attempt to make the best of things."

[*]Newspaper articles set the cost of 127 East 73rd Street, "The House The Gibson Girls Built," at $50,000, and estimates for their total expenditure, including decoration and furniture, traveled to the $100,000 mark. They moved in 1902, and were delighted with the result. In a letter to his architect and friend, Stanford White, Dana wrote, "The beauties of the front occupy my

Irene had 127 East 73rd Street designed for entertaining. The house was her stage, she the central attraction for the many guests who were welcomed by its spacious entrance hall and the openness of the first floor. Local politicians and international statesmen mixed with New York's social aristocracy. Actors and actresses, Drews and Barrymores, Cole Porter, artists, writers, and Dana's associates from the fields of illustration and publishing came. Over the years, the house entertained Georges Clemenceau, the "tiger" of France, Mary Pickford and Douglas Fairbanks, the Winston Churchills, Charlie Chaplin, Roosevelts, countless relatives, and old friends from Virginia and New England.

Dana would have been only too happy to come home each night from an exhausting day's work to a quiet supper with his family, but Irene needed the continual stimulation of talented and interesting people. She relished Dana's and her celebrity and worked hard at being a hostess. Her hospitality was easy and informal - - the sort she had known in Virginia. Guests were comfortable at the Gibsons, embraced by the natural warmth both possessed. One acquaintance, remembering the Gibsons and life in New York City, said, "They were charming - - men like Dana Gibson and his wife, Irene Langhorne. He was the most attractive man, bar none, I've ever met, and Irene - - well you can't just describe her. She *was* the Gibson Girl, and she *stood* so beautifully. It was distinction, that's all. . . . "

Once they were settled into 127 East 73rd Street, Irene and Dana set their sights on purchasing a summer place. For Dana, the decision process had been a long one. Back in 1895 he had pasted into his scrapbook a short article from a Philadelphia newspaper which reported he had been the unsuccessful bidder for Papasqua, an ornately pillared, frame mansion built in 1700 fronting the waters of Bristol Bay in Rhode Island. His bid of $9600 was bested by Middleton cousins from South Carolina who bid $9700. Obvious reasons why they postponed the decision to buy a vacation house are trips abroad, Dana's constant work, and Irene's pregnancies, but my bet is the hiatus was a long, eight-year one because they were at

---

whole attention. . . . There is so much to be thankful for."

odds about the location. Cut off from her roots and her family in Virginia, Irene much would have preferred her own place near Mirador, but Dana was a New Englander who loved the water and boats. Besides, I doubt if he was ever that comfortable in Virginia, having no interest in being a part of Chillie's domain.

During one of their summer cruises along New England's seacoast they stayed at the inn at Islesboro, an island four miles off the coast just east of Camden which, beginning in the 1880s, had become a fashionable resort for wealthy Eastern establishment families. The sloping roofs of huge, shingled "cottages" broke the line of the wooded hills surrounding Dark Harbor, a protected cove shared by great yachts, fishing dories belonging to local lobstermen, and small, racing sailboats. A mile west of Dark Harbor and closer to the mainland, across a narrow strait called Gilkey's Harbor, lies 700 Acre Island. Dana told the story that one morning, rowing a skiff, he spotted a point of land on the southeast shore of 700 Acre Island and fell in love with it. Its plateau with a southern exposure above the rocky shore and pebbled beaches seemed the ideal spot to build a summer house. In August, 1903, they purchased 11 1/4 acres from the Philbrook family.

If there was a battle, Dana had won. Abandoning the happy prospect of long summers spent in western Albemarle County close to her parents and old friends, surrounded by the soft droning of crickets, the red clay soil and purplish evening haze she loved, Irene had to settle for the cool ocean breezes and oftentimes fog-bound shore of Maine's Penobscot Bay.*

Up until the 1880s and 1890s, 700 Acre Island had been the site of a tight, local community of farmers and fishermen who preferred the isolation and quiet of island living. By the time the Gibsons arrived most of them had moved away, unwilling any longer to put up with the harsh environment and the difficulties in educating their children. Besides, the rich summer people were

---

*In her correspondence over the years Irene was always enthusiastic about 700 Acre Island. Grandchildren who spent their summers there say she adored the place. The climate was perfect for her extensive flower gardens, Dana was his happiest on the island, and she had many friends whom she entertained at luncheons and teas.

City Lights

paying handsome prices for land that had little, if any, value a few decades previously. On the island there were not many neighbors, just a few Mainers, two or three modest summer houses, and Miss Rose Cleveland, the sister of the ex-president and the largest landowner. She, with her partner, Miss Evelyn Ames of Boston, farmed the opposite end of the island. Building a house and maintaining a household on an island off an island a good distance from the remote Maine mainland was a daunting challenge - - particularly a century ago - - but the choice of 700 Acre Island was a clever one. While the narrow band of water separating the island from the parties, elaborate picnics, and yacht club activities of Islesboro was Dana's moat, protecting his quiet and privacy, Irene was only a short motorboat ride away from the social action and festivities upon which she thrived.

Again, they commissioned McKim, Meade, and White to design a house. Their architect, a Mr. Albro, designed a native stone and shingle cottage with dormer windows. Its central feature was a large living room with French doors that face south, framing the view of a wide lawn and the broad waters of the Penobscot Bay. Construction started in the winter of 1903-04 with building materials brought over from the mainland on ice sleds according to one family story. Although the material just as easily could have arrived by schooner and been deposited on the beach, this more romantic version is probably correct because that winter was severely cold. Even in March the ice was thick enough for Irene and Dana to go ice boating when they came to check on the house's progress. Skilled local labor under the direction of a man by the name of Glover had the house virtually complete in May, when Dana and Langdon arrived by train at Rockland, Maine. They were met by Dana's captain on board the first of many boats Dana bought over the years, the "Reliance," a 30-foot gasoline-powered vessel that had been an auxiliary launch for an America's Cup defender.

The house was sufficiently habitable by the late summer for the Gibsons to live there. Dick Davis and his wife, Cecil, were among the first guests. If Dick Davis is correct, the original cottage cost $10,000. He said it had nineteen rooms, which is incorrect. Later it did have that many - - and more - - after extensions and additions. Each summer for the next forty years - - excepting one

The Gibson Girl

- - Irene and Dana returned to Maine after impatiently waiting out the long winters in New York City. Preparation for their usual three months stay began in the early spring when they went up briefly, Irene to start her garden and Dana to check on whatever building project was in progress. Most summers in Maine began with a few weeks to themselves, followed shortly by the arrivals of Babs and Langhorne and their friends. In later years, around the first of July, their horde of grandchildren began to arrive, along with numerous relatives and guests.

CHAPTER ELEVEN

CHALLENGES

Most of us do not inquire into the early lives of parents and grandparents before we arrived on the scene. Our impressions of them begin only when we become old enough to form our eyewitness understandings, and by then they are in the middle or ending stages of their lives. Furthermore, parents and grandparents rarely make the effort to relate an honest and well-balanced account of their personal histories, preferring instead to forget much of the detail, or to gloss over any memories having an unpleasant or unhappy ring to them. This dearth of communication between generations is merely an element of human nature, a normal custom in most families, and unquestionably in mine. A few years ago, I, like most of Irene's descendants, if asked to give her biographical sketch, would go into the "belle" part and the "Gibson Girl" part and the grandmother phase of her life, and that would be it. If asked about her difficulties, or disappointments, or challenges, I could not have responded, the thought in my head being, How could this special creature, a grandmother for Heaven's sake, have had any trials or challenges to overcome?

If her story ended here - - around the turn of the century at the age of twenty-seven - - I would judge her life as being as close to ideal as existence on this planet can be. Parts of her childhood had been stressful, but she had sailed through her teens and early twenties on a cushion of approval and recognition. Then she chose wisely a man who gave her the love and appreciation she required. Having married and been blessed with the births of healthy children, she reveled in the role of a prominent, young society matron supported elegantly by a celebrity. Hers would have been a glamorous life fit for the society columns, but not a particularly interesting one.

I liken the challenge to my grandmother at this point in her life to that of the proverbial high-school prom queen, the beautiful, young girl who, having captured the kudos of her peers at an early age, looks around her and thinks, That was easy, but what happens next? Many prom queens - - or football quarterbacks, for that matter - - become bewildered by the loss of their youth and early glory and float through the remainder of their lives, never achieving a great deal more. To enjoy a productive life the early achiever must possess a special brand of character, and the courage to realize and act on the simple truth that life requires more than a pretty face or athletic ability. Irene met the challenge. Irene chose not to languish in the memory of her youthful accolades, and in spite of personal loss, her husband's disappointments, and the loss of financial security, she carved out a life of her own which brought joy and comfort to those she touched.

Keeping peace within the Langhorne family had been Irene's role since her childhood days, when she stood by quietly while Chillie's anger and impatience permeated the atmosphere. Mirador was always Irene's anchor, the one place forever her home. She could climb aboard a train in New York City and after an overnight journey find herself in the one spot on earth where she could be the adored child. Although she was miles away busy with her life and her own family, she continued to do her part as the understanding and conciliatory older daughter called on constantly by her parents and siblings to settle disputes and ease tensions.

But the problems mounting within the seemingly model family life of the Langhornes were too deep for Irene's diplomatic skills to solve. For the "Beautiful Langhorne Sisters of Virginia" the rosy radiance of romance and marriage had dissipated into unhappiness and failure, divorce and separation. Nannie and Phyllis were paying the consequences of marriage for position and money, and Lizzie's and Moncure's marriage long had been one of convenience, kept together for the sake of the three children, Chiswell, Nancy, and Alice. Perhaps, Moncure had a drinking problem; perhaps, he simply was not up to contesting Lizzie's strong will. Within a few years after their marriage, Phyllis and Reggie Brooks were unhappy together and mostly apart, Reggie in Newport and Phyllis roaming the east from hunt to hunt with long stays at Mirador. Nannie was passionately opposed to divorce and attempted to keep her marriage together. But, in 1901 she obtained a legal separation from Robert Gould Shaw and came back to Mirador to live with her parents. Both the Shaws and the

Challenges

Langhornes finally convinced her divorce was the only alternative because her husband was in danger of being jailed for bigamy. In 1903, their marriage was legally dissolved. Of all the first marriages of the Langhorne girls, only Irene's had worked, a fact she spoke of often. Certainly, she was disheartened over the unhappiness of her sisters, but whether or not she felt any responsibility for the failure of Nannie's and Phyllis's marriages because she had encouraged them, I do not know.

Mirador was now overrun with estranged matrons and their children. To alleviate the tension, Chillie encouraged Nanaire and Nannie to take a trip abroad. Chillie was not about to join them. His idea of a good time was not the constant company of a bunch of females with no opportunity for male companionship, poker games, and strong drink. A few weeks after Nannie's final divorce decree, she and Nanaire, together with Bobbie Shaw, Nora, and Nannie's friend, Alice Babcock, took off for Paris and then England. This was Nanaire's first and only trip to a foreign country. In May, 1903, she wrote a letter from Scotland to Buck, who was staying in Richmond with Lizzie. "We stopped at Melrose, the home of Sir Walter Scott, but I am sure you are not interested in our travels, only in our coming home. . . .I hated so much to leave Nannie - - and dear little Bobbie - - but she will come soon."

Nannie did come home a few months later - - in time for Nanaire's death. In October, Nanaire, Chillie, and Keene went to watch Nannie compete in a horseshow in Lynchburg. Nannie recalled Nanaire had complained of a headache when they were on the train that day. "At dinner she looked so pretty and so lovely. Father said, 'You are looking very beautiful tonight, Mrs. Langhorne.' Mother gave him a smile and said she was glad to hear it. Mother suddenly said she wanted some black coffee, so Keene and I went ahead. I remember kissing her and giving her a playful push and telling her to hurry." When Nannie and Keene returned that night, the house in which the Langhornes were staying was dark. Nanaire had died, the victim of a sudden heart attack at the age of fifty-six.

Irene was stunned by the sudden loss of her mother. She hurried down to Richmond from New York and saw Nanaire for the last time, laid out in Lizzie's parlor. According to the Richmond

The Gibson Girl

News-Leader the funeral service in St. Paul's Church was not crowded, ". . . but several hundred people occupied seats on the main floor and there were others in the gallery." "Much weeping" was reported as eight of Nanaire's and Chillie's friends carried her into the church.

Nanaire's death created an immense vacuum in the family. Nannie said of their mother, "She was a wonderful person. She created for all of us an atmosphere of such gaiety and happiness that no matter what happened to us afterward - - no matter if we dripped with diamonds and became great social successes, it never went to our heads. For nothing could be quite as lovely as what we had, those early days, at home." Irene never let the memory of her mother fade. For all her life she took Nanaire as her model, constantly comparing her own life against the wonderful qualities she saw in her mother.

Chillie was bereft and bewildered. His foil through life was gone. No longer would she be there to counterbalance his bluster and arrogance with her grace and softness. He had Nannie to tend to the duties of the mistress of Mirador, but they got along poorly. His sons were close by, but without the presence of their mother, Chillie was even harsher with them. The principal concern was fourteen-year-old Nora, already spoiled as the baby of the family, but now with only sporadic guidance from a covey of older sisters and a father she could manipulate at will. The day-to-day problems created by Nanaire's death would have to be borne by Irene's brothers and sisters. She was moving to Paris.

Dana long had maintained that he did not paint because he could not afford it; yet, success for him was never the accumulation of money. He believed if a person were fortunate enough to earn enough capital on which to live, he should consider that a goal accomplished, and then move on to another stage in life. Dana's own quest was to become a colorist, a painter in oils.

Dana had kept his allegiance to *Life* magazine for the past seven years, spurning the offers of other magazines who wanted him exclusively for as much as $900 a drawing. Then, in 1903, he signed the largest contract ever offered an American illustrator, agreeing to draw for *Collier's* a hundred double-page cartoons to be delivered over a four year period - - total price $100,000. In

1905, when he announced to the media he was giving up his fabulously successful career in order to follow his dream, the reaction was shock. How could he give up an estimated annual income of $65,000 at least - - $25,000 from *Collier's*, $20,000 from *Life*, and $20,000 from book royalties?*

In explaining his decision to the press Dana recalled that Thomas Nast, the great political cartoonist of the 1870s and 1880s, had overworked his artistic formula, and his last years were full of professional sadness and desperation. He pointed out that DuMaurier had given up drawing toward the end of his life and had devoted his labors to writing. Obviously, Dana wanted to retire when he was on top, believing his success with pen-and-ink had peaked. He was burnt out, exhausted from the pressure of deadlines and the need for continuous, commercial creativity.

The press and his friends may have been surprised by his retirement announcement, but they were startled when he told them as soon as he completed his outstanding commissions he was leaving the country for two to three years. The first reactions were indignation and resentment that he would forsake his country's shores, but soon newspaper articles began to appear which saluted him for the support he had given so many of his family, lauding his early success and fame and praising his humility. Reporters acknowledged he was giving up his field only after he felt he had earned the right, and they appreciated the risk he was taking. They, as well as Dana, knew the public had a short memory and could forget him entirely. A comeback might be impossible.

Dana's decision to go abroad was based on his belief that he could paint only if he isolated himself from all distractions and studied intensely. In his illustrative work he had experimented with color, using washes and pastels sporadically, but was dissatisfied with his attempts at oil-work. He threw away almost all of his canvases, fearful of criticism even from his friends. When Dick Davis visited the Gibsons in Maine during the summer of 1904, Dana would not show his oils to him.

---

*Dana's four year commitment to *Collier's* made in 1903 was not completed. I assume he asked to be let out of his contract.

The Gibson Girl

Irene must have been concerned about the prospect of being so distant from her widowed father. Dana's decision meant she had to uproot herself and her now school-age children from their comfortable life in New York City. No memories and no letters record how Irene handled this sudden upheaval in their lives, but I have no doubt she gave Dana her full support. The only hint we have about how she reacted is in an interview Dana gave to the New York *American* on the day of their departure. He said that Irene had always been his partner in all their plans, and she had advised him to forsake the medium in which he was a master and become a student in another branch of the art.

Yet, I wonder what her innermost feelings were. Always the optimist and always reticent to impose her worries on others, she most probably put on a brave face and kept her concerns to herself. She had enjoyed thoroughly their long honeymoon stay in London, and since then they had traveled abroad twice. Most probably, she looked forward to the excitement of a new life and plaudits in other countries. She must have been content because her children would be with her. Nevertheless, three years away from home was a daunting prospect.

On November 30, 1905, the Gibson family embarked -- Dana, not yet forty, Irene, eight-year-old Babs, and six-year-old Langhorne. They spent that winter in Madrid. Dana worked long hours in the dark, musty corridors of the Prado, copying the works of Velasquez and Goya. Babs wrote to Chillie from Madrid, "Mamma and Papa are going to a bullfight tonight that the king Alfonso is giving for Carlos, the king of Portugal, and the queen. Langhorne and I saw him [Alfonso] yesterday. He looks like a ball he is so fat, so is the Queen Amelie. It is lovely here now and Papa is making a portrait of Mamma."

In the Spring they moved to Paris. Irene wrote to Phyllis, "We have a house at 56 Ave. Bois de Boulogne. It is nice for the children. Dana found a studio." Dana's work was well-known in France, and the Gibsons had an entree into its society. A photograph of Irene taken on horseback in the Bois de Boulogne with an unknown gentleman indicates Dana had no problem with her finding recreation in the company of other men while he was busy at work. On weekends they toured the countryside. Irene rode daily in the Bois and took voice lessons from Jean de Reski.

She wrote Nannie, "I would love to see you but am so absorbed in my singing. . . . Tomorrow I have a lesson with 'Jean.' I love them. He is excellent - - as a teacher." The phrase, ". . . as a teacher," is so typically coquettish of her. She felt she had to assure her sister that although her teacher was a man, she saw him only as a teacher. In the same letter to Nannie, Irene wrote, "Pauline St. Lauvenor lunches with us *en famille* tomorrow. Her brother sent you much love and thinks you so attractive. Isn't the little mother funny." Irene saw herself, perhaps uncomfortably, as Nannie's guardian. Both had lost their mother, but she was older and married, and to Irene, Nannie was adrift, divorced from an unhappy marriage and the single mother of a small boy.

Because of his reputation and the artistic acceptance the French gave to illustrators, Dana had the opportunity to know the great artists working in Paris, but there is no record of his studying under one of them. Perhaps, he labored on his own, convinced he had to work out his problems by himself. In the series of interviews with Dana's biographer, Fairfax Downey, Dana revealed he threw most of his canvases away. Americans who saw his work, fellow artists and critics, said it lacked distinction. Dana agreed with them.

Summer in Maine had become the focal point of the past two years, so it might have been in Irene's and Dana's plans to leave Europe for the coolness of 700 Acre Island. As it turned out, they stayed abroad the first summer away because Irene fell ill and was confined to her bed. When she was well enough, Dana sent her and the children to stay at the Hotel de Parame, a luxurious beachside resort in St. Malo on France's northern coast. Babs wrote to her father, "I think Mamma is much better. She is much rossyer (sic)." And, "Mamma goes to bed every night at the same time we do, really not at the same minute, but as soon as she has had her supper. She has a nap every day when we are on the beach."

Irene's illness that summer could explain why they had only two children. Both Irene and Dana came from large families, and the norm in those days was to have a number of offspring. They both adored children; certainly, both were healthy and vigorous. Perhaps, Irene suffered a miscarriage that summer or was afflicted

The Gibson Girl

with some condition that kept her from bearing more babies. Or, an uncomplicated reason for their small family is simply that they wanted no more than two children. In the first ten years of their marriage only Babs and Lang were produced.*

Chillie was still at loose ends even though it had been two-and-a-half years since Nanaire had died. Irene and Dana asked him to stay at 700 Acre Island during the summer of 1906 to look after the place in their absence. This excerpt from a long letter he wrote to Lang and Babs in Paris reveals the doting grandfather they knew, a tender counterpoint to his reputation for gruffness. "Everything reminds me of you children. I went to the bath house and there were your bathing shoes and little blue boat, shells and all sorts of things just as you left them. I went upstairs and there was Babs' doll baby laying [sic] in the crib fast asleep and I am sure she hasn't been awoke [sic] since Babs left her. I did not wake her as she looked so happy and contented and there was no one to play with her."

Dana had ridden through the collapse of the economy and the financial markets in 1893 with ease. His work was in great demand, he was young and a bachelor, and because he liked the good life and was responsible for the support of his mother and sisters, he had not accumulated substantial financial assets whose values would have been ravaged. His circumstances were different in 1907, however. Only because he had saved a large portion of his income over the years of his greatest popularity could he afford to retire from illustration and go to Europe to study. He invested in bonds and stocks through his Wall Street friends and salted away a good portion of his assets in New York's Knickerbocker Trust. His account there was a conservative one, nothing more exciting than a passbook savings balance.

In 1907, all hell again broke loose in the world's economy. A decade of robust markets and financial growth in the United States ended with the Panic of 1907. A sudden lack of confidence sent interest rates in Europe climbing. Great Britain was strapped by the debts she incurred to fight the Boer War; and the earthquake

---

*Although abstinence was still the only effective method of birth control for most Americans because condoms were illegal, Irene and Dana through their European travels and connections always had access to them.

in San Francisco destroyed a great deal of wealth. First a few small banks went under, but the failure of the Knickerbocker Trust was the event that threw the country into a financial upheaval. J. P. Morgan and his associates ultimately rescued the country, but it was too late for Irene and Dana. Every penny they had at the Knickerbocker Trust was lost because in those days there was no Federal Reserve Bank and no insurance to protect depositors. They had other investments, but their market values dropped precipitously.

The Gibsons had to come home. After years of intensive labor, Dana had earned his freedom to paint, but now his dream, his goal to be a painter, had to be put aside. Having renounced his career in illustration, he was faced with the necessity of again carving a place for himself in a field in which he had been the acknowledged star. Dick Davis had said Dana's popularity could withstand his sojourn in Europe; he would have to be correct if Dana was going to shape a comeback. He had a wife, two small children, houses in New York and Maine, other family to support, and an expensive lifestyle to maintain.

Over twenty years had passed since Dana first struggled for acceptance and recognition, trudging up publishers' staircases with his portfolio of youthful drawings under his arm in hopes of a sale here and another there. No stranger to rejection and setbacks, he had challenged the roadblocks in his way and had succeeded. He could do it again. Although he had grown tired of illustration, he had to restart his career to make a living. Endless hours at his drawing board must have been a daunting and difficult prospect to face.

Irene had never been challenged. She had been blessed by Chillie's financial success, then had married a man whom she believed could take over where her father left off. Every stage of their marriage had been upbeat, full of youthful energy, carefree as far as money was concerned. She had been pampered as a child by adoring parents, applauded as a belle, the idol of a public who saw her as America's ideal woman. All of a sudden, her life of plenty and financial security gave way to not knowing whether or not her husband - - whose art and vigor had been the pivots of their married life - - could support her. Her days of belledom were long past, and

The Gibson Girl

it had been years since Dana had used her as his principal model. She was too old now, a matron, though still a young one, whose girlish looks were beginning to fade. Now, she carried the burden of sustaining a husband whose hopes had been dashed. With the comfort of Dana's unquestioned success gone, whatever strength she possessed beneath that exquisite facade she would have to find for herself.

A photograph my father took of Irene, Dana, and Babs on the front porch of their house on 700 Acre Island in 1908 or 1909 helps me to understand the stress and unhappiness my grandfather was experiencing after the rude shock of the Panic. At first glance nothing appears out of the ordinary, only a family scene of chubby Babs sitting on a stone pillar ledge, Irene dressed beautifully in a light-colored, starched shirtwaist, serenely reading, and Dana staring ahead, his hands clasped in his lap. My guess is the camera in my ten-year-old father's hand caught Dana unaware, before he could pose and take that faraway, mournful expression off his face and turn his downcast mouth into a smile. To me the picture is of an unhappy man beset with worry, his mind deep in his troubles and his eyes not really seeing the water and boats beyond.

I doubt if Dana was ever an easy man to be married to in spite of his unquestioned devotion to Irene and the children. He would go for long stretches of time with little energy and time in reserve for the ones he loved. He was an artist and had the temperament of one. He was absorbed in his work, driven by his need to create. By his own admission, he was a worrier. To what degree Dana shared his anxieties with Irene I have no idea, but during this period in their life one letter to Irene expresses his feelings of inadequacy. "I will work hard to make it these next few years and you will work even harder to save some of it so we can have enough to be comfortable in our old age. If you had married a doctor you could be hopeful that some time he could give up having a night bell. A man who works with his hands can only make so much. And there comes a time when he is not wanted. It isn't always easy to be the wife of such a man. . . . I won't send you any more gloomy letters and I will rest easy and trust you to fix up the future. If my spirits are not good my work is bad so I will try not to worry."

Challenges

Dana may have given his wife no public credit for inspiring his Gibson Girl, but he continually referred to Irene as his "main prop," the role she now assumed in the marriage and a reversal of their relationship when Dana was riding high and fulfilled and Irene was content in her more passive status. She had to counter Dana's despondency with buoyancy and hopefulness if they were going to make it through this difficult period. The first few years after Paris were determined, quiet ones for Irene as she concentrated on being the mother of small children and maintained a stable, comfortable home for Dana. My hunch is Irene asked her father for financial help, because it seems implausible that they could have maintained 127 East 73rd Street and 700 Acre Island otherwise.

Dana was too proud to go to *Life*, hat in hand. The magazine was doing well without him, using the work of a number of illustrators who, delighted their popular rival had left the field to them, blatantly began to copy Dana's style as soon as he boarded his ocean liner for Europe. An alert reader could know the *Life* drawings were not Gibsons only if he checked the bottom signatures. Fortunately for Dana, only his style had been duplicated. His imitators in their captions could not match his wit and sense of humor.

Collier's magazine offered a contract Dana accepted. Because he had been out of the public eye for over two years, the first order of business for Dana at *Collier's* was promotion. Reluctantly, Dana agreed to an exhausting, six-week long cross-country tour in the fall of 1908 with the magazine's editor, Norman Hapgood. They visited most of the mid-western and western cities, including St. Louis, Denver, San Francisco, Portland, and Minneapolis. The public relations people at *Collier's* did their work well; local reporters greeted them at every stop.

Although Hapgood was a well-known authority on current events and a recognized political pundit, most of the attention centered on Dana. To the reporters sent to interview him, Dana did not look like an artist. They were impressed with his gentle demeanor, his old slouch hat, and his commanding physique, describing him as a "tall, broad-shouldered man, looking like a Western banker, very friendly, powerful, modest and young-looking." Dana hated the trip and longed for family and home.

161

The Gibson Girl

Dana supplemented his income earned from *Collier's* with book illustration. His distant cousin and fellow artist, William C. Gibson, art editor for *Cosmopolitan* magazine, offered him a commission to illustrate the serialization of *The Common Law*, the newest novel of an old friend of Dana, Robert W. Chambers. The assignment was not appealing to Dana because he did not think book illustration creative, but he needed the money and was paid handsomely - - $900 for each of the eight installments. Other commissions followed in quick succession. The work was tedious - - one novel required fifty-six illustrations.

For the Christmas issue of 1909, *Life* invited Dana back together with his old "friends" of past drawings, his Cupid, Mr. Pipp, some Gibson Girls, and fat old men pictured at a broad dinner table. The composite was pure nostalgia because Dana's Gibson Girl arrayed in the sensuous hourglass styles of the 1890s was a relic of the past, out of vogue. But Dana discovered he was not. He was respected by his peers for his wise and gentle nature as well as for the cleverness of his pen. He had assumed the role of the "grand old man" of illustration. Although he had no enthusiasm for the latest fashions and his work showed it, Dana learned to adjust to the new styles and modernized his Gibson Girl, clothing her in the unbecoming modes of the day - - short, hobble skirts and dish pan and Merry Widow hats with birds perched on top. Under Irene's influence, his creations were sometimes suffragettes on parade, or in business and in the professions, or at country clubs dancing the turkey trot to the loud rhythms of ragtime. Although they were spiritless copies of his youthful inspiration, the public liked what they saw. Dana's popularity had been confirmed.

With Dana driven by his work and fighting hard to meet his financial responsibilities, Irene darted down to Greenwood as often as she could, usually for long visits in the Fall and Spring. My father talked about those visits often. As a city boy he enjoyed the freedom of wandering through woods and pastures, and was fascinated by the farm animals and the process of planting and harvesting corn and grain for winter feed. And he spoke of the wild, and once an almost fatal, carriage rides with Umpty - - as he called his grandfather (perhaps a takeoff on the nursery rhyme character who sat on a wall and had a great fall) - - holding the reins, and the

Challenges

long, horse-drawn adventures to visit Buck and Keene in southern Albemarle and Buckingham Counties. My father forever tempered my romantic visions of old-world Southern elegance with his recollections of floors grimy with red clay dust and the constant shortages of water. He, the youngest family member, was the last to use the bathwater his elders had washed in.

But for Irene the complexion of life at Mirador had changed. Chillie, knowing he would never remarry, gave Mirador to Phyllis in 1908, either a magnanimous gesture on his part and an attempt to salvage Phyllis's and Reggie Brooks's marriage, or a calculated strategy of control to throw a monkeywrench into his daughter's unhappy union. Phyllis had little interest in breaking away from her girlhood home. She preferred the relatively quiet life of the Virginia countryside with her father, while Reggie's need for an ultra-active social life took him on an endless round of visits to society's watering holes. Either Chillie thought ownership of Mirador would temper Reggie's playboy antics and keep him home with his wife, or he thought Phyllis's commitment to Mirador would drive Reggie even farther away, and would more quickly end a marriage which he long had felt was harmful to his daughter.

Chillie moved across the road from Mirador to a white frame, gingerbread-decorated cottage described by my father as ugly and cramped. Chillie named it Misfit[*] and settled in with a couple of servants. According to family stories he spent much of his time sitting on the front lawn with a telescope watching for any changes Phyllis might make at Mirador; then, spotting some activity of which he did not approve, he rushed over to protest and quarrel.

Phyllis began a guestbook in 1909, which chronicles the constant flow of family visitors. Mirador continued to be the magnet and gathering place for the Langhorne children. The sons

---

[*]Two versions explain the name Misfit. Either Chillie thought the house hideous, or he looked upon himself as a misfit in Greenwood because so many of the farms had been bought up by Yankees.

At some point Misfit was torn down. I remember a huge barn behind where the house once stood in which were stored Misfit's columns and other exterior ornamentation. Now the barn is gone, its timbers given to a riding camp near Goshen, Virginia.

The Gibson Girl

- - Keene, Harry, and Buck - - lived close by, firmly under their father's control both as employees of his railroad contracting business and as recipients of his rather sizable gifts. Each summer Lizzie and her children came to stay in Mirador's cottage, happy to be away from Richmond and her deteriorating marriage to Moncure. The only one missing was Nannie. Chillie was wise enough to know it was not good for her to be stuck away at Mirador after her divorce, so he encouraged her to go with Phyllis to England to fox hunt. In the process she might find a husband. Although Nannie made quite a hit and had many opportunities for romance, she was an emotionally bruised young woman and made no serious response to whatever overtures came her way. However, on a second trip abroad she met aboard ship Waldorf Astor, a quiet, sensitive young man who was an heir to one of the world's greatest fortunes.* In 1907, they married in a quiet London ceremony which none of her family attended. Except for infrequent visits, Nannie was lost to Chillie and to Greenwood.

The problem of what to do about Nora was solved in 1909, when she married Paul Phipps. Eighteen when her mother died, Nora's natural tendency to drift through life was encouraged by the absence of discipline and attention from her father who had no idea how to handle her. The family's move from Richmond to rustic Greenwood had interrupted her formal education, and learning was never a priority for her. Nora's daughter, Joyce Grenfell, a successful writer, actress, and monologist, published a piece titled, "My Mother Couldn't Spell," in which she wrote that her mother was not able to concentrate on what her teachers were saying because she was fascinated by their mannerisms, "the pursing of a lip, or the neat moistening of it."

---

*Waldorf's father, William Waldorf Astor, had fled to England in 1890 with his vast fortune after being politically humiliated in his abortive attempt to become governor of New York. As a result of his charitable contributions, William Waldorf was made a peer. When his father died in 1919, Waldorf was required to give up his seat in the House of Commons, which Nannie won in the byelection that followed. After her election Waldorf set aside his political ambitions to further his wife's career.

Challenges

An observer and a talented mimic, Nora had incredible charm, a soft wispiness and sensuality which captivated men. Nannie was little help in guiding her much younger sister through the intricacies of finding a husband because she was weighed down with her own unhappiness. Irene was mostly out of the picture, away in Europe or in New York City, and Phyllis was having a rough time contending with a sour marriage and two boys to raise. Nevertheless, Chillie threw the decisions concerning Nora onto the shoulders of his older daughters, who apparently had little patience with their flighty sibling. They decided the best course was to send her over to England, where Nannie now lived with Waldorf and where Phyllis spent much of her time fox hunting.

Nannie and Phyllis had their hands full, breaking up courtships they decided dangerous for Nora, and at one point unraveling a mess she got into by being engaged to two men simultaneously. Meanwhile, Nora was writing her father plaintive and childish letters full of misspellings and full of physical complaints, of homesickness, and of missing him. Phyllis, in a letter to Chillie reporting on Nora's probable marriage to Paul, a young, aspiring London architect, was hard on her younger sister. She wrote of Nora, " . . . there is charm there," but she believed Paul would get the worst end of the marriage bargain. "Charm ain't anything and I think the young man is going to be deeply disappointed at finding nothing else. Of course she may develop qualities for a man she respects." Phyllis liked Paul and believed he was an exceptional young man, the best Nora was going to get. Sibling tensions were in full flower as Phyllis accused Nora of having a cold, undemonstrative manner while Nora thought Phyllis "miserable and queer."

Toward the end of her life with Dana, Irene wrote that he was the nicest man in the world - - excepting her father. The Chillie Irene was remembering was the father at Misfit, still irascible, but mellowed by age and time, no longer scrabbling against heavy odds to resurrect for himself and his family the ante-bellum life of his childhood, a man who had lost his wife and done what had been his best to raise and support eight children. Never burdened with deep, psychological insight and free from the guilt of later generations conscious of their parenting mistakes, he most likely had few, if

The Gibson Girl

any, regrets. Chillie's happiest times were when Irene came to stay and lavished her attention on him. Each day they enjoyed together the uncomplicated rhythm of their closely bound relationship, riding over Greenwood's dirt roads and woodland trails calling on neighbors, getting the mail at the depot, or leaning against a split-rail chestnut fence to watch Chillie's foxhounds in their kennel. They went to horse shows to applaud Phyllis carrying away the blue ribbons and sat on Misfit's front stoop in good weather eating ice cream and talking.

Irene took side trips to Richmond and Charlottesville to visit friends; but mostly she was content with Greenwood's simple, social pleasures - - "at homes" when she played the mistress of Misfit, tennis parties, and the warm welcomes when she rode over to Mirador to spend time with Phyllis. She wrote Lang when she and Babs were on a visit to Misfit. "Last night we all dressed up in funny costumes and went to supper with Aunt Phyllis. We then called on Mrs. Buck - - and on Algie Craven. Really you never saw anything so funny. Babs was a German professor. I was a country girl from the mountains and so tacky. Genevieve [Harry's wife] was the Mountain Bride. Aunt May was Mrs. Harry Lauder.[*] Aunt Phyllis was a suffragette. Uncle Reggie a negro cowboy. We danced and had a lot of fun. We got Algie out of bed."

Fortunately, Irene could escape to Greenwood and enjoy herself because life at home in New York City was anything but idyllic. Dana was regaining his stature in the world of illustration, but his work load was exhausting and no longer could he command the fees paid him before going off to Europe in 1905. On top of the Gibsons' money troubles came the greatest fright in their lives. They almost lost Babs. Thirteen and very ill, she was diagnosed as having appendicitis and taken to the hospital for surgery. The Gibsons found out later the nurse who prepared Babs for the operation noticed a rash over her body, but failed to alert her doctor. Babs did not have appendicitis, but had contracted scarlet fever. She was brought home, where she developed pneumonia and almost died.

---

[*]Harry Lauder, a popular Scottish performer and the highest paid music hall star of his day, adored his wife, Anne, who was known for her gaudy dress.

Challenges

Dana's sister, Josephine, said she never saw him suffer so deeply. Much rattled by the near tragedy, Dana wrote daily to Babs at Mirador, where she went to recuperate, expressing his deep feelings of gratitude and thanksgiving. Ruth Hapgood, a friend of Babs and the daughter of Dana's *Collier's* editor, Norman Hapgood, was stricken in Europe by the same illness. "I shall never forget her (Ruth) sitting in your room the first day you were ill," Dana wrote to Babs. "Every impression burnt into me at that time will stay with me always. I shall be on the dock to help them off as she may have to be carried on a litter. . . . Poor Norman. I know how he must feel. . . . I might not have been so anxious to meet that steamer a year ago, but I have learned a great deal since then. And I owe more sympathy than I will ever be able to repay." A postscript to this family trauma is a letter Dana received from the financier, Otto Kahn, whose wife was a friend of Irene and who had a summer place at Islesboro, Maine. Kahn was a devoted parent and his letter expressed the relief of a father on the recovery of a child. Dana kept the letter, noting on it he had never particularly liked the man, but, from then on, forever would have a fondness for him.

That same year, 1910, Irene and Dana made the difficult decision to send eleven-year-old Lang off to boarding school. As a child I was always curious about this part of my father's history, fearing somewhere in the back of my brain that my parents might exile me from the home life I adored. To put my mind at ease my father assured me he was sent away only because they lived in New York City, and being out in the country was better for him. I wonder if he believed this explanation; I have trouble with it. Boarding school for young boys in families who could afford it was a normal convention in those days, emulative of the English tradition. Yet, family life in the Gibson household was too important, too close to banish one of its members. His two years at Fay School were terribly unhappy ones because he was acutely homesick. Young Lang worshipped his parents and was extremely hurt he was not allowed to be with his family. I suspect he was sent away most of the year because Dana during this period was incapable of giving the consistent parental attention his son needed. It was best Lang was with his family only for the school year's brief

The Gibson Girl

vacation periods and during the summer break in Maine, when Dana relaxed his frenetic schedule and could focus on him.

Few days passed when Dana did not write Lang at least a very brief note telling his son he was loved and missed. Often he enclosed a comic strip torn from the daily newspaper or commented on the baseball struggles of the Giants and the Yankees. Dana's letters to Babs when she was away from home, however, were more thoughtful and carefully composed, as though he was making a special effort to demonstrate his interest in her life. Some of Babs's children share the opinion that Dana concentrated his affection on their mother because he understood how difficult it was to be the daughter of a woman celebrated for her looks. In terms of looks, any daughter competing with Irene would have had a difficult time of it, but Babs inherited her father's manly, squarish features and as a child and as a young girl was overweight. Not until Babs was in her late teens did she come into her own, possessing an aura of dignity and style which more than compensated for any lack of a classically molded face.

In her dealings with everyone, Irene was most forthright. Her children did not escape her directness, and at times, her thoughtlessness. Irene once told Babs she was not pretty. This criticism, coming from a mother whose beauty was legendary, was a hard blow for a young girl. And when Lang was away at school writing his mother letters gushing with love and his need to be with her, telling her not an hour went by that he did not think of her, Irene wrote back honestly, saying she did not think of him all the time. He was crushed. Once she wrote Lang a particularly insensitive bit of news from Mirador while he was in boarding school longing for his family. Irene told him she and Peter, Phyllis's son Lang's age, were "going to a little picnic and fish in the little creek." In a series of letters from St. Mark's preparatory school, where he went after Fay School, Lang implored Dana to intercede in his behalf to stop his mother from singing solos in chapel every time she came to visit him. He was embarrassed about all the attention directed at both of them. Lang finally asked her not to, and instead of understanding the sometimes illogical insecurities of a teenager, Irene reproached her son, saying she was hurt and dismayed.

Challenges

Money worries continued to plague the Gibsons. In 1911, they made the sad decision to put 127 East 73rd Street on the market. Irene showed a brave face to her son, writing him at Fay School about a much smaller house at 37 East 65th Street they had rented.* "The little house will be very cozy. I would like to feel that you lived in it. I will like it better after you have stayed there." They rented rooms at the Great Northern Hotel while the 65th Street house was being decorated. Irene, certainly upset her home was being taken from her, made a point of being away from the city as much as she possibly could. She and Babs - - whose education was in the hands of tutors - - went to Misfit in September as soon as Lang was put in school; then, leaving Babs in Greenwood, Irene came back to New York for an operation of some sort. Her problem could not have been that critical because in the middle of October she announced to her family she had made a spur-of-the-moment decision to visit Nannie in England. "I am torn between the desire to go and that awful thought of leaving you all," she wrote Babs. "But you don't mind, do you?" Leaving Dana with the problem of finding a tutor for Babs in New York, Irene boarded the *Lusitania* for Southhampton, England with - - I am sure - - the thought she deserved a respite from domestic and financial worry.

Her stay with Nannie at the Astors' London residence, 4 St. James's Square, and at their country estate, Cliveden, was just the tonic Irene needed and yearned for. Her younger sister, now supremely wealthy and certainly aware of the Gibsons' financial straits, took Irene on shopping sprees. Writing home, she described

---

*At 37 East 65th Street Irene had a royal guest. Arthur, Duke of Connaught, a son of Queen Victoria and the uncle of Britain's King George V, was visiting New York City in 1913 with his daughter, Victoria Patricia, a popular and young royal whom the press affectionately called "Princess Pat." The New York papers made quite a commotion over the fact that Princess Pat destroyed one day's carefully planned itinerary by insisting upon calling on Irene at her home. My guess is that Princess Pat met Irene when the Gibsons were in London on their honeymoon. Obviously, the princess, who was only ten years old at the time, had been quite taken with the older Irene. She and her father - - perhaps more attracted to Irene than was his daughter - - had kept up with the Gibsons through the years.

The Gibson Girl

Nannie's gifts, " . . . a lovely black velvet day gown and a purple velvet evening dress (Worth), a white satin evening dress (Worth), and a pale yellow satin evening dress with silver. I feel like Cleopatra. She did not wear so much though."

She and Nannie went to movies and plays and the ballet. "Nannie and I went to the Russian Ballet with the Duchess of Portland who is so like a sheep. . . . There is a new man who dances with Pavlova instead of Nordkin called Nijinsky and you never saw such a dancer." Irene was touched by the attention given her. "You don't know how kind Waldorf and Nannie are. They seem to be just thinking what they can do for me." One evening the Astors gave a dinner party at 4 St. James's Square. One of the guests was Leander Starr Jameson, who led in 1895 the unauthorized Jameson Raid against the Boers, an act that helped to precipitate the South African War. "I sat next to Dr. Jameson and of course it is all settled that we (you all) go to visit him in South Africa. He is delightful."

Irene spent over a month in England, and on her return she and Dana went to 700 Acre Island at the end of November to close the house for the winter. "If you were only here," she wrote Babs. "So cozy and the house so warm. You would never dream such an improvement could be made as enclosing that porch and Pa is going to let me paper all the lower rooms and paint the other woodwork green. We just sit and admire and the little library is fine, all the books I have fixed. . . . Pa paid me a pretty compliment. In my garden there were three rose buds and he said when they saw me they thought it was summer and bloomed. . . . There is a big stove in the hall and the fire's all going. It is very comfortable."

Perhaps my own conservative streak is showing, but I marvel at my grandfather redecorating the 700 Acre Island house when the lack of money had forced them from their New York home. I had always been under the impression my grandparents were, if not wealthy, extremely comfortable. How could they not have been? They owned an elegant house in New York's most exclusive residential area. The place in Maine with its complex of buildings, boat captain, caretaker, gardener, and seasonal summer staff must have taken substantial amounts of cash to operate. The considerable overhead of trips abroad, the entertaining Irene loved, and private schools and tutors must have required a large and consistent income. Saving for a rainy day must have been the last thought in their minds. Instead, they spent what was in Dana's pocket, trusting the future would take care of itself. In a most fashionable manner they lived hand-to-mouth, determined to enjoy what they had at the moment.

By 1913, the Gibsons' economic future had turned brighter. It had taken Dana six long years to finish paying the price for his 1905 retirement from illustration. Financial comfort was restored with more commissions to illustrate books and regular submissions to *Life, Collier's, Good Housekeeping, McCall's* and *Hearst's International*. His popularity was firmly reestablished when he signed an exclusive contract with *Life* magazine, his Gibson Girl once more on its cover, his work once again the magazine's chief feature. He was praised for the distinctiveness of his art. "Other people copy Gibson, but no one comes anywhere near him in results. He is one of the few men who can make pen and ink sketches look like flesh and blood," wrote one critic. Dana was honored by the Luxembourg Museum in Paris with its purchase of "The Champion," a powerful composition of a prizefighter, presumably James J. Jeffries, striding down a city street, a crowd of boys looking up at him in awe.

Life celebrated its thirtieth birthday in 1913. John Ames Mitchell, its founder, proprietor, and still one of its editors, was honored with a large banquet given by the Society of Illustrators of which Dana was the president. Dana's opening remarks as toastmaster were greeted with laughter. "No doubt John Ames Mitchell still has some friends. In fact the Society of Illustrators has gone to the expense of making sure he has them." Dana went on to recall his sale of "The Moon and I" to the magazine and the kind rejection a day later by Mitchell of another six drawings. "I've spent the money I got for that drawing I sold to *Life*, but I kept the hope that Mr. Mitchell gave me the next day."

CHAPTER TWELVE

PRIVATE AND PUBLIC LIVES

Fortunately - - as it turned out - - a buyer was never found for 127 East 73rd Street. The family moved back to their home, and Irene moved on with her life. The bulk of her time was divided between New York City and Maine. She visited Lang at St. Mark's School in Southboro, Massachusetts at least once a month, and on his infrequent vacations home put everything else aside to spend time with him, Dana, and Babs. During the day she lunched and shopped with the children, and at night Dana joined them for light suppers, then the theater or vaudeville. An exciting event in the Gibson family was the purchase of an automobile. Lang was ecstatic over his father's car, and whenever he came home to New York City from school, the family took trips into the country. Dana even hired a chauffeur. Lang wrote to his mother, "I am excited about the chauffeur and I hope he 'makes good' and that you have him fitted out like a Butler in a uniform. . . . You all sound awfully rich going to the theater in our own car but I suppose it was an experiment and it saves taxi money and tips and I think you would always do it."

Irene made regular trips to Greenwood and Chillie, usually taking the Chesapeake and Ohio overnight train from New York, which made a special stop for her at Greenwood Depot in deference to Chillie's long-time contracting relationship with the railroad. Sporadically, Dana came down to Virginia with her, and on more than one occasion made their trips adventures by driving down, a daring way to travel then. Lang described the itinerary of one of their excursions in his diary. They made the 375 mile run in two long days, only because they suffered no blowouts. The trip back to New York took three days because the roads were worse and they had two punctures and a blowout.

Irene and Dana gained another daughter in 1914 under tragic circumstances. Moncure Perkins died, and after his funeral Lizzie came to stay with Irene and Dana in New York City. Nora joined them for a shopping trip one afternoon, and just as the sisters returned to 127 East 73rd Street around four o'clock, Lizzie -- only forty-seven -- collapsed in the ground floor vestibule. Within hours she was dead, stricken with what the newspapers termed apoplexy. After her funeral in Richmond the family met to decide what to do with the two Perkins daughters, seventeen-year-old Nancy and fifteen-year-old Alice. The son, Chiswell, or Chilly, at twenty-three, was old enough to take care of himself. They determined Alice would live with Phyllis at Mirador, and Nancy would go to the Gibsons in New York City. Nancy adored her aunt and uncle, having spent all her summers in Maine. She was fast approaching marriageable age, so what better sponsorship to have than Irene's. Plus, Nancy and Babs were the same age and the closest of friends.

Nancy was a joy to Irene. Exquisitely beautiful with a personality that sparkled and a cosmopolitan air already developed from long visits abroad, she along with Babs was introduced into New York's society, and the young men swarmed around her. Irene did her job well overseeing Nancy's romances, and within two years she met and fell in love with Henry Field, an heir to the Marshall Field department store fortune. Irene's pleasure, however, in having two daughters at home with her was short-lived. In April, 1916, Babs was married to George Post, just two months after her nineteenth birthday, and the following year Nancy married Henry. A month after their honeymoon Henry entered a Chicago hospital to have his tonsils out and died from complications. They were married only five months.*

Nancy, who went on to become one of the most influential interior designers and decorators of her day and owned houses renowned for their comfortable elegance, attributed her early awareness of taste and style to her mother, whose house in Richmond was full of beautiful furniture and immaculate linens. Her education continued under Irene's roof. Nancy was less impressed with the formal style of the New York house than with the simple way Irene decorated 700 Acre Island -- with inexpensive, local pine furniture and subtle colors on the walls. Perhaps Nancy developed her interest in gardening from Irene as well. She

---

*Unfortunately for Nancy, Henry's trusts provided that if he died without children, his brother, Marshall, would be his beneficiary.

The Gibson Girl

remembered her aunt's beautiful garden, ". . . mostly annuals, enclosed from the wind by a hedge of arborvitae, and the beds were set off from the grass paths by white, inch-wide boards attached lengthwise to four-inch stakes. She always had the entrance beds planted with heliotrope and lemon verbena. The sea air made monkshood, raspberries, and green peas grow enormous." Nancy recalled Irene sending the children out to "dead head" pansies and nasturtiums while she arranged flowers in glass bowls for every table in the sitting room, described by Nancy as ". . . painted green with white woodwork and contained white furniture. French windows opened on to a brick terrace, and there was a stone fireplace with a ship's model on the mantelpiece. My aunt was one of the first summer people to have hooked rugs on the floor."

Though Irene and Dana had tried to sell their house in New York City when their financial outlook was at its most bleak, they never considered selling 700 Acre Island. It was too much a part of their life. Their children considered the island home, where they could be a family, together for a portion of each day, enjoying the windswept blue waters and cool summer breezes of Penobscot Bay.

Irene closed 127 East 73rd Street each summer and went about the complex task of relocating the family to 700 Acre Island. From New York, she brought with her a housemaid and a parlor maid, as well as Emma, her personal maid. When June came, the ice house was full of blocks that had been cut in the winter and covered with saw dust. Outdoor bins held logs carried from the woods by sled that winter, split and ready for the fireplaces. Below the waters around the island lay crab and lobster pots to furnish meat for cold salads and whole lobsters for roasts on the beach. A large vegetable garden had been planted to provide peas and beans, carrots, onions and lettuce - - enough for the Gibsons and the people working there. Apples picked the previous fall were spread out on cellar shelves under a dusting of lime. After a thorough spring cleaning and airing by the wives of the Gibsons' local staff, the main house was ready for the Gibsons' arrival.

Irene and Dana left from New York by train to Boston. Sometimes they switched to the Bar Harbor Express, leaving their Pullman sleeper at Rockland, where their boat captain picked them up. They preferred, however, to board a steamship in Boston for the overnight run to Camden, taking an outside cabin to enjoy the refreshing sea breezes. A walk around the deck preceded supper in the gilded dining room, served by stewards in white coats; to bed, an early breakfast, then a seven o'clock arrival at Camden's pier.

The first summer weeks were quiet ones before the July and August season began. Dana had built a studio down the hill from the main house close to the shores of Cradle Cove which formed the northern edge of their point. As he set up his space for the summer's work, Irene stocked the larders and organized the help in preparation for the onslaught of guests which packed the house for most of the summer. Soon Lang came from school, and the arrival of Nancy and Babs, finished with their parties and rounds of visits to friends after the school year's end, made the family complete.

Dependence on servants required a strict household routine. Breakfast was served punctually at eight-thirty. As at Mirador everyone was expected to be on time, fully dressed. Irene had already taken her morning swim in the icy water off the sandy beach below the house. Afterward, she wrote letters, picked and arranged flowers, and gave instructions to the servants before putting on a heavy veil and a great straw hat to grub in the garden. While Dana worked, some mornings she sailed with Lang or went with him across to Islesboro to play golf. Other days, friends arrived for late morning tennis parties on the hard-surfaced court by the shore. At some point Dana might wander down to watch before ginger ale and sarsaparilla were served; if the guests stayed for lunch, the *piece de resistance* was often a soufflé.

Dana's exercise was his building projects. The large undertakings, such as additions to the rambling house and the construction of a front dock and a protective log-and-stone breakwater to shelter his small fleet of boats,[*] he left to local contractors. But each afternoon after his nap, trowel in hand and wearing a white shirt and a black four-in-hand tie, he satisfied his

---

[*]In an appendix to his diary, Lang in 1920 listed nine of them, from small racers to work boats to Dana's favorite, the "Javelin," a mahogany and teak speedboat, long and narrow with gasoline motors mounted in tandem.

The Gibson Girl

creative urge with stone, brick, and mortar. He built walls and paths leading from the house to the water, an octagonal tool house with a cone-shaped, shingled roof, and later, when they had grandchildren, an exquisitely detailed and proportioned stone play house on the front lawn. His grandest project was the chapel faced with curious patterns of stone and brick. Its small nave is overwhelmed by his version of a square Norman keep with steps winding up one side to a tiny bedroom with fireplace where Irene sometimes took her naps.

The evening routine at 700 Acre Island rarely altered. Before dinner, Irene took long walks, often with Lang and Babs, up the hill beyond the house and onto the paths that wound through the dark, mossy woods covering most of the island. After quiet family dinners, Irene read as Dana sat in his green armchair telling stories to the young for only as long as they tickled his ankles. Sundays, Irene went to church, leaving Dana home because he was never a churchgoer. Nancy remembered. "No automobiles were allowed on Islesboro at the time, but one could rent a horse and buggy 'with a fringe on top.' That is what we did on Sundays to go to church, where Aunt Irene led the hymn singing, dressed to kill and ready for all the admiration she received. After church everyone met at the swimming pool located in a tidal pool below the Islesboro Inn."

Irene's relatives and Virginia friends flocked to 700 Acre Island to join with Dana's sisters and mother, Langdon and his family, and Babs's and Lang's friends. The only important people in Irene's life not in Maine were her sisters, Nannie and Phyllis, both in England and unable to visit because of the Great War raging in Europe. These summers were important to Irene, the special times when her family was together, she and Dana isolated from their many commitments in New York. In Maine she had Dana close at hand to make certain he took care of himself and not overwork. Again, their lives would change, and Irene had no way of knowing that these tranquil, uninterrupted Maine summers would be their last for many years.

During the trying years since the return from Paris Irene had concentrated her energies and her concerns on supporting Dana. Now that his career was back on track she was free to act on political and charitable causes, which had begun to absorb her

Private and Public Lives

interest. She and Dana personally had been untouched by the massive social, economic, and political changes taking place around them during the 1890s and the early years of the twentieth century. Caught up in the lavish lifestyle of the Gilded Age, neither of them had been greatly concerned by current events because life had been too full and too successful. But after 1907 both began to see themselves as two of the many victims of the political authority in control of the country - - the Republican party - - with its power, graft and corruption. Rampant speculation and the abuses of the money trusts had destroyed the Gibsons' handsome nest egg. They believed the moral abuses of the unfettered industrial society had targeted them, and Irene began to feel a kinship with the deprivation and need she saw. While Dana began the tedious process of restarting his career in illustration, Irene launched her commitment to the world around her.

The year 1913 - - which marked the rebirth of Dana's success - - also brought Irene's entry into the rough-and-tumble political life of New York City; she received her first press coverage for active political involvement. The Tammany Hall machine had a vise grip on New York City, and the best that could be said about Boss Charles F. Murphy's leadership is he held down graft and corruption. He was definitely a cut above his predecessor, John Croker, who publicly stated, "I am working for my pockets all the time." But fraud and police corruption in New York City were still rampant. In the 1913 New York City mayoral campaign, Irene joined with Independent Democrats, Republicans, and Populists united in a fusion movement to back John Purroy Mitchel, a young man not yet forty who had been appointed by President Wilson to the post of Collector of the City of New York. Pitted against Tammany's Edward E. McCall, Mitchel had a reputation for straight dealing, a quality that commended him to this coalition of political interests that wanted good government.

Irene's efforts on Mitchel's behalf were featured in a newspaper article captioned "Society Women Out On Mitchel Carts: Mrs. C.D. Gibson and Mrs. Harriman[*] Take the Stump and

---

[*]More than one Mrs. Harriman was active in New York City's political life at this time. I could not determine who she was.

The Gibson Girl

Argue with Longshoremen: Talk of Milk and Parks: With a Third Speaker, They Win the Crowds Away from McCall and Delight Them." Irene's cart was parked at the corner of South and Fulton Streets, its side emblazoned with the Women's Fusion League banner as well as pictures of Mitchel. "It was Mrs. Dana Gibson's maiden political speech and the beginning of a practical political campaign by the New York women who are following English women in working for the men of their families and the politics they advocate."

Irene was driven by automobile to each stand. Between speeches she mingled with the crowd of burly and raucous longshoremen. The reporter commented if women were going in for cart-tail oratory, either the carts would have to be changed or the new skirts. " 'Come up,' said Mrs. Harriman, hospitably from her cart to Mrs. Gibson, who had just made her appearance at the Battery. Mrs. Gibson was wearing a trim tailored suit with a very modern [tight] skirt, and she smiled up from beneath her little round hat. ' I can't get up,' she said. But some one gave her a hand from the cart, some one helped from the ground, and with a brave little jump, she was there."

Mrs. Harriman spoke first, lauding Mitchel for his stand on pure milk and city parks. Irene noticed the men smiling when her turn to speak came. " ' Gentlemen, I'm not a speaker. This is my first speech,' said Mrs. Gibson. 'You will know in a minute that it is my first speech. We are here in a good cause - - don't laugh, for this is very serious.' "

Irene talked about the pure milk stations. " 'Perhaps you aren't all of you married,' she said, ' but you will be some time, and you will be interested. Then there were the parks that we got through Mr. Mitchel. (Irene obviously was enjoying herself, very comfortable atop that cart. She forgot the parks' names, and in a very loud aside to Mrs. Harriman asked her what parks she was speaking about.) . . . And you mustn't forget about industrial education he got for the children of the city. And I'm not talking about politics, but I am not a suffragette if that interests you. And now won't you please all raise your hands who are going to vote for Mitchel?' "

Private and Public Lives

The crowd listened with great interest and smiling, pleased attention. Around the street corner, the drums of McCall, Mitchel's opponent, tried unsuccessfully to drown Irene's voice, and in the end gave up, leaving Irene the "victor in the field," according to the reporter. Mitchel was elected mayor of New York City, and his record was one of clear and efficient municipal government. Theodore Roosevelt cited him as the best mayor New York ever had.

In telling the crowd she was not a suffragette, perhaps Irene was not being completely truthful. She could have been under the influence of upper-class activists and anti-suffragettes such as Mary Augusta Ward and Pearl Craigie, who had befriended her in London almost eighteen years before. These women were leaders in a broadly organized movement of progressive reformers who thought women could champion charitable, philanthropic, and educational causes more effectively without the ballot and as a non-partisan body of impartial workers. Popular history, of course, tends to forget the anti-suffragettes and their now sacrilegious beliefs, naturally preferring to recall the militant and forceful efforts of Susan B. Anthony, Elizabeth Cady Stanton, and other fighters for women's rights. Nevertheless, the "anti-" point of view dominated the elitist society of which Irene was a member.

It is difficult to reconcile Irene's personal denial of equal suffrage with her past involvements. In January, 1911, the Equal Franchise Society, together with the Women's Political League, staged a tableaux at the Maxwell Elliott Theater to demonstrate women both needed and deserved the vote. Living images portrayed the accomplishments and heroism of women, showing them as homemakers at spinning wheels, and as ragged creatures outside a factory building, gaunt and tired looking. In one tableau, Irene - - certainly a member of either the Society or the League, or perhaps both - - posed as "Motherhood" in the style of a Raphael Madonna. She wrote her son, Lang, about it. "Did you hear about my posing as a Madonna with a baby, and the baby yelling? It was very funny." Also, an article in *The New York Times* of March 30, 1912 covered a night at the Women's Industrial Exhibition sponsored by the Federation of Women's Clubs, an equal suffrage organization. The extensive program featured Irene's singing. "The

The Gibson Girl

crowds at the Grand Concert Palace, both afternoon and evening, were larger than on any previous day of the show. Mrs. Gibson's program, which was for the benefit of the George Junior Republic, was greatly enjoyed."

Suffrage probably was not a burning, personal issue for Irene, and most likely she was ambivalent on the question. Later she endorsed the suffrage movement. I know this only because one of my father's favorite stories was watching his mother marching in a suffragette parade, one hand holding a placard, the other holding up her bloomers, which had become unsnapped or unbuttoned, threatening to fall around her knees.

The years leading to the United States' entry into the First World War were vibrant ones for Irene. She was constantly on the go, traveling to Washington to keep in touch with politically influential people and to attend Democratic Party conferences. She enthusiastically wrote about teas with generals, luncheons with senators and ambassadors, and dinners with admirals. Irene's concentrated efforts to become involved in national politics by making political trips across the country were rewarded in 1916, when she was named chairman of the Eastern Women's Bureau of the Democratic National Committee during the presidential election. In 1918 the mayor of New York City appointed her the chairman of his Committee on Local Defense.

She was in her element, enjoying the effects of her charm on powerful men. She collected politicians. Her old beau, Nicholas Longworth, was Speaker of the House of Representatives, and Irene and his wife, Alice, the daughter of Theodore Roosevelt, became quite friendly. President Taft and his wife came to 700 Acre Island on the presidential yacht, "Mayflower," to have lunch with the Gibsons. The Theodore Roosevelts came to dine. Often, Irene and Dana were invited to the White House by the Woodrow Wilsons. In 1921, after Wilson's presidency, Irene wrote to Phyllis, "We were in Washington Sunday, had tea with Mr. and Mrs. Wilson, which was most enjoyable. He looks better and of course is an old man, so witty and wise. She is an angel to him." A notation in my father's diary, "the Churchills came to lunch," made me wonder if he meant the future Prime Minister of Great Britain. I asked my mother about it, and she remembered my father telling her

Private and Public Lives

he was astonished Churchill could talk to him and read a book at the same time. Perhaps, Churchill was not enthralled with his conversation with a twenty-year-old college student.*

The summers before America's 1917 entry into the Great War, my father's daily entries into his diary chronicled Dana's almost weekly trips to New York City from Maine and back again a few days later. Dana had taken upon himself a personal crusade against the country's isolationist stance, and with his pen ridiculed the absurd idea America could escape involvement in the war that was tearing the western world apart. His was one of the earliest voices in favor of preparedness and intervention. Always fiercely proud of being an American, he was incensed at the lackadaisical attitude of his countrymen toward the suffering in Europe and, to him, the barbaric actions of the Hun. His deep patriotism was aroused; his sense of what was fair and right enraged. He put aside his social commentary and concentrated on convincing Americans to join the fight against Germany and her allies. Years before, his sensitivity had put an end to a possible career in cartooning. Now he had the passion and the scorn and the conviction to draw powerfully and emotionally.

Dana had made the comment, "Humor is the only way in the world to kill war, hatred, envy, spite, and ignorance." But after the German atrocities in Belgium and the sinking of the *Lusitania*, the time for humor was over. His pen dripped with his hatred and disgust for his favorite nemesis, Kaiser Wilhelm, in a series of anti-Hun cartoons in *Life* magazine. Ironically, Wilhelm was a fan of Dana's. Dana's mother in 1905 was on one of her long trips abroad which he financed and wrote her son from a friend's boat anchored close by the Kaiser's royal yacht, *Hohenzollern*, at Kiel in northern Germany. Somehow, Wilhelm discovered that the mother of the famous illustrator, Charles Dana Gibson, whose books he owned and whose pictures he admired, was nearby, and he asked her to

---

*Years later, Irene was not too enthralled over a visit Winston Churchill's daughter, Sarah, made to 127 East 73rd Street in 1936. Her behavior irritated Irene. In a letter to Phyllis she wrote, ". . . she ran off, quite attractive and intelligent but an ass to run off."

The Gibson Girl

come and see him. Obviously, Kaiser Wilhelm had not seen or remembered the unflattering caricatures Dana had drawn of him for *Life* before the Spanish American War. Nor could he have known that with the outbreak of the Great War in 1914, he would become the main target of Dana's pen.

When the United States finally declared war on Germany, Irene poured her energies into the war effort. She participated in war bond rallies, was active in the Red Cross, and for a time managed an officers' club in Manhattan. But Dana made the greater commitment. He helped to create the Division of Pictorial Publicity, a coalition of artists who wanted to contribute to the war effort. The problem was how to corral a collection of artistic temperaments into a coordinated propaganda machine. After much infighting, and after many artistic egos had been bruised, Dana, because of the respect his fellow artists had for him, emerged as their leader. He calmed his peers and massaged the government's bureaucracy until he and his fellows were pouring out a prodigious volume of work designed to make the anti-Germany pulse of the nation race.

Posters being the main propaganda vehicle, the artists dubbed their effort, "The Battle of the Fences." Painters, designers, illustrators, cartoonists - - and even sculptors - - joined the concentrated effort. Crowds gathered to watch a succession of well-known artists ply their talents on huge canvases hung on the facade of the New York Public Library. The Division of Pictorial Publicity participated in all the Liberty Loan drives. Much powerful work familiar to us today came from this effort, the best known being James Montgomery Flagg's Uncle Sam pointing his finger and saying, "I Want You." Dana's most poignant effort was a picture of a mother giving her son to Uncle Sam. Lang posed for the drawing.

In an interview Dana gave in 1942, he said, "If a poster doesn't make you want to go out and kill a German or a Jap - - if it doesn't make you dig deep in your pocket to buy a bond - - then it's a waste of paper and paint."* Dana continued. "In 1917 thousands

---

* ". . . it's the punch that counts," said Dana. "The greatest word-wallop of the war thus far is, 'Sighted sub, sank same.' Some difference from Admiral Sampson's long-winded report of his naval battle [in the Spanish-

of pictures of all kinds poured into Washington. I was one of several artists chosen to pick out the best ones. It was a terrible task. We found only one or two that hit the nail on the head. Of course there were some magnificent things that you remember, those by James Montgomery Flagg, Howard Chandler Christy, Leyndecker and others. But, by golly, there were thousands, including the cartoons, which were just ordinary, and it broke our hearts to send most of them back."

The war struck close to home when Lang, eighteen years old and a senior at St. Mark's school, decided to enlist in the Navy. He needed, however, parental permission, which Irene and Dana were reluctant to give because of his age. Under his incessant pressure they finally gave in after his graduation, and Irene decided to call in some political chips to make sure her son got the destroyer service he desired. Lang's diary entries for June 23-24, 1918 were, "Arrived in Wash. with Ma at 2 A.M. and went to the New Willard. . . . Saw Sec. Daniels and Franklin Roosevelt in the A.M.. Left on the 2 P.M. train for Greenwood." Irene was not in the least bit bothered that the Secretary of the Navy, Josephus Daniels, and his Undersecretary, Franklin Delano Roosevelt, had a war to run and had better things to do than discuss the enlistment of a raw, seaman recruit. Lang got the assignment he wanted, a berth on a recently commissioned destroyer, the U.S.S. *Evans*.

At least in the beginning, politics for Irene was a stage. In an interview she gave toward the end of her life she admitted as much, saying she first went into politics for the "fun" of it. She was having a glorious time atop that cart in lower Manhattan and she relished the opportunity to sing in the Grand Concert Palace and to pose as the Madonna. But as the years went by, she became adept at the political game. She used politics, aware that her friendships and alliances with important and powerful men and women could further the causes she believed in. The root of Irene's political commitments was her intense belief that government should come to the aid of the disadvantaged. She was a progressive who

---

American War]. He said, 'We make you a present of the Spanish fleet, etc.,' and wrote himself right out of history."

believed hands-off, conservative government bred corruption and exploited those not able to fend for themselves - - particularly children. Her political efforts were sporadic, mainly centered on election campaigns, but her altruism was continual and intense as she used her political connections and wealthy friends to help promote her charitable interests.

As a young woman, Irene most probably was not particularly sensitive to the world beyond her family, friends, and social activities. The only piece of evidence that argues otherwise is a mention in the social columns of Richmond's *Dispatch* noting her chairmanship of the ladies' auxiliary of Summer Rest. As a child I remember Summer Rest as a rundown, clapboard inn near the railroad tracks in Greenwood. In Irene's day it was maintained by the Episcopal Church as a place where Richmond working girls could go for a few weeks each summer to experience a semblance of the mountain resort life their more fortunate neighbors enjoyed at spas such as Hot Springs and The White. Her involvement in Summer Rest could have sprung from a heartfelt concern over the welfare of the working class or it could have been merely a polite activity for a young society woman in Richmond during the 1890s.

Although Chillie used political friendships to further his business interests, he was not a political animal, and instilled in his children no strong political leanings. The Langhornes were ardent Democrats, however. Almost all white Southerners hated the tyranny of the Radical Republicans, who were blamed for all the abrasions of Reconstruction. Irene was eleven in 1884, when Grover Cleveland was elected the first Democratic President since the Civil War. She witnessed the joy of Richmond's white population, the ringing of bells, the impromptu demonstrations, the parades and bonfires that celebrated Cleveland's election. These impressionable childhood memories most likely forever endeared her to the Democrats, in her lifetime the party of change and reform.

Irene married a man with no strong political convictions. As a young artist, Dana's pen supported the editorial policy of whatever magazine employed him. If he had a political mentor, it was *Life's* editor, John Ames Mitchell, a staunch Republican who abhorred the Populist movement, William Jennings Bryan, and free-silver Democrats. Probably just for the fun of it, Dana, with Stanford White, Richard Harding Davis, and 300 employees of the publishing company, Harper and Brothers, put on a yellow sash and a four-inch goldbug hatpin and joined 100,000 other "sound money" Republicans in a parade down Fifth Avenue in 1896, shortly before the McKinley-Bryan election. Davis reported that he, Dana, and several other friends on election night were "on our feet from eight until two in the morning, cheering all the time and trying to find a Bryan man to lick."

With his pen and his popularity, Dana had the opportunity to comment on and influence the social and political issues of the day, but he rarely did. Even when success earned him the liberty to draw what he wanted, his themes were not the criminally absurd machinations of New York City's Tammany Hall, for example, or the ravages of poverty. Rather, his social commentary continued to be confined to lampooning the rich and the Anglophile. Although the Gibson Girl opened people's eyes to the fact that women's capabilities were equal to those of men and women's roles were changing, Dana was a conservative and did not campaign for equal property rights and suffrage for women. The Gibson Girl gets very low marks from many ardent feminists who maintain, and correctly so, she was still fettered by the collective restraints of the previous generation of women. Besides, Irene, his model and inspiration, was no liberal. She savored her womanhood and enjoyed the power of her own femininity. Moreover, when she was a young woman around the turn of the century, it was not yet the vogue for society people like themselves to reach out beyond their comfortable cocoon to sponsor and work for "good causes."

It is difficult to track the routes of Irene's early charitable associations because little media attention was given to altruistic efforts in the first decades of the century, and Irene in her letters rarely mentioned activities beyond home and family. In 1902, she was one of a group of women who visited the new Children's Court in New York City. Her intent was "to learn the cause back of the problems which brought these children to the court." Seeing the need for role models in their lives, she was later instrumental in founding the Protestant Big Sisters, Inc., and served on its board for many years. In 1935, Irene gave a fund-raising radio talk on

The Gibson Girl

behalf of the Catholic, Jewish and Protestant Big Sisters, reminding her audience the three Big Sisters groups sprung from the 1902 court visit. She said the movement was spawned "to guide and befriend inexperienced children, whose unsupervised and thoughtless acts were leading them toward danger and serious misdemeanors."

Irene's involvement in charity work in New York City was first publicly noted in a 1909 *The New York Times* article captioned "Society Girls Dance And Beg For Hope Farm." The Farm was a home for children whose patrons included some of the most fashionable of New York's ladies, women such as Mrs. Robert Goelet, Mrs. W. K. Vanderbilt, and Mrs. Arthur Iselin, as well as Harrimans and Woodwards and Kahns and Roots. The event was a garden fete on the Lonox Library field, which, according to the paper, had been transformed into a "bit of Versailles." Irene's job was to sell hats from one of the booths. Babs and Ethel Harriman were flower girls.

In 1923, Irene and Dana were trustees of the Heckscher Foundation, which ran a home for children at Fifth Avenue and 105th Street. On a Thanksgiving visit to the children, it was not part of the program for Irene to sing to the 150 children there, but she did - - songs they had never heard, songs from her childhood days in Danville and Richmond that had never been written down. The reporter must have asked Irene for the lyrics:

"If I was an elephant
How happy I would be,
I'd lock Malinda in my trunk
An' throw away the key!

Doo-da, Malinda! Doo-da, my Jane!
I'm gwine away to leave you,
But I'm comin' back again!"

He described Irene's performance. "In a rich, clear voice she sang the wonders of Malinda while 150 enchanted children listened with faces beaming and with shoulders that were tempted to sway.

Most of them had never heard songs like this before. The lilting voice went on:

> *An' if I was an alligate*
> *How lightly I would swim,*
> *I'd open wide my alley gate*
> *An' take Malinda in!*
>
> *Doo-da, Malinda! Doo-da, my Jane!*
> *I'm gwine away to leave you,*
> *But I'm comin' back again!"*

Her great pleasure was not the bureaucratic, organizational side of charity work, but the intimate, one-on-one contact with children. I remember her complete inability to ignore any child, black or white, powdered and dressed "to the nines" in a lavish party dress, or grubby and well in need of a bath. From Mirador in 1911 she wrote to my father, "I am teaching Florence, a little negro girl, and Lang, you should see her. She loves her lessons, and gets so excited, and is very bright. I am teaching her some poetry now." One of my favorite stories is the time she was traveling by train on a sleeper car, not in a private compartment, but one with rows of upper and lower berths, a person's privacy protected only by canvas curtains. A mother sharing a neighboring berth with two children was having a difficult time of it, so Irene invited one of them to spend the night with her. The point of my grandmother's story was not to note what I take to be an offer also impossible to imagine, but to describe the child bringing with her a packet of crackers whose crumbs made for an exceedingly miserable night.

Irene's work with the Child Placing and Adoption Committee of New York's State Charities Aid Association gave her the opportunity to change the lives of many children. In 1923 she assumed the Committee's chairmanship, and for twenty years thereafter she oversaw the process of finding adoptive homes for thousands of children. On average, the administrative staff for which Irene had responsibility effected 150 placements a year. She filled her committee with financiers and politically powerful people who stood behind her in the continual effort to keep the agency

The Gibson Girl

going with both private and public contributions. Irene was the very visible spokesperson for the organization, posing frequently for newspaper and magazine photographs with children clustered around her, speech-making, and chairing fund-raising campaigns for which she was not the least bit hesitant in recruiting her wealthy friends. Her appeals were very personal, offering to intervene for particular prospective parents and singling out children no one could possibly refuse.

At a dinner in her honor in 1943, Irene was presented with an antique silver tray and praised for her unfailing sympathy, her charm, and her ability to achieve results. Bernard Baruch, the "lone wolf of Wall Street," an advisor to American presidents on economic matters for forty years, and an old friend said, "It has been my privilege to know Mrs. Gibson for many years. I have seen her in association with the great and the near-great, with the mighty and with the weak. With all of them she has always been the same. She has a certain inborn, innate nobility. Her sweetness and understanding have endeared her to all of us who know her and have made happier those who have touched upon the radius of her activities."

In 1948, - - four years after Dana's death - - " the stately and still handsome" Irene at seventy-five was again honored for her work with the Charities Aid Association. So many of the elements of Dana's and her lives came together as *Life* magazine gave extensive coverage to the Gibson Girl Ball in the grand ballroom of the Plaza Hotel. Again, Irene was the "belle of the ball" as she led the grand march with Winthrop Aldrich, a prominent New York banker. The magazine reported the ball a "smashing success" with the rich and famous of two continents well represented, and women with their hair swept into pompadours emulating the Gibson Girl style, its "mixture of opulence and gaiety, haughtiness and coquetry."

Irene appeared frequently on panels comprised of politicians and welfare leaders to promote spending for the needy. She spoke against child labor and advocated proper food, clothing, shelter, education and health services. She used the radio to appeal for the approval of a $40 million New York State bond issue for unemployment emergency relief, and was involved in Roosevelt's

Private and Public Lives

New Deal initiatives, teaming up with Frances Perkins, Roosevelt's Secretary of Labor, to expound against the sufferings of children.

Children's causes were not Irene's only interest. Virginia and the South were dear to her heart. She chaired New York's branch of the Southern Women's Educational Alliance, which worked to find opportunities for deserving Southern girls to obtain college educations. In 1929, Irene was elected the national publicity director of the Robert E. Lee Memorial Foundation - - her job to raise $500,000 for the acquisition and restoration of Stratford Hall, Lee's birthplace in Virginia. Nancy Astor directed fund raising in England. Among the kudos Irene received for her philanthropic work were an honorary degree from Russell Sage College in Albany, New York and an appointment by Governor Herbert H. Lehman to the board of Letchfield Village, a state home for children. Years later, a former superintendent of the institution said, "every visit of hers was worth a million dollars to Letchfield Village."

Throughout the Depression, she worked for unemployment relief and for the passage of child labor legislation. The Roosevelt administration recognized her efforts when Secretary Perkins named her to a committee to study immigration and naturalization. John W. Davis, a powerful Wall Street lawyer, a former Presidential candidate, and another transplanted Southerner, best encapsulated Irene's work for the less fortunate with an elegant tribute at the 1943 dinner in her honor: "The hand that hath made you fair, hath made you good."

CHAPTER THIRTEEN

POLITICS

It had taken a decade and a war for Dana to regain the popularity and the financial rewards of his talent that he had cast aside in 1905 to follow his artistic dream. Drawing exclusively for *Life* he rode the crest of the magazine's pre-war success as his patriotic drawings time and time again graced its weekly covers. Plaudits were many after the war's end. His fellow artists presented him with a bust of himself and a leather-bound volume of reproductions of war posters. The French honored him as a member of the Legion of Honor, and the Belgians admitted him to their Order of the Crown. Dana had earned again the chance to retire at the top, to leave his successes and get on with the business of learning to paint. His income for the past six years had been handsome, and according to family lore, stock market tips from influential Wall Street friends helped in his accumulation of a substantial nest egg.

The Gibsons' economic revival was given a further boost by Chillie's death in 1919. To the end, Irene's father was feisty and flamboyant, noted for the ever-present, bright-red carnation in the lapel of his swallowtail coat and his chauffeur-driven, long, black Cadillac. He divided his time between an apartment in Richmond and Misfit, where Genevieve, Harry's widow, looked after the house. On pretty days he rode his favorite horse, Blackbird, around Greenwood, often accompanied by his valet, a retired British seaman. Chillie had given magnificent gifts to his children and had supported countless relatives; nevertheless, he died a rich man, not among the richest men in Virginia as his obituary declared, but his estate came to almost $2 million. Irene's one-seventh share generated an annual income of $10,000, a comfortable sum in those days and enough to eradicate any financial pressure Dana may have felt.

Dana was now over fifty years old, and Irene, at forty-five, was soon to be a grandmother. Although Irene knew her husband's consuming need to work would never be satisfied, only diverted from pen-and-ink to painting in oils, still the coming years would be more relaxed with long, uninterrupted summers in Maine and extended trips to England and Virginia. Plus, Dana no longer would be shackled by financial worry and illustration contracts and deadlines. Irene's plans for the coming years, however, were wrecked by the greatest mistake Dana made in his life. The chain of events leading up to it began with the death of John Ames Mitchell in 1918.

Andrew Miller, Mitchell's long-term junior partner, took over the helm of *Life* and appointed Dana as art editor, a post Mitchell had held since the 1880s, when he founded the magazine. A year and a half later, Miller died, and his estate put *Life* on the auction block. The family-like staff looked to Dana for leadership. A victim of his scrupulous sense of duty and responsibility, he could not resist their entreaties, and called on his friends to join him in a syndicate to bid for the magazine against the only serious competitor, Doubleday, Page and Company. The *Life* syndicate's bid of $1 million bought the magazine, and Dana, in control of the majority interest, was named the magazine's president. He was responsible for the administrative, creative, and marketing headaches of a periodical whose circulation stood at one-half million.

Dana had no desire to become a businessman and an administrator, but had not the heart to let *Life's* staff down when they asked for his leadership. After his successful stint at coordinating the war's massive publicity effort, he may have thought he had the experience and the know-how to be a manager, but magazine publishing was a far cry from the patriotic intimacy of the Division of Pictorial Publicity. Dana assumed he could be the benevolent father figure to his large, happy business family. He soon discovered command at *Life* was not so simple. Naively, he assumed everyone at the magazine would continue on and work as one, big happy family. The squabbles, the infighting, and the strong personalities of the staff needed the dictatorial leadership of a Mitchell, not a man like Dana who was uncomfortable with conflict and controversy.

While in Dana's control, *Life* kept its slick, sophisticated format. The magazine captured some of the finest talent of the day,

The Gibson Girl

cartoonists like Norman Rockwell, H.T. Webster, creator of "The Timid Soul," and John Held, Jr., soon to be famous for his flapper cartoons; and the literary staff hired top writers - - Will Rogers, Dorothy Parker, Robert Benchley, and Ring Lardner. Nevertheless, *Life's* circulation began its plummet as soon as Dana assumed the presidency. *Judge*, its principal rival, surged past it in sales, and by 1922 circulation dropped to 227,000, less than half the post-war level. The problem was *Life* and its president were not keeping up with the times; both were too genteel and too old-fashioned for the new breed of readers, the free-wheeling, speakeasy generation.

Dana did his artistic part in resurrecting circulation by contributing drawings, but his output was dated with no heart behind it. The reign of the Gibson Girl was over, replaced by John Held's Flapper, a skinny, flat-chested working-class girl with short, cropped hair and heavy makeup who was full of fun and freedom. She danced the Charleston, smoked cigarettes, and wore short dresses. Dana valiantly tried to draw America's new ideal woman, but she was denounced as "a pathetically insolent and slimsy person, vaguely drawn." He brought back Mr. Pipp, but the old man was a dismal failure. Dana's talent which for years made *Life* a success was now powerless.

Shortly after Lang graduated from Yale, Dana brought him in as treasurer in hopes he would take an interest and carry on the magazine, but the display of nepotism was a failure - - Lang did not have the experience or the inclination. Dana's troubles intensified in 1925, when Andrew Miller's heirs brought suit against *Life's* owners. They had loaned money to Dana and his syndicate to finance the sale of the magazine and were concerned the loan would not be repaid. The suit was eventually dropped, but not before Dana suffered the humiliation of having his $20,000 salary - - plus the $30,000 *Life* paid for his art - - challenged.

The successful artist had become an unsuccessful businessman. Immersed in the failing magazine and depressed by his inability to help the staff and financial backers, Dana's health began to show the effects of his stress and work overload. Overnight, he seemed to age. Irene twice carted him off to Europe for needed rests with Nannie and Waldorf in England, but it was impossible to escape the worry and pressure of business. Daily, Lang wrote to keep him abreast, letters which were full of optimism and encouragement, but invariably containing depressing financial reports. Dana was more withdrawn from Irene than he ever had been. Shut out from his life and powerless to influence this course she knew to be destructive to her husband's welfare and happiness, she immersed herself in her own interests. She revived political and charitable involvements which had been only peripheral during the years when Dana had spent more time with her. As a result, the decade of the twenties, which should have been a time of tranquillity for them both, became ten years of frantic activity.

Irene's new commitment to politics coincided with the victory of nationwide suffrage for women with the passage in 1920 of the Nineteenth Amendment. Women's votes had to be captured and the political power structures had to be retooled to accommodate the demands and needs of a broadened electorate. Irene had been a dedicated soldier in New York's Democratic Party for years and a delegate to national conventions. Her labors already had been rewarded with a committee chairmanship. Now, the party powers in Albany and Washington employed her to win over women to the state and national Democratic Party, sending her all over the East to stump for local candidates and to speak before women's groups.

Irene found herself in a curious personal position during the nomination process before the 1924 presidential election. She was a close friend of two of her party's contenders, Alfred E. Smith, the governor of New York, and John W. Davis, a successful corporate lawyer who had been a Congressman from West Virginia, then the nation's Solicitor General and ambassador to Great Britain's Court of St. James's.

Irene's political relationship with Smith went back at least fifteen years from the beginning of his career at the local, ward level in New York City. The two had developed a warm friendship in spite of their disparate personalities - - Irene the gentle beauty in contrast to his raw, unpolished manner. As a New York delegate to the Democratic convention, she was committed to Smith, heavily involved in his campaign, and considered important enough in the Party to be considered for the privilege of seconding his nomination. A month before the convention a reporter wrote, "It

The Gibson Girl

seems pretty well agreed that a woman should make the seconding speech, and there is talk of Mrs. Charles Dana Gibson being chosen for this honor." As it turned out, Irene was not asked.

Irene wrote to Phyllis before the convention telling her she had run into "Bernie" Baruch on the street and he said to her, "We have to get a man entirely unknown and as pure as snow." Baruch got his wish, at least as far as the "unknown" part was concerned because John Davis, after long steamy days of political maneuvering in Manhattan's Madison Square Garden, was nominated on the 103rd ballot to oppose Calvin Coolidge in the Fall election only because of the convention's inability to chose one of the party's front runners.

The Davises and the Gibsons had been close friends for years, even enjoying the ritual of celebrating Christmas together at 127 East 73rd Street. After Davis's victory Irene and Dana extended the exhausted nominee and his wife an invitation to visit them on 700 Acre Island for a week to ten-day rest. The reporters swarmed over to the Gibsons' island even before the candidate arrived, one of them catching Irene off guard, a paintbrush in her hands. They wanted to take her picture, but she coyly demurred, saying Dana would not approve. "I shall do all I can to elect Mr. Davis. That'll be a good time for you to take my picture. Get me when I am standing on a soap box exhorting the Populace to vote for him. Wouldn't that be killing!"*

The next highlight in Irene's political life involved the presidential candidacy of her old friend, Alfred E. Smith, the man Franklin Roosevelt proclaimed "The Happy Warrior" at the 1924 Democratic Convention. In spite of being a Roman Catholic, Smith made a strong showing against Herbert Hoover in the 1928

---

*Although Dana was in terrific pain from a boil on his backside, he gamely went with Irene down to the dock to greet the Davises and pose for the cameras. The Davises were easy guests with only a few reporters to disturb the relaxing atmosphere of 700 Acre Island after the initial flurry of press activity. One newspaper photographer posed the presidential candidate in front of the playhouse Dana had built for his grandchildren, and captioned the doll-like structure the Gibsons' home; then he sat Davis in front of the round tool shed and labeled it the Gibsons' guest house. The Davises' visit was uneventful and quiet, as colorless as his unsuccessful campaign against Calvin Coolidge.

election. Irene went to the 1928 Democratic Convention in Houston, Texas as a delegate-at-large from New York.* She was instrumental in putting into the platform a general declaration for the outlawing of war. Speaking to a reporter she said, "It [the anti-war declaration] is thoroughly in line with our policy, although we had carried it a bit further in our Women's Democratic Union plank."

After his nomination, The Happy Warrior's first campaign tour was launched on September 16. A special train crowded with newspaper correspondents, stenographers, mimeograph operators, speech writers, and advisors took off to the West from Albany. In Smith's personal party were his wife, two children, and ten friends and advisors, among them Irene. His daughter recalled, ". . . Father, along with the rest of us, was happy to have her [Irene] as a member of the party. She joined the train in Baltimore, and from that point on was a most delightful addition to our group. Virginian that she was, she constantly called Father 'Cousin,' and she followed his speeches and activities with great interest."**

Irene gave radio talks on behalf of Smith's candidacy. On September 25, she wrote Phyllis that Al Smith had been pleased about her radio show, and that she had to return to New York

---

*Smith asked Irene to give a nationally broadcast radio talk in August after his nomination, her task to discuss the personality of Mrs. Smith while another lady talked about Mrs. Hoover. Irene told her audience that Al Smith's mother "died happy in the thought that her son was in the keeping of a pure and tender wife." Irene recalled going to a meeting with Al Smith back in 1911 after which he invited her to his house to meet Mrs. Smith. Irene said she was charmed by her gracious manner and tact. She told of taking Mrs. Smith to call on Mrs. Woodrow Wilson. "There were two women destined to play very important roles in their husbands' lives."

**In his autobiography Al Smith recounted an incident in Missouri that must have been very entertaining to him. "Norman H. Davis [former Acting Secretary of State under Wilson] and Mrs. Charles Dana Gibson were in my party. Mrs. Gibson asked Mr. Davis to take care of her money for her and he put it with his own in a wallet in his hip pocket. At some time during the evening, whether in the meeting hall or in the crowds outside of it, somebody relieved Mr. Davis of the purse. It furnished much amusement to the people on the train. They said he went all the way from Broadway to Sedalia to have his pocket picked."

because they needed her "to do some speaking." In early October, she embarked on a whirlwind swing through the Southern states with Frances Perkins, who would be in Roosevelt's cabinet. Their first stop was in Baltimore, where they addressed a luncheon meeting of 600 men and women. Frances Perkins wrote that part of Al Smith's campaign strategy was to send out "Protestants of old American stock" into areas where there was the most prejudice against his Catholicism. She, Irene, and others told their audiences they knew the man well, and they knew him to be honest, independent, competent, and intelligent.

Al Smith's strategists teamed Irene with Eleanor Roosevelt. "I remember one trip I took with Mrs. Charles Dana Gibson to New Hampshire," Mrs. Roosevelt wrote. "I was to give the facts and figures and she was to charm the audience. Mrs. Gibson carried out her part of the program. . . . She has always been a loyal Democrat and has taken part in nearly all the campaigns, but I do not think she found overnight jaunts as easy as I did. She rose to the occasion, however, telling Southern stories aptly and well to illustrate the political points she wished to make. Everyone applauded loudly and whatever shortcomings were mine, she made up for them."

Nancy Astor in 1919 had been elected a member of Britain's House of Commons; by the mid-1920s her role as a contentious and controversial political figure was firmly established.* In 1928, Irene wrote to Phyllis in England, "Don't let Nannie come over before Election Day. She will just lose her head and attack Smith the way she does in her letters. I don't mind but she has a following in Virginia. It will do a lot of harm! Don't tell her I said this for then she will surely come. I hope you like Al - - he is a fine creature I think and very necessary. The Democrats should get it. If Al is not elected we will not see a Democrat in our own time. Then all the crooks of our country will adhere to the Republican party like barnacles on a boat which has not been taken

---

*She was also firmly anti-Catholic.

out of the water for many a day. It will be destructive for our country."

Irene was a campaign worker rather than a political soothsayer. Herbert Hoover won the 1928 election, but the Democrats came to power four years later with Franklin Delano Roosevelt. In the 1932 race for the Democratic nomination, Irene backed Smith again in a bitter fight. Before leaving for the convention in Chicago, she wrote, "Went to see Al yesterday. There is an honest man and wish we could elect him. He made a wonderful speech on the radio which many think will nominate him. I fear not."

Al Smith had come out of political retirement to make one more stab at the Presidency. Roosevelt was the front runner, and William Randolph Hearst the prime manipulator at the Chicago convention. Fearful that Roosevelt was losing his lead after a number of ballots, Hearst decided to throw his weight to him, thinking Roosevelt a lesser evil than Smith. Roosevelt got his nomination and the leaders of the party wanted it to be unanimous. Smith was recalcitrant, refusing to shift his votes to the winner. James W. Gerard, treasurer of the Democratic National Committee, went down on the convention floor to find Irene. "You're a great friend of Smith's. You go up there," he hurriedly told her, pointing to the gallery where Smith was sitting with his arms folded, a look of defiant disappointment on his face, "and tell him he has to come down here to the floor and move to make the nomination unanimous." Irene agreed to go and returned a few minutes later to report Smith's reply, " I won't do it . . . I won't do it. . . I won't do it. . . I won't do it." And he did not.

Smith's political career was over, and Irene warmly embraced the candidacy of Franklin Roosevelt. As a vigorous partisan member of the Women's Division of the Democratic National Committee, she lashed out at President Hoover in October, 1932, a month before Roosevelt was elected president. "Women, however, will not be deceived by these latest and most flagrant attempts by Mr. Hoover to exploit humanitarian causes to further his political ambitions. . . . Nor can they forget that while the President gave lip service to the children's cause for two and a

The Gibson Girl

half years he let the depression bear its heaviest on children without lifting a finger for their relief."

Dana's and Irene's friendship with the Roosevelts went back a long way. She had no qualms about using this important connection to discuss Lang's wartime service. Throughout Roosevelt's years in the White House she kept in touch with him, writing letters of encouragement, which Dana urged her not to send because he felt she was wasting the President's time. Irene thought nothing of asking him to use his power to get money for the library at the University of Virginia. "Just tell Mr. Ickes [Secretary of the Interior] to appropriate the sum for it. If he wants to look about the University, two of these 'Langhorne Sisters' will with great pleasure take him down." She asked herself to tea at the White House: "Could you see Phyllis and me if we 'dropped' in on you next Sunday afternoon?" Irene posted a flurry of letters to President Roosevelt during a period of attack on the Cliveden Set, a group in Great Britain before the Second World War that often assembled at Nannie and Waldorf Astor's country place and who were accused of having strong pro-Nazi leanings. Nannie had asked her sister to defend her, so Irene wrote to Roosevelt, "I feel very badly that the 'Cliveden Set' should be thought and alluded to as disloyal to what is right."

Irene's assertiveness was at least partially based on her friendship with Eleanor Roosevelt.* One of Mrs. Roosevelt's syndicated newspaper columns began, "We were joined at luncheon yesterday by Mrs. Charles Dana Gibson, who is in Washington on her way back to New York City from Virginia. The younger members of the family were fascinated by her, because she is still the Gibson Girl of her husband's drawings; and though some of the children had never heard of the Gibson Girl, they fell a victim to her charm of manner and her beauty."

Beneath Irene's frenetic political and charitable pace of the 1920s was a sadness and a frustration she probably did not admit

---

*Periodically, Irene went to Washington to visit Mrs. Roosevelt, accompanying the First Lady to luncheons with Cabinet wives and to teas, one with "thirty Admirals."

fully to herself. Always in the role of the caretaker to Dana and others she seldom complained. In her letters full of cheer and optimism she consistently gloried in her life, particularly in her good fortune to be married to such a good man. But in one letter to Phyllis she let down her defenses, revealing a discontent she hid from Dana. Admitting the fast life she sustained was not her ideal, she wrote, "I have a longing to live in or near a small city. I am 'Main Street' and there is no doubt about it. I like the cozy life." And, "I am fed up with New York, can't abide it." Her fantasies pictured the two of them away from New York and the exhausting pressure of *Life* magazine, at Mirador, where she could have Dana to herself. Her Virginia home was on the market, and if they sold 127 East 73rd Street, Irene believed Dana could afford to buy Mirador - - but knew he never would.

Dana's natural inclination to remain quietly to himself intensified, and after exhausting days at the office and at the drawing board he wanted only to stay home in the evenings, listening to the radio and getting to bed after an early supper. For long stretches Irene shared his hermit-like existence and declined most of the countless social invitations they received. Even with her heavy charitable and political obligations, Irene had plenty of excess energy. "But Dana has turned like that old worm and refuses to go out," she wrote Phyllis in 1927, "so in spite of my new trousseau, I have been quieter than I have been for a long time. The other night, though, I thought I'd get a gate on and 'grandma' went to four things in one evening. She ended home at 3 a.m. and found a note pinned on her pillow which said, 'I bet I feel better tomorrow morning than you will,' and other tender messages."

At *Life* Dana hired new talent and constantly reshuffled his staff, determined to build back the magazine's popularity, but by 1929 circulation had fallen to 113,000. He stepped down from the presidency, finally accepting the fact he was not the man for the job. With Dana as chairman, a new leader came in who threw away all tradition and created a zany format geared to youth, full of risqué jokes and New York nightclub recommendations. Sales shot up briefly, but at the expense of advertisers. One of Dana's editors commented, "Their howls of anguish could be heard way up in Maine where Charles Dana Gibson spent his summers."

The Gibson Girl

For the second time in his adult life, Dana found himself almost broke. Embarrassed by the 1925 lawsuit, he had cut his salary at *Life* dramatically and charged very little for the drawings he sold to the magazine. He turned to a competing magazine, *Cosmopolitan*, accepting a long-term contract which paid him the highest prices of his career for pen-and-ink double pages. From 1927 to 1929 he drew for *Cosmopolitan*, but his work was not good, and he tore up the contract, not wanting to be a burden. Charles Dana Gibson, the most famous and celebrated illustrator of his time, had overstayed his welcome. In late 1931, Dana resigned from *Life*, once the country's leading humor and satiric magazine, and now a struggling monthly periodical barely able to hang on.*
For most of its fifty-year existence Dana's talent as an illustrator had been a dominant part of its success; his ineptitude as a businessman was a major cause of its downfall.

Toward the end of his life, Dana, acknowledging he made a stab at oils in 1929 as he had in 1905, said with his usual wit, "You can always tell when a panic is coming by when I start to paint." Along with the rest of America, the Crash of 1929 set Irene and Dana back on their heels. Fortunately for Dana, his financial responsibilities were limited to supporting only the two of them; his sister, Josephine, was happily married and on her own; his mother had died in 1922; and his children were grown. In 1922, just five months after his graduation from Yale, Lang had married Marion Taylor and had two sons, Dana and Harry.**

Babs's marriage to George Post lasted only through the births of two children, and soon after her divorce she married Jack Emery,*** a successful businessman who expanded a small family

---

*Life survived for a few years after Dana resigned. In 1936, the name was sold to Time, Inc. for $92,000. The old *Life* was replaced by the still popular photographic version.

**In 1936, Lang and Marion divorced, and he married Parthenia Ross. They had five children, Parthie, Mark, Lang Jr., Renee, and Diana.

***Nancy and George are the Post children. The four Emerys are Rene, Lela, Melissa, and Ethan.

Politics

business in Cincinnati, Ohio into a conglomerate that included hotels, downtown real estate, and chemical companies.

Dana felt beaten. Again in their life together Irene needed all her strength to prop up her husband in the leaner years ahead of them. Having given up his life-long routine of strenuous exercise, Dana gained weight and was susceptible to colds and ear infections. Irene worried about him. "His legs are not good. He is tired, working every day since July. I can't leave him. He depends on me so and oh! how lonely he would be."

In 1931, she wrote to Phyllis, "Dana can't stay at Islesboro and is very worried and depressed. It is not easy to pull in at 62, especially after he has worked so hard to see it [*Life*] through. I hate him to have disappointments. He has been a grand provider. Life has been graced and very satisfactory. We were prosperous at the right time, when the children got the benefit of it and charming homes." Irene did not fully appreciate the extent of their financial plight when she wrote, "We have to live within a budget, go down to three servants and shut off the top floor [of 127 East 73rd Street]. It will be exciting to see how we can do it. I shall market and then I think of what one could have saved."

Life in the thirties did not turn out to be that easy. They could not afford to keep 127 East 73rd Street, much less pay the servants needed to keep the house operating. Again, they regretfully decided to sell, and, again, they found no takers for their townhouse because of the Depression. So 127 stood vacant while Irene and Dana extended their months on 700 Acre Island from early Spring until the onslaught of winter drove them back to dreary hotel rooms in New York.

700 Acre Island became the permanent home they determined not to lose. Although the large complex with its many dependencies required continual maintenance, it was a practical place during the Depression years as their long-time neighbor, William Astor Chanler, explained. "His property in Maine was no white elephant, but rather self-sufficient, his little farm by the waterside producing the wherewithal to survive comfortably. A permanent crew of three ran the place. . . . Between the three of them, Dana Gibson rarely had to pay a plumber, painter, plasterer, mason or mechanic during the lean years of the Depression. His

own crew could do it all. The farm horse plowed, harrowed and carted. Two cows gave milk, butter and cream for four households. Two calves supplied veal and beef. Some three dozen eggs a day were guaranteed during the laying season in the hen-house. In a second poultry yard three hundred broilers were more than enough for the Gibson table and the help besides."

New York City was a depressing place for Irene now that the pinch of economics kept them from their home. Less active in politics and charity work on a day-to-day basis, she was becoming impatient with the many demands on her in New York to serve on committees. "I can't bear them, just sit and people's minds seem so slow." No longer able to entertain at home, she kept up with her friends at lunches and teas at restaurants and at the Colony Club, while in his Carnegie Hall studio, guarded by a woman he called his Watchdog, Dana labored, completely absorbed in his painting.

Irene's last active political involvement was in 1933. In the New York City mayoral race, Joseph V. McKee ran as an independent against the Tammany Hall incumbent, John P. O'Brien, and the Fusion candidate, Fiorello LaGuardia. Irene backed Tammany Hall, but convinced O'Brien could not win, joined McKee when he asked for her support. She chaired the women's division of his campaign committee, and mobilized her fashionable friends. Their Tammany Hall opposition charged campaign snobbery, referring to the "nice people" in McKee's campaign and "afternoon tea" at his headquarters. Irene "expressed indignation" according to the newspapers, saying the women she had recruited were not only "nice," but were the most intelligent. "Are we snobs because we like Al Smith?" retorted Irene. The split in New York City's political establishment paved the way for LaGuardia's election and long occupation of the mayor's chair.

Finally, after twenty years Dana's time to paint had come; however, his freedom was a result of the end of popularity and financial failure, and not wholly his choice. The man who had led his field in the art of illustration certainly had the drive to excel in another medium, but a part of his dream had never been to paint to support himself. Irene had envisioned his transition from illustration to oils to be a restful retirement for Dana. But Dana knew his paint brush - - not his pen - - was now the only instrument with which he could earn the income they needed.

Irene's hopes - - great quantities of time together in their autumn years with visits to see children, grandchildren, relatives, and friends - - again were dashed as Dana threw himself into his work with renewed intensity. She discovered she was married to the same compulsive workaholic who in New York still arrived home each evening, sometimes after dinnertime, weary from long hours standing in front of an easel and preoccupied with his next project. At least in Maine, Dana relaxed his intense schedule, painting only in the mornings. In New York all she could count on was the brief time after dinner with the radio or when Dana let her read to him from the latest novel.

Irene was well aware that Dana's dream had been denied him for many years, and long ago she had accepted the difficulty of dealing with his artistic temperament. She had indulged his narrowly channeled commitment to his work because their existence was dependent on his skill. She did not appreciate that he was painting to survive, and she was tired of accepting his lapses in attention. For the first time, at least in her letters, she began to express her resentment at his thoughtlessness. Dana promised he would go with her to visit relatives in Virginia, for example, and then, at the last moment, pulled away from his pledge. "It was unkind of him to chuck me and Aunt Liz at the last moment. She was so looking forward to his coming."

One Christmas, he decided not to go with Irene to Cincinnati to spend this important day with her and Babs's family. Dana knew he was not being fair to Irene and wrote her from New York. "Everything is lovely and there is light in every window to guide you back. I had every intention of going to Cincinnati but wasn't quite up to it at the last minute. I want to (and will be) right when you get back so I am taking it peacefully and quietly. From now on I am going to . . . feel confidence that in the long run I can make you like me better. But I will see your dear face before this reaches you so no more. Ouch! How I love you!" The next Christmas Dana again backed away from going to the Emerys. He told Irene to tell everyone he was in Cincinnati so people would not bother him in New York.

The Gibson Girl

Dana's initial goal after severing his ties with *Life* was to create a body of work which, when shown, would establish a place for him in the field of painting. Knowing his limitations and that he had much to learn, Dana was unsatisfied with his efforts. He seldom allowed Irene to view his work. "The portraits I was not permitted to see as Pa said they were not good enough so he was not going to look at them for a year - - of course, to 'get something,' " she wrote Babs. "Artists are like that." Not until 1936 did Dana give Irene paintings to hang on the walls of their house. She was ecstatic. "Pa has given me nine paintings," she wrote Babs. "You never saw anything so lovely. Three in the library . . . and six in my room."

Dana's earlier paintings from his Paris years are precise and realistic, even dainty; but now his brushwork was confident, rough and robust, full of strong colors and heavy contrasts in light and shadow. In New York he limited his subjects to portraits of models and friends, and in Maine he painted what he loved - - his family, his place - - and seascapes, landscapes, Maine watermen and farmers, mountains and flowers. His captain, Merrill Young, took him to the wildness of Matinicus Island in Penobscot Bay, where he captured the stark beauty of lonesome beaches, the barren shores, and fishing nets hung to dry against brightly colored village buildings. Other times, Young chauffeured him on week-long trips through the New England countryside. Covered bridges and rural homesteads filled his canvases.

He got his chance for an important showing when New York's Academy of Arts and Letters chose him to exhibit at its annual show in 1934. He hung eighty of his paintings together with a retrospective of his pen-and-inks which stretched back to 1888. The reviews were mostly positive, his talent described as "vigorous, forthright and underivative." One critic described his ". . . exuberance, the blithe letting go," but cautioned that his knowledge of the craft was not "infallible." Fairfax Downey, Dana's biographer, expressed the significance of the exhibition to Dana, ". . . a dream come true, a high adventure after cruel disappointments, the promise of a rainbow fulfilled at last." Throughout the 1930s and into the 1940s he promoted his work with retrospective exhibitions in cities across the country in which he incorporated his recent paintings with pen-and-inks and even his boyhood silhouettes.

Family members were asked to loan oils that he had given them, oils that he thought particularly fine. His primary interest, however, was in the works for sale. In his copies of the exhibition catalogues, he meticulously noted the prices of the few paintings that sold.

CHAPTER FOURTEEN

SISTERS

Irene had no intention of succumbing to the advancing years or of letting the disappointments in her life knock her down. Confident she was still an attractive woman, she took excellent care of herself by working hard in her Maine garden during the summers and by taking long treks on New York's streets. She was proud of her figure, particularly of her slim and well-shaped legs; she held her back ramrod straight and never was there a hint of a tummy beneath the swaying folds of her immaculate dresses.

When she was fifty, she wrote Phyllis, "Bill Wheeler came to see Nannie and he looked at her very lovingly I thought and so did she I think. We all like a little of the 'Yearn.' " With relish, Irene reported to Babs in a 1941 letter a proposition she received. "----- Bernstein made a Bee Line for me. [I am] 67 and I find him most interesting to talk to. But apparently he has such a bad reputation that I feel ashamed. He said he had a charming apartment at the Waldorf and that I must lunch with him there. I said I am not old enough, something foolish like that. When we parted, several people, among them your ardent admirer, Wm. Murphey, said 'disgusting man,' so I let it drop at that."

Irene was still the flirt. She wrote, "A man told me yesterday, 'Madame, you are beautiful.' I had a lovely reaction and bounced down the street, like a ball!!" She adored the attention of the opposite sex and brazenly approached strangers when the mood came over her. She told this story on herself. "In a shop the other day I asked a stranger what his chest measured. He got red and began to move on. Said I, 'Mister, I am not picking you up. Were that the case I would choose someone lighter in weight, whom I might carry off.' He said, 'Excuse me, I am not too heavy to be carried by so strong a Lady.' 'You win,' said I. And so it goes."

Dana always understood Irene's need for attention and knew he had no cause for jealousy. Long ago he had stated he was married to a canary who must be allowed to sing. He told this story. One summer in Maine they had a luncheon guest, a very attractive

Englishman with whom Irene flirted during the meal. When it was time for him to go, Dana offered to walk with the two of them down to the dock rather than take his nap. Irene gave the man a good-bye kiss. After he left, she asked Dana why he had taken the trouble to see their guest off. Dana replied, "I knew you wanted your kiss, and would not take it unless I was with you."

Occasionally, the press remembered Irene's past role as the Gibson Girl and as an arbiter of fashion, and she was asked for interviews, once by London's *Daily Express*. Approached by a female reporter, Irene weakly protested, "I am much too old to be interviewed." The reporter was most gracious, declaring Irene had grown more enchanting with the years, ". . . for she leaves the most casual acquaintance with the feeling the day is nicer and filled with a sense of excitement." She described Irene's dignified carriage, the graceful set of her head and a complexion a girl of twenty-five would envy. She asked Irene to compare the modern woman to the girls of her day. "Girls today are not as pretty as their mothers," Irene replied. "They lack the dignity their mothers had. I suppose it is because the tempo of life is so much faster. They cannot wear the right type of clothes to show off their beauty. Besides, they do not walk properly. I suppose they think the slouch is really becoming. It needs leisure to create beauty. Everyone works nowadays. And the things that keep you young? I have seven grandchildren, my dear. You simply have to become young again - - to keep up with them."

As the years wore on, Irene looked more toward her sisters and her Virginia roots. Thinking of Nannie and Phyllis in particular, Irene wrote Babs in 1935, "How as we grow older we cling together - - those of us left." Her parents were gone and so were Lizzie, Harry, and Keene. Although Nora and Buck were her only siblings living in the United States, she was not close to either. She loved and enjoyed Buck, a humorous man, full of light country charm; but she never took him seriously, and they had little in common.

Nora was a vexing problem for both Irene and Dana. She left Paul Phipps for Maurice, or "Lefty," Flynn, a big, attractive man who had been an All-American football player at Yale and a silent film cowboy star. At least twice the family asked Dana to chase after the two of them and cajole Nora into coming back to her husband. She did once, but then ran off again with Lefty and married him in 1931, much to Irene's chagrin.

Irene could not abide Lefty. "His gall mystifies me. I am sick of their guitar and harmony." Irene tried valiantly to conquer her negative feelings toward him, but with small success. "Well, we went to Nora's. She has as you know a charming house and I felt quite friendly towards 'The Man From The Golden West' and I made a real effort, and now they are here. He walks around [at Mirador] so familiarly, singing, I feel I shall die. This is the same meanness I am trying to overcome." Irene believed Nora had "such a lack of feeling," that she was selfish and did not care how she treated others. However, Irene was incapable of harboring a long-lasting, serious grudge against her youngest sister. "Nora is just so sweet and so intense. She seems so happy." Both age and dissimilar personalities separated the two. Nora was the Peter Pan of the Langhorne children who never grew up, who never cared for responsibility of any kind. She lived for the moment, a "will o' the wisp" who flitted from one pleasure to the other, unmindful of the consequences.

Lefty Flynn had no intention of supporting his wife. For years the sole support for the couple's lavish life was a generous monthly allowance from Nannie, which Nora always outspent, constantly asking her wealthy sister for more. This uncomfortable dependence was a continual source of discord and resentment between the two sisters, and Irene was asked to intervene and calm ruffled feelings. Once she contrived an ingenious - - though financially absurd - - scheme to solve the problem of Nora's need for more money. She suggested Nannie loan to Nora the money needed to pay off her debts. Then Nora would pay back the loan with an increase in her monthly allowance. Nannie made the loan.

In the mid-thirties, the Flynns were close friends of Zelda and F. Scott Fitzgerald in Tryon, North Carolina, a small, horsy town in the western part of the state. In interviews for Fitzgerald's biographers, Nora came very close to admitting she and Fitzgerald had an affair. Nora was a tonic for the writer's depressions. To Fitzgerald, she was bold and exciting, a woman who in his words "never looked behind," whose attitude toward life was "tighten up your belt, baby, let's get going. To any pole." He thought Nora ". . . one of the world's most delightful women."

Nannie had been the scrawny baby sister whom Irene nursed during her many childhood illnesses. Irene was Nannie's ideal. She compared herself to Irene, knowing people wondered if she would turn out to be as beautiful and as charismatic. It was Nannie who kept count of Irene's sixty-plus marriage proposals, while she credited herself with only sixteen. Phyllis cried at Irene's wedding, not Nannie. Nannie recalled, "Phyllis had the day off from school and her first grown up dress. I remember her walking [down the aisle] beside me, looking lovely, with tears running down her face. Phyllis was always the sentimental one and cried easily." Nannie was pleased Irene was married and gone from the Langhorne household; not only would she get more attention from her father, she could move into Irene's bedroom that night.

Understanding Nannie's deep unhappiness, Irene wrote Phyllis, "I reckon she would do much of her life over could she go back." Nannie's disastrous marriage and wrenching divorce from the playboy, Robert Gould Shaw, had marked her as a woman determined not to be hurt again - - by anyone. Her protection was a quick mind and a glib tongue, a defensive screen of sarcasm and biting wit she erected against both political opponents and those she loved. Masking her own insecurities with excessive judgment and contempt of others, outwardly she appeared supremely confident. Nannie's girlhood friend, Ella Gordon Smith, wrote in her book, *Tears and Laughter*, "Nannie had little tolerance for human foibles and frailties," and was "dedicated to correcting people's faults."

By divorcing Bobbie Shaw, Nannie had failed - - miserably - - after so many childhood years of trying to show Chillie she was worthy of his approval. Nannie clamored for the attention of her father, attention Irene received so easily. Frail as a child and tiny in stature, she had to prove to her father she was worthy of notice. Chillie admired a person who rode aggressively and with wild abandon. So Nancy did. Chillie was gruff and opinionated. Nancy emulated him.

Nannie's particular frustration with her big sister was that there was so little to criticize. In her memoir Nannie aimed heavy amounts of faultfinding at her family, sparing only two - - Nanaire

The Gibson Girl

and Irene. Almost reverently she wrote of Irene's "sweet nature" and "wonderful charm," and that she was "completely unspoiled." Yet, beneath Nannie's adoration of her sister lay a distinct strain of jealousy. Nannie had to find some fault in Irene by saying she "had no literary talent whatsoever." Nannie did acknowledge the example of her Aunt Liz Lewis, an ardent suffragette and pioneer in the field of education, for her own political inclination, but never saluted the fact that Irene was stumping politically in New York City's lower East Side long before Nannie had a thought of running for Parliament in England.

Another slight Nannie aimed at Irene was that she "was never much of a horsewoman . . . ." True, Irene did not ride recklessly like her little sister, but she was an accomplished rider and was cited in the Richmond *Dispatch*, along with Phyllis and Nannie, as being among the "crack riders" of the Deep Run Hunt Club who "follow the hounds and are never far behind at the finish." An article in the *Virginia Cavalcade* magazine describing an incident before Irene's marriage further refutes Nannie's criticism. "She [Irene] was as courageous as she was gorgeous. They tell in Richmond how her dogcart drawn by two thoroughbred horses, harnessed tandem, became trapped one day in the narrow, but adequate space between a passing train and lowered gates. Onlookers screamed in terror, but Irene Langhorne coolly restrained the nervous animals until the train had passed. When the gates went up, she continued on her way, to the accompaniment of a tremendous cheer from the crowd."

Irene was confident in her status of older sister. Her strategy in holding her own against the combative and powerful Nannie was to remind her often of her superior Langhorne family role. "You are always to me a little sister," she wrote Nannie. "But I have great admiration for you." Nevertheless, Irene's feelings could easily be hurt, and she was far from being impervious to Nannie's assaults. At times, Nannie did her best to wound her sister - - striking where she knew Irene would be stung the most - - by criticizing Babs relentlessly and unmercifully for divorcing George Post. Her censure was particularly mean spirited because of Nannie's own divorce from Shaw. To dig even deeper at Irene,

Nannie continually sang the praises of her other niece, Nancy Perkins.

Irene wrestled strongly with herself not to rise at Nannie's bait, and to concentrate on the feelings of love she had for her sister. " . . . and Nannie has been so sweet lately," she wrote to Phyllis in 1926, "and I am sure feels badly that she said what she did and has not the slightest idea that she hurts me so much or made me so angry. Be that as it may I love her so devotedly." And, "Would that my dear little sister would think more kindly." Irene reveled in her sister's success, writing when Nannie entered the House of Commons in 1919, "I am just thrilled over Nannie's election. I think it is the greatest thing that has been done since the war and as for that a great triumph." And Irene was full of compassion during the rough times. In 1931, Nannie's son, Bobbie Shaw, was jailed for homosexuality. Irene wrote Phyllis, "Oh Phil, aren't you glad Lizzie, Keene, and Harry, Mother and Father were spared this. It is seeing those one loves suffer that kills us. Nannie must be heartbroken."

Ella Gordon Smith commented that Nannie was "particularly nice to those she could help." There is no doubt Nannie Astor was generous with her wealth, but in her munificence she satisfied her need to control others. Nannie's long-lasting defeat was Irene's refusal to be dependent on her. However, Irene had accepted Nannie's gifts of clothes in the 1920s, and did so again during the Depression. One of Nannie's happiest moments in their relationship must have been when Irene accepted a large check from her. On a trip to the United States, Nannie saw that the Gibsons' townhouse needed decoration and Irene's wardrobe was inadequate. "Nannie wrote me the sweetest letter you ever read from the steamer going to Bermuda," she wrote Babs. "She wanted to give me a present to spend on myself and my house and I was honor bound so to do." With Nannie's gift, Irene bought two suits and an evening wrap, new curtains and slipcovers, and fixtures for Dana's bathroom. She painted the house and replaced an eiderdown quilt.

Irene had been left out of the special relationship Nannie and Phyllis had shared since childhood because for years she was too much the majestic, older sister. Phyllis, too, was made of different fabric from Irene. Where Irene was extrovertive and

The Gibson Girl

direct, Phyllis was shy, unassuming, and contemplative. But each shared a sensitivity and a tranquillity their sister Nannie lacked.

After Phyllis divorced Reggie Brooks, she spent most of her time in England, where she fell in love with a British army officer. They were to be wed, but in 1914 he was killed in combat fighting the Germans on the Western Front.* Nannie wrote, "Poor Phyllis. She had a sad life. She didn't like Reggie Brooks. He was just rich, the only reason she married him." Phyllis did find happiness with a kindred spirit, Robert Brand,** a sensitive and kind Englishman whom she married in 1920. Phyllis lived in England with her husband, and was not a close mother to her two boys, David (or Winkie) and Peter, who, in spite of her entreaties, chose to stay in America with their father.

Irene saw Phyllis as an understanding person, full of patience and tolerance, and exposed her deepest emotions in letters to her. She wrote about her cares and happiness, her frustrations for and love of Dana, and the pride she had in her children. "Such happy days I had with you. You are my closest companion. I wish I had been closer to you as a child." Irene declared this expression of Phyllis's importance to her in November, 1935. In a year Phyllis would be dead.

Phyllis's death was linked to that of her son, Winkie. With his bride of five months Winkie came back from a party to their fourteenth floor apartment in Manhattan's Mayfair House at Park Avenue and 65th Street. Complaining the apartment was hot and stuffy, he went into the bedroom to open a window, and either losing his balance or jumping out, was killed instantly when he struck the sidewalk. "It has been a shock to her too hard to bear," Bob Brand wrote Irene, "the actual character of his death making the shock greater. But you know it is hard for her not to think of all

---

*Captain Henry Douglas-Tennant left Phyllis $300,000 in his will.
**Robert Brand, son of Viscount Hampden, headed British economic missions to the United States during World War II, including food and lend-lease. He also negotiated loans from both the United States and Canada. After the war, he was involved in the creation of the World Bank and the International Monetary Fund and was created Lord Brand.

the things which might have been different, if she had never left Mirador.... But he [Winkie] felt too drawn to the U.S.."

The remorse Phyllis felt for the years of being away from her son, together with her chilling fear his death had been suicide, plunged her into a numbing depression. On the hunting field she began to ride recklessly, completely unconcerned with her own safety. Her last hunt was on her favorite horse, Mirador, at Cliveden where she arrived for the weekend, sick with influenza. The weather was cold and damp, and her niece, Alice Winn,*begged her not to ride, warning, "You will kill yourself with flu." Phyllis replied, "I probably will, but it is worth it." Flu developed into pneumonia and after a torturous week of suffering, Phyllis died.

Irene was devastated. "I know she loved me and that is comforting. Her lovely rare qualities, so peaceful and understanding. So pretty and so gay and so charming. Sweet Phyl, never to see her again. Never have we had cross words or even impatient ones." Irene immediately left for England. "I need a lot of strength when I get there. I will feel close to her because I will be near and with the people and things she loved," she wrote Babs.

She arrived at Eydon Hall to find Nannie exhausted after her bedside vigil. Irene wrote, "Nannie sang Negro songs to her. She was able to give Phyllis confidence and for one week stayed with her night and day. Nannie's pins are knocked out from under her. Poor Nannie, they had been like twins all their youth and really loved each other. I can't remember when they weren't coupled together like a pair of horses." And, "Bob [Brand] is absolutely broken hearted. He comes up to my room all the time when I am dressing or in bed. It is touching. He seems to get a great deal of comfort out of being with Phyllis's sister."

Irene stayed at Eydon Hall over a week to comfort the family. She "ordered" Nannie to spend a quiet weekend away with Waldorf. Then she went with Nannie and Waldorf to visit Nannie's son, Jakey,** in Munich on the way to St. Moritz for a long rest. "Nannie has been in bed 36 hours and looks rested," Irene wrote

---

*Phyllis's niece and Lizzie's daughter, formerly Alice Perkins, had married an Englishman, Reginald Winn.
**John Jacob, the youngest Astor son.

The Gibson Girl

Babs. "Bibles everywhere on her bed. She is kind and generous and always thinking what she can do for me." In a letter to Dana from Switzerland, "I look to Heaven and see these majestic peaks. Yet they don't touch the Blue Ridge. Lordy! If I could see my grandchildren skating and skiing I would give the World!"

Babs and Irene were extremely close, but in their letters filled with family news, servant problems, and decoration ideas they shared little in the way of feelings and introspection. Perhaps because Nancy Perkins entered Irene's family as a somewhat sophisticated seventeen-year-old and neither was burdened with any deep-rooted baggage of child-parent roles, Irene was much more open with Nancy - - at least in her correspondence. Aunt and niece had much in common - - stunning looks, animated personalities, a zest for life, and a love of Virginia and Mirador.

Nancy was born at Mirador in the brick cottage to the west of the main house reserved for Lizzie and her family on their long, summer visits. A good part of her childhood was spent in Greenwood, years she carefully chronicled in a series of short, family essays. With her share of Lizzie's inheritance from Chillie, Nancy purchased Misfit from his estate three years after Henry Field's death. In 1920 she married Ronald Tree, a wealthy Anglicized American, also a descendant of Marshall Field. With Ronnie's money and the architectural services of a family friend, William Adams Delano, Nancy bought Mirador from Phyllis and completely revitalized and modernized the house and gardens.

They carved out its center, creating a grand circular hall that reached to a skylight above. The wings Chillie built were extended backwards to enlarge the kitchen and dining room. Out went the dark, musty furniture from Nanaire's and Chillie's days, the antlers and the faded prints in ornate frames. Bright chintzes, pastel colors on the walls, and needlepoint rugs created a light and airy feeling. Bathrooms were added, an elegant stairway constructed. The simplicity of Nanaire's garden was replaced by complex patterns of flowers, shrubbery, paths and secret places cooled by arbors of grapevine and wisteria. Away from the house to the east, past the new outside terrace, a walkway enclosed by brick serpentine walls on either side led to the pond surrounded by willow trees.

Irene, delighted Mirador had come alive again, rushed down to Greenwood at every opportunity to enjoy the open, urbane hospitality of the Trees. Once more, the house was filled with guests as family members descended in droves to mix with politicians, industrialists, poets, and novelists. She and Nancy worked together in the gardens during the days, forming a strong bond of shared pleasure and creativity.

But Ronnie had political ambitions, and in America his Englishness was a hindrance. He decided to try his hand at politics in England, and they moved from Mirador in 1926. Although the Trees managed to come back to the United States twice a year until the onset of World War II, Nancy's new focus became Ditchley Park,* a mammoth English country estate that she transformed with superb taste and innovative ideas into a showcase of comfort and luxury.**

Nancy's marriage to Ronnie Tree began to sour in the mid-1930s, and she turned to her Aunt Irene as her confidante, sharing her most intimate secrets and frustrations. After Phyllis's death, Irene wanted Nancy as a surrogate, younger sister to whom she could pour out her own feelings, but Nancy's problems forced her into the position of the mother figure, dispensing advice and admonitions. Irene's letters attempting to guide her niece through a difficult period in her life open a window to Irene's innermost thoughts during her older, more reflective years.

Urging Nancy to decide whether or not to stay with and commit herself to Ronnie, Irene expressed her own approach to life. "But dearest. You must take hold of yourself - - and look things squarely in the face. I do not mean that I for one moment do not think you are not making an effort. . . . But what we all want and

---

*During World War II Winston Churchill and his staff spent weekends with the Trees at Ditchley Park when the moon was full. Chequers, the country house of British prime ministers, was known to the Germans and an easy bombing target on bright, moonlit nights.

**Nancy went on to become one of her era's most influential interior decorators and designers, the style she created known as the English Country look. Her story is told delightfully by Robert Becker in *Nancy Lancaster: Her Life, Her World, Her Art*.

The Gibson Girl

should want is Peace and we alone can make it for ourselves and it can be made only by just deciding what is best for those we love and who are affected by our behavior - - of course if it is at the cost of our nerves and inability to find any happiness and be always disgruntled and miserable - - and impossible to do, then do the thing that will make it better for all concerned."

Irene continued. "Life is not a bed of roses for anyone. There are ups and downs. Don't join that array of women who 'can't keep step' and fall by the roadside. You are not one of them. I know you too well. Get something to do that is worthwhile. Choose friends whom you might think right. I sound horrible. But these are the pleadings of a devoted mother to her child, as you are to me. Don't judge me too quickly and say, 'Sst! Aunt Irene is old and foolish.' I am not. I am 'young and gay.' " Firm and supportive, and ever the optimist, believing each is the master of his or her destiny, Irene admonished Nancy, "We just have to take hold of ourselves. No one can do it for us, and besides we are all getting older and it is what we put into life that counts. You are generously endowed with an excellent mind, good looks, charm, generosity and kindness. Just turn the page and see how fine it will be. You will get so much comfort and the clouds will roll by quickly."

Irene tried to make peace time and again between Nancy and Nannie Astor. Nancy Tree was as strong-willed and feisty as her aunt; they were too much alike to have a harmonious relationship. To Nancy, Irene implored, "I am distressed to know that you and Nannie came to such serious words. I never dreamed it was that way. Now listen to the pleadings of your old aunt. Do forget it and send her a nice letter. In spite of all you say and think, Nannie really loves you and admires you." Irene understood the defensive and sometimes angry shroud Nannie put over herself for protection against people who had the power to hurt her. She understood the mixed emotions her sister had toward their niece, a combination of love and envy. Irene explained the dilemma in their relationship to Phyllis. "She [Nannie] seems to have a terrible rush on Nancy. She sees in her all the qualities she was so long in finding out she possessed." Irene saw her niece as the stronger of the two, and expressed her worry and sorrow for Nannie in a letter to Nancy written in 1936. "I am so sorry you think Nannie is no better and looks so peeked. Poor little soul, her heart is really of gold. She doesn't mean it. She sees things passing her by and that is sad. But she is a wonderful person! Stick by her, give her affection." In order to maintain her role as peacemaker between the two women, Irene warned Nancy not to show her letters to Nannie because she would be resentful of their intimacies.

When the clouds of war began to gather over Europe, Nancy was not able to come to Virginia to tend the gardens she had created at Mirador, and Irene came often to monitor the progress of Nancy's instructions to her staff. "Nance! I have bowls of honeysuckle in my room and the night breezes waft in over this old face of mine. We are having waffles and turkey hash for supper. Wouldn't you love some?"

In long letters Irene created word pictures of the gardens. "The flowers are rampant and so colorful. All is growing. This morning before breakfast I walked down the walk and as I came up I could not see the library windows. Box so tall. The Serpentine Walk is lovely and every bush in back there full and fat - - and that round place as green as the Emerald Isle. The willows are huge and all from bushes and as you walk down those steps to the lake it is divine and in full bloom." And, "The Birds knew me and that Oriole was in the Tulip Tree where his forebears had always dwelt. . . . I have just had a walk all over the place alone - - a perfect afternoon in the mountains, so clear and so sad and so still and so comforting."

Irene desperately wanted Dana to share her happiness at Mirador. The one time in the 1930s he came down to paint, Irene happily wrote Nancy, "He is painting all the day and loves it. . . . But thank you for letting us be here. No one has ever enjoyed or appreciated it more. We only wish you were here." They remembered his proposal to her on Mirador's lawn over forty years earlier. "He hugs the big sycamore tree every time we pass it in the 'back yard' and I am made to see if we two can still span it."

With Nancy away from Mirador during the war, Irene thought she would have the opportunity to spend more time there alone and with her friends. Dana supported her plans to open the place every Spring, but Irene's desire to have Mirador to herself was thwarted by Nancy's offer of the house to members of the

The Gibson Girl

British embassy as an asylum away from the pressures of wartime Washington. Irene visited anyway, thoroughly enjoying the attractive Britishers who took full advantage of Nancy's largesse, among them Lord Halifax[*] and Anthony Eden. "The Halifaxes are here," she wrote her niece. "As I walked up the walk I just hollered, 'You all come on down and greet me,' and I was Home."

On one of her wartime visits Irene was startled by a conversation she had with one of the English ladies staying at Mirador. "I asked her about Desmond [an old friend of Irene's] and she said, 'Oh! yes. He was with my husband at Dunkirk and while walking on the beach they were blown up, only their hats left.' That did kinder give me a shudder! But this terrific war certainly has made people seem strange about sick things when underneath I know their hearts are aching and breaking."

During the war Mirador was no longer full of gaiety and crowded with relatives and close friends, and Irene became more and more nostalgic and reflective in letters about her girlhood home. Finally, she began to admit feeling the advances of age. "Life goes on and I grow older. But I am well, very happy and so grateful for all my blessings and Heaven knows I have had and do have so many and I wonder why! I should do much more than I do. But the old engine runs down and I have to slow up. I just long for another Spring at Mirador. But how I long for the hot smell of honeysuckle and roses and that great droning about 3 p.m. and the tree frogs at dark. I am sure that's the music I like best. I yearn for it.

"Mother thought I was the Junoesque type. I was really soft like. . . . You would laugh at me June 19th with a red woolen shawl over my old shoulders and the shawl was the one Mrs. [Fitzhugh] Lee loaned to mother. We had dinner down there to call on her and it was chilly. So we took the shawl and never returned it. When we got home a trained bear was on the lawn with an old Italian. I think our excitement was too much. At the same time a mirror to go over

---

[*]Edward Frederick Lindley Wood, 1st Earl of Halifax and former Viceroy of India, served as Britian's ambassador to the United States throughout the war years. He had a withered arm, and when my parents took us children over to Mirador to call, my mother was fearful one of us would point to it and ask what was wrong with him.

the mantelpiece had arrived which our darling little mother had bought in Richmond and she did not want Dab [Chillie] to see it before it was put up. So up it went and was a great success. You must remember the mirror.

"I am now just an elderly lady of dreams when I am here. I see Mother and Father and all their children and some grandchildren sitting about talking, sewing, up and down the front steps. Now we have all gone separate journeys, some to the Promised Land and us left to carry on as best we can and this terrific war to conquer which we will do. Think of all the dear ones who have lived are parted from all they cherished.. But good times are ahead and a better world I feel sure. Changed yes! But the young can become adjusted and do them well I know.

"I now live in the past. It is the only thing that makes me feel really good."

CHAPTER FIFTEEN

THE FINAL SEASON

"I shall hold classes in saneness," Irene wrote Nancy Tree one autumn day in 1941 from Maine. "People are so queer and so dissatisfied and restless. Thank God the Earth stands firm!!! I look out my window as I write this. The wind is blowing pretty strong and [it is] low tide. I see rocks that people would strike (where they are not good navigators) at high tide. But the old land stands. It has a winter to combat with - - snow and ice." Perhaps Irene saw her life out there in the dangerous but challenging windswept waters beyond her window. She too had been a good sailor. She sensed her time with Dana soon would end, that their final season together was upon them.

Those summers in Maine before the outbreak of another world war were good times, summers surrounded by family, the grandchildren - - the two Posts, Nancy and George, and the Emerys, Rene, Lela, Melissa, and Ethan, and Lang's Dana and Harry - - swarming around them. "I never knew a man who enjoyed children more," Irene wrote of Dana in 1935. The grandchildren came, with or without their parents, joyfully embraced by Irene and Dana and not abandoned to the servants' wing to be looked after by governesses.

Life on 700 Acre Island was quiet and orderly. Some mornings the children piled in Irene's bed to hear the latest installment of her Jack and Dick stories, magical tales, full of brave feats and adventures. Then Irene, regardless of the weather, took a swim off the little beach below the front lawn. Breakfast was seated and served at 8:30 with johnniecakes and batterbread the main staples. Everyone was expected to be on time, properly dressed, to discuss and decide upon the plans of the day. Some mornings Irene found flowers at her place put there by Dana. Once, he cut off a good portion of a favorite rose bush. "Pa had a lovely branch of yellow roses at my breakfast plate. But I cherished that branch. It is the old-fashioned yellow rose."

The Final Season

Periodically, Dana gave his lesson in "honeyology," demonstrating to the youngsters how honey could be applied to toast and biscuits without being dripped all over arms and hands and onto the rug. Each child at the table fervently hoped he or she would not be called on to pose that day. Dana's invitation - - or command - - meant a tiresome, boring morning with frequent "That's it's" and "Don't move's." Dana was well aware of their distaste. "I like to do portraits of my grandchildren, but the trouble is that while they would gladly pose for a stranger, they consider it a task to do it for me."

After breakfast, Dana, wearing an old tweed coat, a black tie, and gray trousers, with a gray fedora on his head, walked down to his studio close to the water, its northern wall almost completely glass. He clasped his hands behind his back, oftentimes holding a sheaf of flowers he had purloined from Irene's garden. Irene spent the first hour or so of each day chatting with friends on the telephone in the library. Then the gardeners arrived, and with them she worked the morning away, a straw hat on her head with its veil pinned below her mouth to keep the sun from her light complexion. She hummed or whistled softly through her teeth as she grubbed and weeded.

Dana acquiesced to Irene's desire for formal luncheons, which were served promptly at one o'clock. Again, everyone sat down at the dining room table. Sherry might be served, but the Gibsons did not drink. Dana referred to cocktails as "sheep dip." If there were no guests, Dana gave lessons in sailing to the grandchildren, using knives and forks to show wind direction and how the sail should be angled. His game of substituting trick collapsible utensils at a child's place at the table worked only for the most forgetful or gullible. Even if they had guests, Dana left the table immediately after dessert to take his nap.

When the Gibsons entertained, Irene led the conversation, keeping the table amused with her sparkling personality while Dana sat quietly, enjoying the attractiveness of his wife. Sometimes Dana gently chided Irene when she got a bit carried away lauding the accomplishments of one of the family. Bill Delano, the architect who remodeled Mirador, remembered such an occasion. "Once, dining at his house when some distinguished foreigners were

The Gibson Girl

present, his charming wife had been expatiating longer than he thought tactful on the virtues of their son Langhorne's book, *The Battle of Jutland*. She told how writers and naval men alike had agreed what a wonderful book it was. In a lull, Dana quietly said, 'When my brother was 21 years old he shot a polar bear. The polar bear was six feet long from the tip of its nose to where its tail should have been. For a year my mother said the bear was six feet long; at the end of 18 months the polar bear had grown to 12 feet, and at the end of two years, believe it or not, it was 18 feet long.' This story put an end to further remarks on *The Battle of Jutland*. "

Dana's friends appreciated his uncanny ability to sum up a situation briefly. Delano was with Dana and Irene two months before Dana's death. He asked Dana his thoughts on President Roosevelt's seeking a fourth term. "Now look here," Dana said. "There's a poker game going on; Stalin, Chiang-Kai-shek, Churchill and Roosevelt are sitting around the table; suddenly Roosevelt gets up and another takes his place; Churchill cups his ear and says to the newcomer, 'Excuse me, what's your name?' " Delano voted for the fourth term.

Yet, Dana's commentary and observations were not limited to the profound and the succinct. He had made his living with his wit as well as his artistic talent, and for years he had poked fun at people and society. By nature, he was a teaser, and Irene, his children, and grandchildren did not escape his gentle barbs made in jest and in the spirit of good fun. Delano classified his laughter as always "good-humored." "He laughed with me and at me," Irene wrote after his death.

Nap time for Dana after lunch was Irene's quiet period, when she read and wrote letters. The grandchildren do not remember Dana ever raising his voice in anger, but George Post has a story about Dana's nap time when George's Uncle Lang was a boy. Apparently, Dana took his nap in the raw, and Lang thought it a great prank to smother his father's bed with a thick layer of flour. Dana lay down, looked down, got up and tore after his son, broom in hand, "mad as Hell."

Irene had a complex household to run on an island void of grocery or any other stores. She compiled long lists of essentials needed in mainland Camden, a good hour's boat ride away, always

The Final Season

buying two of everything, a practice learned from Nanaire. Sometimes she entrusted a servant to buy the provisions, but she often went herself, a covey of grandchildren going along in hopes of a treat after the shopping was over.

Both grandparents devoted a portion of their afternoons to the children. Irene played with them and Dana instructed. Dana gave George boxing lessons. Each grandchild was taught to sail - - how to come to a dead stop, how to make a mooring. The children thought it odd Dana's hat was always blowing off into the water when they had the tiller. Later on in life, they realized the maneuvering to pick it up was all a part of his instruction. Irene helped the children rearrange the furniture and clean the playhouse Dana had built for them. "I really think I am more a child than they are. Yesterday Nancy, George, I and Mildred made a fire on the beach and played Indians. I felt cheated as I had not had a go at them." Sometimes she allowed them to sail her across Gilkey's Harbor for a game of golf on Islesboro's nine-hole course.

Most late afternoons, Dana could be found seated in a wicker chair looking out over the water, armed with binoculars and a glass of iced tea, watching sailboat races and mostly worrying about his children and grandchildren, not happy until everyone was back safely. At times, Irene became particularly annoyed with his worry. "But he gets quite nervous over unnecessary things." Lang and his new wife, Parthenia, had gone off in a boat with Merrill Young on a foggy day. They did not return when Dana expected they would. "Pa pranced up and down in the front. He thought they had been shipwrecked," Irene wrote Babs. "I said come right in and be sensible." They were late because they had gone for the mail.

Dana enjoyed the male prerogative of being with his family on his own schedule, while Irene had the responsibility of keeping the entire enterprise running smoothly. "Irene ran things her way with queenly yet practical thoroughness," wrote William Astor Chanler. She was on continuous call, and on occasion she tired. "Age is coming upon us. I love that quiet hour on a foggy day when the children go to supper - - or to nap!! Don't tell," she told Babs. "They are sweet." Irene was in charge of a menagerie. She wrote Nancy Tree, "I wish you could see this place - - 7 grandchildren, 2 great nephews, 1 great niece - - 3 dogs, 3 ponies - - meals at all

The Gibson Girl

hours. I never step that I don't put my foot in it. But that ceased today. I have had created a run and 3 little houses way down in the garden and the dogs can come out when the children play with them. Islesboro is really like the Islesboro of old days, very simple, picnics with children."

To the grandchildren, Dana was very puritanical; Irene, very proper and protective. Dana could not abide short shorts on his young granddaughters. Red polish on Irene's fingernails was unacceptable. "He gasped," wrote Irene when she came to dinner wearing bold crimson. He could not stand for dogs to sleep in the children's bedrooms and bodily hurled them out when the children sneaked them in. Chanler told a story about a teenager working on his boat at Norton's Yacht Yard, which adjoined the Gibson place. Irene climbed up the ladder to the deck of the boat to see what the boy was doing. Inspecting the cabin, she saw on the bulkhead a picture of a nude standing ankle deep in water. "Young man! You must raise your mind to a higher plane." Irene's sense of propriety was disturbed by an attractive and young, but unmarried couple summering on 700 Acre Island. She never invited them over because they were "living in sin."

Her granddaughter, Rene Goodale, recalled what appeared to be Irene's startling naiveté. Young Ethan, Rene's brother and Babs's youngest child, angry at his grandmother, aimed at her a coarse expletive, a word whose meaning he did not know. Rene was there and remembered their grandmother turning to her to ask what the word meant. Perhaps, Irene was not that ingenuous, but she was a good actress.

In his youth Lang had not escaped the sometimes overprotectiveness of his mother. He was captain of the Yale varsity crew and had given his miniature golden oar to his current girlfriend. Irene noticed it was not hanging from his watch chain, and she asked him where it was. She was furious. Calling for the captain, she set off across the water to the young lady's house, where she confronted the frightened girl. She demanded the return of the golden oar. "You have no right to keep the Yale memento -- and Langhorne had no right to give it away."

Evenings were strictly family times. A fire blazed in the living room's large stone fireplace. Before they ate, Dana sat in his

The Final Season

chair, leaning toward the cabinet which housed the radio, his ear cocked, listening to the news, for which he had a passion. The children ate earlier, and after Irene's and Dana's light supper, everyone met in the living room to listen to Irene play the piano and sing. Dana turned his armchair slightly to watch his wife. At times, he brought out his art books, challenging the children to recreate the poses painted by the great masters. The grandchildren remember the safe aura of the house, the accessibility of their grandparents, being made to feel grown-up and special. Occasionally, a lucky child got to sleep with Irene all night, snuggled up against her as Dana snored away in an adjacent bedroom.

Those family-filled summers in Maine ended with World War II as Islesboro almost closed down because summer people feared being close to the water and targets for German U-boats. "Islesboro will be quiet I hear - - as many are afraid to be on the coast. I am not!!" wrote Irene. They could no longer staff the place because the local men had been drafted or called away to war-related work. Their children could not come. Babs was having difficulty at Peterloon keeping her huge house going, and was adamant that her children should participate in the war by staying at home and growing a victory garden. Gas was rationed, so nonessential travel was next to impossible. Lang had enlisted in the Navy.

Irene was frightened for her family in England. She urged Nancy Tree to come to America to escape the danger of air raids and a possible German invasion. She wrote her niece, "Please come on over - - we all long to have you. Let's you and I establish kind of a nursery for little children whose mothers are working and see what we can do. Ask Waldorf to lend us a house. How lovely that would be." At sixty-eight, Irene still had the energy to be active in war work. A driving force in the Maple Leaf Fund, a Canadian relief organization, she also participated in the American Air Raid Relief Campaign as a division leader with four captains under her who in turn were each responsible for nine workers.

The winter of 1941-42 Irene and Dana did not open 127 East 73rd Street and moved into the Westbury Hotel on Madison Avenue and 69th Street. "A very nice and attractive apartment. But

The Gibson Girl

a hotel!" she wrote Babs. "Two rooms with a large kitchenette. It is so nice. Went home and got a few things and my tea-set - - a very few things. Don't think I am blue. I just feel funny. So near home and not in it. And I shall never stay for any time in a hotel." Irene admitted she was disorientated and concerned about Dana. "I feel so queer and lost. It must be because Pa feels so miserable. Is a bit of a crank. It pulls him down and makes him depressed and he coughs all the time. Will go away to a dry climate. But don't know where. Ssh to the expense, much cheaper than opening 127, but steps would be too much for him."

Dana again volunteered his pen to the production of war propaganda, and began to stay on in New York when Irene went to Maine. From 700 Acre Island Irene wrote in June, 1941, "I've not seen him for two months." Then, "What a joy to have Pa and he is so happy to be here. Says he is almost sorry he came as he hates to go - - which he must do on Thursday. He returns 7/1 for good. He is a charming companion."

Dana's oils were gaining more attention, and fearing they would run out of money, he painted furiously. He promoted his work with retrospective exhibitions in Boston, Cincinnati, Richmond, Chicago and Santa Barbara, California. Once more they tried to sell 127 East 73rd Street, and again there were no buyers. "How I love 127," Irene wrote in 1942. "So many happy days - - worthwhile days have been spent in it. Even though houses are selling for nothing we would be spared the taxes."

Jack Emery had built a cottage on the lawn in Maine, ostensibly for his family, but in reality a generous gift to his in-laws so they could continue on in Maine without the expense of opening up the big house, which had no insulation to combat the chilling cold of the early spring and late autumn months, much less the numbing winters. Irene felt the young bride, so pleased with herself to be fully capable of housekeeping duties servants always had performed for her. To Babs she wrote, "Now, Darling. Let me explain our life here. It is bliss. I've never been happier, never seen Pa in such good spirits and when he tends his 'stones' with a scuttle it is a lovely sight. He does butt in over the cooking, but I love it and we do eat well. First our breakfast at 8. I have the night before my coffee in a Pot! Percolator. My orange juice is all done in the ice box - - and I am all set. . . . Tonight we have soup - - lobster salad - - with lettuce and your apples. We love them raw. We cannot bare to bake them. Pa says I do the best he ever ate." At 5:30 in the evening Irene took "a lovely hot bath," assuring Babs she "dressed" for dinner, a light supper on tray tables set before the roaring fire. "Then to my mail - - papers, news and music and a book in bed, and so it goes."

But Irene's happiness was marred by Dana's visible physical decline, and she vented her frustration and inability to do anything about it by complaining to Babs about his loss of hearing. "Your Pa is so deaf. He hears nothing unless one yells. Won't let me use the bowl of water and syringe and clean out his ears. He says 'Give it time.' I am furious. My voice is gone. A guest came to lunch and she yelled her head off. Radio goes on blasting. . . . I love the man but I hate to yell." Dana was racked with continuous bouts of cold and flu. "Pa has not been well all winter. Has not been himself, but [has] not complained. . . ."

Although her health was good, Irene, affected by her husband's age and infirmities, felt her own mortality. Buck had finally succumbed to tuberculosis and only she, Nannie and Nora were left. Her thoughts were of the past, and she began to write her memoirs. "I don't want to leave this world," she wrote Nancy Tree. "It has been so kind to me and so much beauty in it. If one could grasp it all and just be lovely and kind and peaceful and entertaining."

Irene wanted Dana to spend as much time as possible on 700 Acre Island. There he came to life, reinvigorated by the calm and beauty of the place they had shared for forty years. A Boston *Globe* reporter arrived on the island during the summer of 1942. His account is a testament to the recuperative power of the place for Dana. Having noted the orange awnings over the windows of the house, he said, "A tall, handsome chap in a snappy blue serge suit waved a stylish gray fedora in our direction. He bounded down the steps three at a time, made fast the boat to the wharf, said something about it being a fine day, picked up my carrying case and tripod, and then it dawned on me this was our host, Charles Dana Gibson himself." They walked up the steps and Irene greeted him, "A tall, graceful figure in a blue dress and a straw hat."

The Gibson Girl

Dana told the reporter, "I knew I would never be happy without this island so I bought it and built this place." He pointed to the structures of rock and brick and slate which he had fashioned with his own hands and which symbolized his love of his family and chronicled its growth - - a cottage for Babs on Ensign Island close by, the chapel on the point for marriages and christenings, and playhouses for the grandchildren.

"This place is my net. You know people in my line of business need nets just as much as trapeze artists. We may seem to swing through the air with the greatest of ease, but no one who has ever drawn knows the nervous tension under which we work. Every now and then we suddenly lose our grip. Our hands slip and if there isn't a net to catch us we are in for a terrible fall. When I feel myself slipping in my work, I drop in here and rest a while and then I'm ready to swing out again."

In the same interview Dana said, "The only fault I have with life is that it is too short. If I could live but a few hundred years longer, I would show you some painting for I am now beginning to feel I am getting the hang of it." He looked forward to the war's end, writing Irene from New York, "When peaceful days come again, we will have no more partings until the big one. We will often go to Greenwood, Ramsay [Lang's home] and Mirador. Sit under those trees and look and talk it all over together. . . . I may be tempted to keep you as much as possible to myself." And, "I live entirely in the days ahead when we will be all together up there in Maine. This war has cut our lives up into small chapters."

Irene knew the danger to Dana in spending the summer of 1944 on 700 Acre Island alone except for a few grandchildren and possibly cut off by bad weather in case of an emergency. Dana had suffered what Irene called two serious heart attacks. He had lost weight. The chiseled features of his face now were drawn and aged. She was determined they spend what could be their last days together where he wanted to be, but she feared another heart attack and formed a plan to get Dana quickly off the island if it occurred. On August 2, 1944 she wrote President Roosevelt. "I feel sure that you understand my asking you what I am doing. . . . and [if he] can leave here, the Doctor suggests he could go in a Hydroplane right to New York. . . . I am asking through you when the time comes

The Final Season

could he have one? He could be carried right down the jetty aboard one. If my asking you is wrong, I don't mean to take any liberty with you. But you know, 49 happy years and such a man as Dana is, I feel nothing can be wrong in the asking."

A month later, Dana had his third attack. Lela Emery heard her grandmother talk to the President. The plane was summoned, and the twin-engine Grumman amphibian swooped down as Dana was gently carried down to the dock. As his stretcher was lifted into the plane, he turned his head toward the men there and said, "I'll be back." It was not to be.

Roosevelt wrote to Irene the day after Dana was flown to New York. "Dear Irene, I am distressed about Dana but I am so glad our people succeeded so quickly in getting the plane to Dark Harbor. . . . and I am so sorry that he is really so sick." Dana entered Doctors' Hospital. Seeming to recover, he was sent home to 127 East 73rd Street. From there he wrote to thank the President. "I am ashamed to have caused so much trouble. Thanks to the generous help you gave me at the time, we got to Doctors' Hospital in 2 hours and 45 minutes and the old heart is plugging along as good as new." Dana died two days before Christmas. He was at home, Irene beside him.

Irene wrote to her friends, "I shall always be lonely - - without him. But he leaves me and the children so enriched with glorious memories." She was seventy-one years old, and had before her more than eleven years. Most of them would be good ones. 127 73rd Street was finally sold and Irene moved into an apartment at 876 Park Avenue, where grandchildren came to stay with her. I remember long walks with her down city sidewalks. When I - - or she - - tired, she stepped to the curb to hail a taxi. Placing her forefinger in one side of her mouth, her little finger in the other, she let go a piercing, high-pitched whistle.

Babs and Jack Emery took over 700 Acre Island. Irene went there in the summers but it was never the same for her. She made her life in New York City, lunching with friends and going to plays and to the movies. She last signed the Mirador guestbook in 1948. The place she loved the most, her home, was lost to her soon after when Nancy finally sold it. Every year she visited Babs in Ohio, Lang in Virginia. A few of her friends in Richmond were still

The Gibson Girl

alive, so she took pilgrimages there. They were quiet years for Irene. The oldest grandchildren, the ones she knew the best, visited her in New York only occasionally. They were busy building their own lives - - they had grown up.

Babs and Lang worried about their mother. On that wonderful, wintry night when she was honored for her many years at the helm of the State Charities Aid Association, she tripped and fell going into the Plaza Hotel. The family saw she was failing. All her life she had reveled in bringing together interesting and talented people. She still tried. George Post was at a large luncheon in his grandmother's apartment when she featured a radio personality, a talk show host, whom she thought would be charming. He was not. He was crude and rude and brought out a cigar at the dining room table. The lunch was an embarrassing fiasco for Irene.

Irene still relished the spotlight, but opportunity was mostly confined to private dinner parties where she recited the Uncle Remus fables of Joel Chandler Harris in impeccable Negro dialect. Her last public appearance occurred in 1951, when she attended a dinner at Luchow's Restaurant honoring the founders of the American Society of Composers, Authors and Publishers. A newspaper reported, "Mrs. Gibson delighted the audience by singing the old popular song, 'Why Do They Call Me A Gibson Girl.' "

My grandmother was too old to stay in New York City any longer. She and Babs came to Greenwood to look for a spot on Lang's farm where a house could be built for her. After the architect completed his drawings, my aunt constructed a cardboard model of the interior in order for my grandmother to better visualize the floor plan. The shingled, modest cottage with its steeply slanted roof broken by three dormer windows was simply designed. It had only a kitchen, a large living room and a short hallway going to two bedrooms and baths. A slate-floored, screened-in porch was attached to the north side where Irene could sit on good days and gaze over the fields and the white Mirador barns to the Blue Ridge mountains beyond. I was amazed at how frustrated and confused my grandmother became when Babs explained the layout to her. She just could not understand.

The Final Season

My siblings and I impatiently waited for her moving van. The two Irish maids, Fanny and Jenny, who came to care for her, helped my mother make the house ready. The children participated, unpacking large crates full of her beautiful possessions, everything smelling wonderfully of lavender, lilac, and rose. I walked over to visit my grandmother the day following her arrival, and she let me loll on her bed, which was completely covered with a sable fur bedspread, the soft thatch of its fur tickling my nose. I noticed she was not as lively and vibrant as she had been on her past visits.

Her cottage was warm and cozy, filled with the things she loved, her elegant furniture, linens and crystal, china figurines and bric-a-brac. Dana's paintings and drawings hung on every wall, reminding her of Maine, picnics on the beach, tennis parties and sailboat races. As she slowly failed, everyone worked to maintain her dignity. During the first few months of her life in Greenwood there were callers almost every day. Then they stopped coming. My older sister remembers feeling sad seeing our grandmother arrayed in a lovely tea gown, propped in a chair with a view of the driveway, waiting for people who never came.

During her last months Nannie came to be with her, sitting on a low stool by her bed, reading hour after hour, hoping the power of her own Christian Science faith would bring her older sister back. But Irene was ready to go on. Her mind drifted away to her past lives, to Virginia long ago, Maine and New York. A light smile came across her face as she wandered through the years, reliving somewhere deep in her brain those glorious times when her beauty equaled any other of Nature's creations. Nanaire and Chillie were with her, also Lizzie, Phyllis and Buck; Babs and Lang as children, grandchildren, old servants and old friends; but, especially Dana, the love of her life, her partner in so much happiness, so much accomplishment.

Irene had come to Greenwood to die, to be as close to her home, to Mirador, as she could. She chose the Springtime, when the redbud trees were in blossom and the daffodils clustered in bunches of yellow and white. She died with no regrets because she had left nothing out of her life. Her legacy remains -- kindness and love, strength and passion. April 20, 1956 was her last day on earth. She died as gently as she had lived.

The Gibson Girl

I served as the acolyte at her funeral at Emmanuel Episcopal, a beautiful country church with brick colonnades she and her sisters and brothers had rebuilt in memory of Nanaire. I stood near the altar, in full view of all my older cousins, embarrassed to be crying during the service. Everyone went over to our house across the road afterwards. For hours, people told wonderful stories about her. Most everyone laughed. Some cried. Some did both.

Granny was cremated. My father took her ashes to Massachusetts to bury them beside Grandpa. Not too many years after she died, my sister moved into her house and lives there now. She says when she opens a closet door or walks into Granny's bedroom, she still smells the fragrant perfumes.

ACKNOWLEDGMENTS

This book is the product of cooperative family effort. My mother, my brothers and sisters, and a host of cousins enthusiastically opened to me their memories, their scrapbooks, photograph albums, and letter boxes. Their interest and encouragement were my main support during the three years this project has been under way. My thanks go out to Renee Darrell, Ethan Emery, Josiah Emery, Elizabeth Ferry, Sir Edward Ford, Diana Garner, Betsy Gibson, C. Dana and Kay Gibson, Mark Gibson, Parthenia Gibson, Tanner Gibson, Rene Goodale, Dan Knowlton, Melissa Lanier, Chill Langhorne, Harry and Liz Langhorne, Chill Perkins, George Post, Parthie Shields, Lela Steele, Ross Stevens, Lang Talley, Penelope Tree, Betsy Varner, and Alice Winn.

Many people helped in the research process. The staffs of the Virginia State Library, the Valentine Museum, the Alderman Library, Michael Bott at Reading University in England, Frances Pollard at the Virginia Historical Society, and Lewis Averett at the Jones Memorial Library were particularly helpful. Gary Grant in Danville shared his historical insight, Robert Becker his source material, and Robert Conte of The Greenbrier his library. Hope Burghardt opened her home, Mirador, to me.

Each manuscript revision was patiently read, commented upon, and corrected by my wife, Sara. My daughter, Dana, a gifted writer and artist, gave me crucial direction. The guidance of Nelson Lankford, Laurie Spratley, George Longest, and Roger Hailes was invaluable to the writing process, and Anne Freeman made herself available whenever I needed her. Steve Martin and George Lee added their expertise. My editor, Elizabeth Pope, with her strict pencil and knowledge of the English language, brought order to the words.

To all of you, my thanks.

SOURCES

Primary sources include family letters in the hundreds, diaries, interviews, and unpublished remembrances written by Irene, my father, Nancy Astor, Alice Winn, Nancy Lancaster, Robert Brand, William Delano, William Astor Chanler, and Angus MacDonnell. Deedbooks and records of Virginia communities revealed glimpses into the lives of ancestors long dead.

The following books about my family were invaluable: *Portrait of an Era*, Fairfax Downey's biography of Dana, Michael Astor's *Tribal Feeling*, *Nancy, The Life of Lady Astor* by Christopher Sykes, *Always A Virginian* by Alice Winn, and Josephine Knowlton's two books, *Longfield, The House On The Neck* and *Butterballs and Fingerbowls*.

Numerous references furnished historical, biographical, and cultural information. Those particularly useful were *Adventures and Letters of Richard Harding Davis* edited by his brother, Charles, *The Gilded Life of Stanford White* by Gerald Langford, Dan Beard's autobiography, *Hardly a Man Alive*, Cleveland Amory's books, *Who Killed Society?* and *The Last Resorts*, *The Springs of Virginia* by Percival Reneirs, and *Famous Belles of the 19th Century* by Virginia Tatnall. Also helpful were *The Life and Times of Theodore Roosevelt* by Stefan Dorant, *One Woman, One Vote, Rediscovering the Woman Suffrage Movement* edited by Marjorie S. Wheeler, and the autobiographical writings of Al Smith and Eleanor Roosevelt.